ALEXANDER HAMILTON

Alexander Hamilton
From a portrait by James Sharples
Photo courtesy of The New York Public Library

ALEXANDER HAMILTON

A Concise Biography

Broadus

Mitchell

New York   OXFORD UNIVERSITY PRESS   1976

973.40924
M69a
100187
Mar.1977

Foreword

Alexander Hamilton, our first Secretary of the Treasury, was an artillerist in the early part of the American Revolution. It is appropriate therefore to speak of his trajectory—not of cannonballs, but of policies for his country. His proposals describe today's economic and political developments. He rejected the agrarian society which his opponents favored, and he urged a combination of farming, finance, industry, and commerce. He would bring about these varied pursuits by concerted effort. Not for him the passive government of the Antifederalists, weakest at the center. Instead he magnified the national authority, made it the engine of improvement.

To be sure, the states had as their province local concerns, but the sovereign power was in Congress and the executive and judicial branches of the general government. Hamilton did not leave progress to inclination of the individual citizen; he created facilities that encouraged prosperity. Of chief influence was restoration of public credit, which imbued the country with confidence and furnished the means of private enterprise. His national bank was an active supplement, providing a dependable paper currency. He systematized import duties on foreign wares to protect infant manufactures at home.

For half a generation America lapsed from Hamilton's plans. This was from the advent of the Republicans (the Jeffersonians) in 1801 to the sequel of the War of 1812–14. Thereafter those who had neglected Hamilton's advice returned to his promptings. In 1816 a truly protective tariff was enacted, the

Second Bank of the United States was chartered, and a national system of turnpikes and canals was promoted. Soon the industrial revolution which Hamilton had solicited took vigorous hold. During the following hundred and fifty years, with reversals from time to time, the national authority expanded and corporate forms of business became dominant.

The Great Depression of the 1930's marked a new departure from these developments, for the New Deal then inaugurated the welfare state. The national government was obliged to rescue agriculture, industry, transportation, banks, and insurance companies, and it reached into local communities with relief for the unemployed and loans for homeowners. The Democrats who sponsored these remedies continued to honor Jefferson and Jackson as patron saints of their party, but in fact they were encountering the forecast and celebrating the policies of Alexander Hamilton.

Hamilton was a zealous champion of individual rights. He urged manhood suffrage, a numerous House of Representatives, and was, of course, the foe of slavery. In the maturing of his plans for material advance, he would be the first to protect personal freedom from bureaucratic presumption. The friend of effective national instruments, he would guard against their demonstrated tendency to use authority for usurpation.

Alexander Hamilton's passionate commitment to America is vivid in our country today, and the story of his career is worth retelling.

New York City   B.M.
October 1975

Contents

To L.P.D and J.B.M. with love

ALEXANDER HAMILTON

Chapter 1

PRECOCIOUS CLERK

Alexander Hamilton was born on January 11, 1755, at Charlestown on the island of Nevis in the British West Indies. His mother was Rachel Faucette Lavien, the daughter of John Faucette, a planter of French extraction, and Faucette's wife, Mary Uppington. His father was James Hamilton, fourth son of Alexander Hamilton, Laird of "Grange," in Ayrshire, Scotland, and his wife, Elizabeth Pollock.

His birth date has been given as 1757, but recent evidence indicates that he was born two years earlier. This difference is significant, for it has a bearing on his precocious youthful performance and his later life; he was probably thirty-four when he became Secretary of the Treasury, not thirty-two. He himself mentioned his age in several connections, but always approximately; in effect, he assigned different years for his birth.

Although Hamilton's life was to influence a continent, it began in a miniature world. Nevis, five miles in diameter, is a volcanic cone, its peak usually wrapped in cloud. The village of Charlestown, which lies on the island's crescent beach, has not changed much in two centuries. The reputed site of Ham-

ilton's birth is a walled yard beside the sea; a double flight
of stone steps is all that is left of the house. Hamilton's mother
was a native of Nevis. She was born on a plantation there. It
may be that at the time Hamilton was born his father was
employed, as he was later, on the adjacent island of St. Kitts.

Nevis is an island of surpassing beauty, its green mountain
lifting from a sapphire sea and profound silence reigning over
all, but this paradise is marked by historic violence. French,
English, Dutch, and Spanish adventurers contended for foot-
holds here, and they strewed the beaches with bones that are
turned up to this day. Worse was the harsh treatment of the
black slaves who labored in fields of sugarcane and cotton. The
sensitive boy Alexander knew Nevis' loveliness and its evils at
first hand.

In 1740, when Rachel Faucette was eleven, her parents were
legally separated. The reasons for their breakup after twenty-
two years of marriage can only be guessed. Five of their seven
children had died, three of them in an epidemic a few years
before. Mary Faucette appears to have been John's second
wife, and she may have been considerably younger than he,
for he died five years later, in 1745. Mary's annual income, £53
a year, agreed to at the separation, probably ceased at his
death, but she had property of her own. John Faucette's will
left all that he had to his daughter Rachel, then sixteen.

Mother and daughter moved from Nevis—or St. Kitts—to
the near-by Danish island of St. Croix. There, in November
1745, Mary Faucette was godmother at the christening of the
son of her stepdaughter, Ann Lytton. Ann, Rachel's half-sister
and fifteen years her senior, had married James Lytton of
Nevis. Because of drought on Nevis, the Lyttons, with relatives and friends, moved from that island to St. Croix in 1738,
and there Lytton bought a plantation, "Grange," in Company's Quarter. The Lytton family, prosperous and reliable,
became the anchor of Mary Faucette and Rachel on St. Croix.

Another who had transferred from Nevis to St. Croix was

the merchant John Michael Lavien; the name was variously spelled, and it is uncertain whether he was Danish or German-Jewish. He bought a sugar plantation in Company's Quarter, and James Lytton was a witness to the deed. This place was soon sold at auction, and Lavien then bought half a cotton plantation, "Contentment," in the same Company's Quarter. This was in February 1745. In that year he married Rachel Faucette.

The belief of the Hamilton family historian that Lavien "received [Rachel's] hand against her inclination" is borne out by her unhappiness in the union. Their home, "Contentment," had not that meaning for Rachel. Here their son Peter was born in 1746. Three years later they moved to "Beeston Hill." Lavien's fortunes worsened. He was in heavy debt to the company, failed as an independent planter, became overseer for others, was later superintendent of the hospital at Frederiksted, and ended his days as a mere roomer there. He seems to have been almost twice Rachel's age, which may have added to their disharmony. On the other hand, Rachel's relatives remained on good terms with Lavien.

In any event, Rachel, according to Lavien's complaint, became so unwifely that he had her imprisoned in the fort at Christiansted. He must have charged that she had "twice been guilty of adultery" and declared that he was no longer living with her; so the Danish law required. He thought better of jailing her in one of those narrow, dark cells, and released her in hopes she would mend her ways. His story was that, instead of returning to him, she went off to "an English island" where she begot two illegitimate children. Lavien sued for divorce especially because if he died she, as his widow, might claim for her illegitimate children what rightly belonged to his son Peter. This was in 1759, about nine years after Rachel deserted him. Rachel and three witnesses were summoned to the divorce hearing. The papers were attempted to be served on her at either one of the two places where she last lived in the island, the Fort where she was in jail and the plantation of Town Captain deNully, who may have secured her release from prison. Rachel did not respond to the summons. The court then dissolved the marriage, declaring that "said Rachel Lewin shall have no rights whatsoever as wife to either John Michael Lewin's person or means. . . . Also, Rachel Lewin's illegitimate children are denied all rights or pretensions to the plaintiff's possessions." Lavien was free to marry again (which he did), but Rachel, as the offending party, under Danish law was forbidden to do so.

Rachel and her mother probably left St. Croix when Rachel separated from Lavien in 1750. Her mother and the Lytton family thought no worse of her for her marital troubles. Where the two went—except to "an English island"—is unknown. It is likely that they returned to St. Kitts, though Mary Faucette was living on the Dutch island of St. Eustatius in 1755.

About 1752, two years after quitting Lavien, Rachel had begun to live with James Hamilton, an attractive Scotsman ten years her senior, whom she probably met on St. Kitts. A younger son in an ancient landed family, he had served a commercial apprenticeship in Glasgow and had come to the West Indies seeking his fortune as a merchant. Their elder son James was born in 1753, Alexander two years later. Rachel, of course, was forbidden to remarry, but aside from that justification, her informal union with James Hamilton was not unusual or socially reprobated in that part of the world. There is no reason to believe that the community took seriously Lavien's stigmas that Rachel was "shameless, rude and ungodly" and "gave herself up to whoring with everyone." The common law marriage of Rachel and James endured for fifteen years or more, in honorable distinction to the frequent casual connections of white planters with their slave women. "James Hamilton and Rachel Hamilton his wife" were godfather and godmother at a christening on St. Eustatius in 1758.

The Hamilton household was on St. Croix in the spring of

1765, when Alexander was ten. James Hamilton had come from St. Kitts to collect a debt for Archibald Ingram, whose head clerk he was. Moir & Gordon refused to pay Ingram £807 11s. 11d., and James Hamilton was obliged to recover the amount in a Christiansted court. When he returned to St. Kitts he did not take his family with him. This was the "separation between him and me, when I was very young," of which Alexander wrote in later life, and which "threw me upon the bounty of my mother's relatives, some of whom were then wealthy." Alexander explained it to his cousin in Scotland: "my father's affairs at a very early day went to wreck; so as to have rendered his situation during the greatest part of his life far from eligible."

Against the supposition that James Hamilton deliberately deserted Rachel and their young sons stands Alexander's continuing affection for his father. Seven years after the separation he wrote to his father dutifully, and later he informed his father of his marriage, adding that he hoped his wife would esteem him. At the close of the Revolution he inquired of his brother James, "what has become of our dear father? It is an age since I have heard from him. . . . Perhaps alas! he is no more, and I shall not have the pleasing opportunity of contributing to render the close of his life more happy than the progress of it. My heart bleeds at the recollection of his misfortunes and embarrassments." Afterward he had news of his father, sent him money, and planned for the old man to come and live with him in New York. But by this time, the 1790's, James Hamilton, Sr., was on the island of St. Vincent, in failing health, and afraid to risk the voyage during the war between England and France. He died in 1799, at the age of eighty-one, and was buried on St. Vincent. More than five years later a line was added on his tombstone, describing him as "Father of General Hamilton in America killed by Col. Baird" (Burr).

We know that James Hamilton, Sr., was employed on a

plantation on St. Vincent and that a friend assisted in settling his affairs (paying his debts) before his death. We assume that he had drifted through the islands, somehow supporting himself, except for occasional help from Alexander. For long periods his son in America was ignorant of his whereabouts. There is no evidence that he was ever able, or cared, to be of assistance to Rachel and the boys, though when he parted from them he probably did not intend that he should never see them again.

If Alexander's father was irresponsible, his mother was not. When left in Christiansted she at once opened a little provision store to support herself and her sons. She had to be self-reliant because the Lytton family was falling apart. James Lytton had sold his "Grange" plantation and he and his wife had returned to Nevis. Their sons and daughters had fared badly. Their eldest daughter had married a merchant who borrowed from her father and died in poverty; she and her second husband survived only briefly. The second daughter, Ann, was Alexander Hamilton's favorite cousin; she and her bankrupt husband had left the island. James Lytton, Jr., suffered business losses and he and his second wife absconded with slaves belonging to his first wife's estate and wound up at the Bay of Honduras. Peter Lytton sold his plantations, invested unwisely, quit the island, and returned only to commit suicide.

But for these misfortunes among his mother's relatives, Alexander Hamilton might have been absorbed into their varied enterprises of planting, commerce, and banking and never have sought the continent for his future. The ill wind blew him and America good.

Alexander's grandmother Faucette had died, and Rachel was renting out the services of three or more slave women she had received by her mother's will. Alexander may have helped in the little store, for he was quite capable of waiting on customers and keeping simple accounts. If so, his business experience began when he was ten.

For something more than two years Rachel acted as an independent provider, but then she fell ill with fever. Alexander had the same complaint. It was only after they had been in the care of a practical nurse for a week that Dr. Heering was called. He bled the patients and gave them fever medicine and emetics. "Elicks" responded to medicine and nourishing diet, but after two days Rachel died, on February 19, 1768. Relatives and friends provided the funeral next day. The nurse laid out the body, a merchant with whom Rachel had dealt furnished eggs, white bread, and cake, an uncle of the boys bought black cloth to cover the coffin, and the Town Judge advanced money for a pair of shoes for James and black veils for both brothers. The parish clerk of the English church summoned pallbearers and other mourners to the ceremony. Rachel's body was taken in a hearse to the Lytton grave plot on "Grange" plantation and was there buried by the Reverend Cecil Wray Goodchild.

The disappearance of all who would have cared, and two centuries of neglect, have all but erased the signs of that spot in the thin woods. Several who in late years made pious search for it failed. A score of graves there are distinguishable only by brick borders or covering. No headstone is standing; a broken one is thrown down, others have been taken for other uses. Which grave is Rachel's cannot be told. Neither can the sadness of the orphan boys, black-veiled beside it, be known. Gertrude Atherton, the novelist who did much to make a generation of admirers of Alexander Hamilton, erected a monument to Rachel near the plantation house on top of the hill under the ancient mahogany trees. Rachel's age, taken from the St. John's Church register, is mistaken; she was thirty-nine, not thirty-two, when she died.

The probate court found Rachel's property to consist principally of slaves: five women, a girl, and three boys. The stock in trade of salt pork, butter, and flour belonged to wholesale merchants, but the only bills presented were for recent orders, showing that Rachel had been nearly current in her payments.

Little can be judged of Rachel from her scanty personal and household effects. She had six silver spoons, seven silver teaspoons, a pair of sugar tongs, two chests, a bed with feather comforter and bolster, and thirty-four books. Her wardrobe consisted of four dresses, one red skirt, one white skirt, and a black silk sun-hat.

In preparing to divide the inheritance, the court noted that Rachel's children "are 3 sons." First was named "Peter Lewine, born in the deceased person's marriage with John Michael Lewine." Then the record designated "also two sons, namely James Hamilton and Alexander Hamilton, one 15 and the other one 13 years old, who are the same bastard children born after the deceased person's divorce from said Lewine." "Present for the two minor children and heirs was Mr. James Lytton on behalf of Peter Lytton, who is a son of the minor children's mother's sister." Lytton, recently returned from Nevis, attended the probate proceeding to protect the interest of the Hamilton boys pending the arrival of his own son, Peter Lytton, who was appointed the boys' guardian. Surely it was the older Lytton who gave the ages of the boys; he knew James and Alexander intimately, was in every way a responsible man, and often served the court as guardian of minors.

However, the young Hamiltons got nothing when the estate was settled. John Michael Lavien produced his divorce decree and claimed the net amount, 632 rigsdaler, 6 real, 5½ styver, for his son Peter, Rachel's only legitimate child. Later Peter Lavien, now twenty-two, returned from South Carolina to sign for his inheritance. The Hamilton boys' guardian bought the thirty-four books at the auction. The titles were not given, but from Alexander's writings, set down shortly afterward, we know that the small collection may have contained Machiavelli's *The Prince*, works of Pope, and some volumes of sermons.

Alexander and James had the protection of their older relatives for little more than a year, for both Lyttons died in the summer of 1769. The deterioration in the Lytton family was evident in the long wrangle over the division of James Lytton's considerable estate. Alexander receipted for sums going to his cousin Ann Lytton Venton, who was probably helping him with money when others had forsaken him.

The brothers had to earn their own keep. James was apprenticed to a carpenter, Thomas McNobeny, and Alexander worked in the business establishment of Nicholas Cruger. The choice of occupations for the two, one to be an artisan, the other a merchant, reflects their aptitudes and likes. In Alexander's earliest preserved letter (November 11, 1769), written to his young friend Edward Stevens, several circumstances appear. Alexander doubts whether he will be on St. Croix when Edward returns (from the continent or, possibly, Antigua), "for, to confess my weakness, Ned, my ambition is prevalent, so that I contemn the grovelling condition of a clerk or the like, to which my fortune, etc., condemns me, and would willingly risk my life, though not my character, to exalt my station." He had been with Cruger for some time, for the absent Edward knew of it; if Alexander had commenced as errand boy he had not tarried long in that employment, but was already concerned with accounts and correspondence. Probably he started with Cruger shortly after his mother's death, when he was thirteen.

His maturity to that point, obviously beyond his years, is linked to his education, about which almost nothing is known. As a small child he had been taught, he said, to recite the Decalogue in Hebrew in the school of a Jewess. Instruction at home by his mother and grandmother seems likely; if so they must have been good teachers, because as a young man he was able not only to speak but to write accurately in French. There is evidence that he was an eager reader. The earliest samples of his handwriting, in letters he copied for Cruger, are similar to his later script; though the characters are rounded and he was being careful, there is nothing childish in his youthful penmanship.

Cruger was involved in exporting island products and importing provisions and other plantation supplies, and Alexander's practical commercial education was of value later, when Hamilton came to transact economic affairs of a nation. As a very young man he dealt with merchants, planters, sea captains, lawyers, government officials. As he had sole responsibility for several round-trip voyages of Cruger's vessels, he had to apply knowledge and use judgment. The scene of his business training was peculiar to the Caribbean. St. Croix, along with other islands in the group, had been acquired by Denmark from France in 1733. It is roughly twenty miles long east to west and five miles wide. The island's 50,000 acres were intensively cultivated, mostly in sugar cane. In Hamilton's boyhood the population was 24,000, all but 2000 black. Christiansted, the capital, had 3500 people, three-fourths of them black. Fredericksted, on the western end of the island, had 500, only 200 white. On the plantations slaves outnumbered whites by more than twenty to one. The officials and soldiers were Danes; the other whites were mainly English and Scottish.

Christiansted was a half-mile square, its principal streets converging at the waterfront. Unfortunately, the coral reef three-quarters of a mile out blocked the entrance to the harbor for all but small, skillfully piloted vessels. Heavier cargoes were landed at Fredericksted, where the anchorage was open but unprotected. Today the waterfront of Christiansted is the same as that young Hamilton knew, it has been declared a National Historic Site. The stone houses are fortress-like to withstand the hurricanes; those remaining from French occupation are of the seventeenth century, and they are more elegant than the solid Danish structures. The little sloops and schooners tied along the wharf are not different from those which fetched and carried for Cruger.

By crown regulation the staple exports of St. Croix—muscovado sugar, molasses, and rum—went mostly to Denmark, whence came manufactured wares and some meat and fish. The colonies on continental America furnished lumber, staves, and hoops for casks, livestock, and most foodstuffs. The economy of the island, which was based on sugar, some cotton, and less coffee, was speculative, which put the planters in fealty to Dutch bankers. The planters' luxurious habits of living led to heavy debts.

Nicholas Cruger, a dozen years older than his clerk Alexander, was of an old New York merchant family with representatives elsewhere in the Caribbean and in Bristol, England. In all likelihood his close ties with New York determined that city as Alexander's destination when he was shipped to the American continent. That chance circumstance had much to do with American history. Cruger had one of the few stores in Christiansted which kept stocks always on hand; it was common for planters to turn merchants temporarily or for captains to sell cargoes from the holds of their vessels. Cruger's store was in one of two old buildings which still stand in King's Street; conflicting evidence has been resolved in local lore in favor of the larger structure nearer the waterfront.

When Cruger, years later, transferred his business to New York, he figured in public life, but, more important to us, he continued to be the firm friend and admirer of Alexander Hamilton. Historians guess that one token of his affection was a gift to Hamilton—a sheaf of seventy letters, mostly in Hamilton's hand, lifted from the records of the old store in Christiansted. All are copies; they cover eleven months, from August 1771 to July 1772. Of special value are a score of letters written by Hamilton between early November 1771 and February 1772, when he was left in charge of the business in Cruger's absence on a visit to New York. The "clarke," or "young man," as Cruger called him, lacked three months of being seventeen, but surely he had already proved his supe-

rior capacity; his readiness to be given full responsibility was
subject only to the final judgment of Cruger's "attorneys," two
older merchant associates.

All we know of Hamilton's services to Cruger is in these letters, particularly those written as proxy for his employer. They
are youthful in their eagerness, but if one did not know the
age of the writer he would suppose them the work of a mature
man, perhaps Cruger himself. Doubtless it was the capability
Alexander displayed in this interval of Cruger's absence that
won him his chance in life. His famous letter to his father describing the hurricane the following autumn was a striking
single performance, but the demonstration of day by day ac-
complishment over a period of months was likely what rallied
supporters of his adventure on the continent.

Alexander immediately finished off old business and began
with new, keeping Cruger in New York informed of all he did.
He reported that he had "sold about 30 bbls flour more &
Collected a little more money from different people." He was
impressed with the need of quick sale: "Your Philadelphia
flour is . . . of a most swarthy complexion—& withal very un-
tractable; the Bakers complain that they cannot by any means
get it to rise. . . . I have observ'd a kind of worm . . . about
the surface—which is an indication of age—it could not have
been very new when shipd." Also, the market was over-
stocked; he was prepared to accept eight pieces of eight from
any buyer of good credit who would take forty or fifty barrels.

Soon he dispatched Captain William Newton in the *Thunderbolt* to Tileman Cruger at Curaçao. He took pains to salvage
casks and staves on board and to give Newton defense against
the Spanish patrols when he continued to Venezuela for
mules. "Captain Newton must arm with you," Alexander told
Tileman, "as he could not so conveniently do it here. Give me
leave to hint . . . that you cannot be too particular in your instructions to him. I think he seems to lack experience in such
voyages." On the other hand, perhaps the Guarda Costas were

a competitor's trick. The captain of a large sloop with seventy mules from the Main "talks largely of Danger & Difficultys upon the Coast—but no doubt exaggerates a good deal by way of stimulation."

There was "not a moment of time to spare" in speeding Newton's voyage, for the crops were forward. Alexander wrote three business letters one Sunday. He was pressing because the new *Thunderbolt*, though "a fine vessel indeed," was "not so swift as she ought to be."

Alexander's next to Nicholas Cruger in New York was cheerful. He had sold candles, hoops, codfish, alewives. The new superfine flour so delighted the bakers that he thought of raising its price. "Believe me Sir I Dun as hard as is proper." But this was sunshine before the cloud. He was compelled to inform Tileman Cruger: "Two days ago Capt. Newton delivered me . . . 41 mules in such order that I have been obliged to send all of them to pasture—and . . . I expect at least a third will die—the highest offer made me for 20 of the best was 70 ps [pieces of eight]—whereas if they had been in good order I could readily have obtained £40 round. . . ." Seven of Newton's mules had died on the slow passage; on landing eight could hardly stand, "& in spite of the greatest care 4 of them are now in Limbo."

Nothing daunted, Newton was commanded back with codfish, bread, and rum, and with warnings to take in enough grass to feed sixty mules on return from the Spanish Main. Alexander must have been pleased to have Nicholas Cruger present to welcome the *Thunderbolt* with fine mules that sold for £36 average. Secretary of the Treasury Hamilton learned early all about frauds on the customs, and how to guard against them. Cruger freighted his vessel with sugar and cotton for New York, and cautioned the consignees, "No. 1 to 6 ST are . . . Hhds Clay'd Sugars, that you'll have carted up immediately for fear of a Discovery . . . have them Enter'd paying the same Duty as Muscovado." And another time he explained that to evade the import duty of 25 per cent on rye flour, "we enter it as corn meal and give the [tide] waiter a fee. . . ." The copy of this is in Hamilton's hand.

Alexander, while in Cruger's employ, wrote of other things besides smoked fish and wormy flour. In the spring of 1771 the young man's fancy turned to thoughts of love, but quite lightly and in images only. Verses signed "A.H." with an apology for his youth, were published in the island newspaper. The original of his pastoral may have been any one of the mannered lyrics in favor at the time:

> In yonder mead my love I found
>   Beside a murm'ring brook reclin'd;
> Her pretty lambkins dancing round
>   Secure in harmless bliss.
> I bad the waters gently glide
>   And vainly hush'd the heedless wind,
> Then, softly kneeling by her side
>   I stole a silent kiss—

There is more, a bit more carnal. Other rhymes describe a capricious mistress. Throughout his life, from time to time, Hamilton indulged his muse. Most of his lines have not survived, with small loss, unless, perhaps, they had some biographical value.

He promptly shifted from poetry to politics, for a week after romping with his love and her lambkins he offered in the newspaper "Rules for Statesmen." He pretended to be a correspondent in London; from "some years gleaning from Machiavel, Puffendorf, &c," he advised "by what means a Premier may act most to the honour of his Prince, and the enlargement of his own power." His earliest views of authority were his latest. He praised the British system of confiding in "a Prime Minister like a Commander in Chief; . . . I think this wise regulation a wholesome restraint on the people, [whose] turbulence, at times, . . . require[s] a Dictator."

Alexander's apprenticeship with Cruger was cut off by the hurricane that desolated St. Croix at the end of August 1772. The storm, which lasted six hours, was the most violent in memory. The sea rose a dozen feet, casting vessels on shore; thirty people were killed; crops were uprooted. The King's Magazine at Christiansted sold provisions at reduced prices; emergency loans were to be opened at Copenhagen and Amsterdam, and help was expected from North America.

On the Sunday following the hurricane, in the midst of dire distress, the Presbyterian minister, the Reverend Hugh Knox, preached to the community. Inevitably, he rehearsed the wrath of the Almighty and the need of human repentance. With Knox's exhortation ringing in his ears, Alexander Hamilton wrote to his father a description of the catastrophe, with appropriate reflections. His purple prose outdid the clergyman's sermon, though Alexander had the excuse that he was impressing one who had not experienced the terror. "Good God! what horror and destruction. . . . It seemed as if a total dissolution of nature was taking place. The roaring of the sea and wind—fiery meteors flying about in the air—the prodigious glare of almost perpetual lightning . . . the ear-piercing shrieks of the distressed, were sufficient to strike astonishment into Angels." Then came his "self-discourse. 'Where now, oh! vile worm, is all thy boasted fortitude and resolution? What is become of thy arrogance and self-sufficency? . . . how contemptible you now appear . . . Oh! impotent presumptuous fool! How durst thou offend that Omnipotence, whose nod alone were sufficient to quell the destruction that hovers over thee, or crush thee into atoms?' " He was moved to pity for "tender infancy pinched with hunger and hanging on the mother's knee for food! . . . her poverty denies relief . . . her heart is bursting—the tears gush down her cheeks."

Doubtless Alexander showed his imitative letter to Knox, for that clergyman, at length overcoming the author's objections, published it in the *Royal Danish-American Gazette* as the work

of "a Youth of this Island." As no one had earlier appreciation
of Alexander's promise or fuller pride in his after-career, Knox
should be identified at this point. He came to America from
northern Ireland, taught school in Delaware, graduated from
the College of New Jersey (Princeton), and remained there for
an additional year of theological study with President Aaron
Burr, the father of Hamilton's enemy. Knox was ordained by
the New York Presbytery in 1755 (the year Hamilton was born)
and was then dispatched to the Dutch Reformed church in the
island of Saba, Netherlands West Indies. For seventeen years
in this singularly isolated and tiny community he industriously published devotional works and remained in active correspondence with religious colleagues on the American continent.

Knox visited St. Croix in the autumn of 1771 and, in May of
the following year, in response to a cordial invitation, he became minister of the Presbyterian church there. A quick sympathy ran between him and the aspiring youth in Cruger's
store. Knox loaned Alexander books and gave him welcome
intellectual companionship. He showed Alexander's hurricane
letter around to friends, with the proposal that the youth
should be sent to the continent for his education. The disaster
had stirred generosity. The plan was to ship island products to
New York to be sold for Alexander's benefit. Probable contrib-
utors were Nicholas Cruger, Cruger's sometime partner Cor-
nelius Kortright, and Town Captain DeNully, who had befriended Rachel in years past. The merchant Thomas Stevens,
father of Alexander's friend Edward, may have helped; Edward was already studying in New York and Alexander seems
to have been at times a guest in the Stevens home in Christiansted. James Towers, the probate judge, and Governor Van
Roepstorff may have chipped in. Alexander's cousin Ann Venton in all likelihood shared what came to her from her father
James Lytton's estate, but other relatives were unable to assist.

Hugh Knox wrote to Hamilton long afterward, "I have

always had a just & secret pride in having advised you to go to America, & in having recommended you to some [of] my old friends there." This was a modest statement of Knox's part in the charitable enterprise. Hamilton sailed in September or October 1772, and surely Knox, Cruger, and others named were at the wharf to bid him Godspeed. This was Hamilton's permanent farewell to his island home, for once he arrived on the continent he never left it. Knox, having been a teacher, knew that his protégé would need preparatory schooling before he could enter college, but in other respects Alexander was already equipped with experience and independence of action rare in one of his years. His upbringing in an isolated society fitted him to view the continental colonies with detachment, and his contacts on St. Croix with the principal persons of the island enabled him to be easy in the presence of their more important counterparts on the mainland.

The fact that Alexander landed at Boston rather than New York indicates that his friends put him on the first vessel available. "Waters from St. Croix" reached the New England port some time before October 22 and may have brought Alexander as a passenger.

Chapter 2

STUDENT INTO SOLDIER

In Boston young Hamilton was in the right place to witness the rising spirit of American rebellion. During the few days he may have tarried there the removal of the judges from popular control fetched the "Freeholders and other Inhabitants" to Faneuil Hall "to Enquire into . . . a Report . . . that Salaries are annexed to the Offices of the Judges of the Superior Court . . . whereby they are rendered Independent of the Grants of the General Assembly . . . contrary to . . . invariable Usage." A less considered protest against royal authority was made by "a mob of upwards a thousand people Hallooing in the street" after they had tarred and feathered an informer and burned contraband at the beacon on the Common. On the other hand, "Hon. Col. Hancock" commanded his uniformed company of cadets in evolutions in honor of the thirteenth anniversary of George III's accession to the throne. Undoubtedly Alexander approved of the demonstration of Hancock, not that of the hallooers, for he came to the continent with crown loyalties.

Whether Alexander reached New York by vessel or by Nicholas Green's "first stage coach that ever was improv'd on the Road," he presented himself at the countinghouse of Kort-right & Company, Cruger's friends, to which West Indian sugar was to be consigned for his benefit. He was placed in the care of Hercules Mulligan, younger bachelor brother of one of the partners. Hercules's tailor and haberdasher shop and home were in Water Street, "next door to Philip Rhinelander's china store, between Burling's Slip and the Fly Market." Here Alexander must have lodged in the few days before he moved over to New Jersey. Mulligan took him to meet Dr. John Rodgers and the Reverend John Mason, leading Presbyterian clergymen of the city, to whom Hugh Knox had given him let-ters soliciting their good offices for the young stranger. He also had letters addressed to Elias Boudinot and William Living-ston, principal Presbyterian laymen of Elizabethtown, New Jersey. Under these auspices Alexander was placed in the academy at Elizabethtown to prepare for college, which in his case meant acquiring a fair knowledge of Latin and Greek and of mathematics beyond arithmetic.

The academy was a product of the Presbyterian community. The building was on the grounds of the Presbyterian church, of which the Reverend James Caldwell was pastor. The head-master was Francis Barber, a Princeton graduate. Boudinot and Livingston were trustees. Friends and relatives of these figures were all of the same stripe in religion, dissenters against the Anglican church, of which Dr. Thomas Bradbury Chandler was rector. The Presbyterians, at the time Alexander was in their care, were prepared to be patriots in the coming break from the mother country, but they were still hoping for conciliation and would seek independence for America only as a last resort. Chandler and his supporters were assertive loyal-ists.

During his year of study in Barber's academy, Alexander was often a guest in the homes of Livingston and Boudinot, especially of the latter, probably for months at a time. His no-table piety at this stage would have sat him on Sundays before

Caldwell, from whose pulpit flowed emotional "New Lights" eloquence. Boudinot was painfully religious, if anything about that warmhearted man can be called painful. Alexander could not have had sponsors more intelligent and friendly for his introduction to America. He was impressed with their merits and he and they worked affectionately together in after years in the national arena.

Alexander cut through his studies; after staying up until midnight with his books he would be seen early next morning in the churchyard, still getting his lessons. In less than a year Barber wrote Mulligan that his pupil was prepared for college. Alexander "came to N.Y.," Mulligan recorded, "and told me he preferred Princeton to King's Colledge because it was more republican." Evidently, the young man had by now given over his royalist leanings. All of his associations were with Princeton people; he knew Elizabethtown boys who were studying at Princeton, and they would report on debates there. President John Witherspoon boasted of Princeton's democratic atmosphere; he had numerous students from the West Indies and was angling for more. King's College in New York, on the other hand, was Anglican and loyalist. The president of King's College was Myles Cooper, an Oxford graduate who had been chosen for his post in America by the Archbishop of Canterbury. Morning and evening, Cooper intoned prayers to which his students made responses. A year after this Cooper, in a remonstrance against the Continental Congress, blasted "these rebellious Republicans, . . . hairbrained fanaticks, as mad . . . as the ANABAPTISTS OF MUNSTER."

So Mulligan took Alexander to Princeton and introduced him to President Witherspoon. Witherspoon's house is still there, just as it was then, with the little study at the back. In that study the doctor gave Alexander an oral examination. He was quickly convinced that the young applicant was fully fit to enter the college. Then Hamilton explained that he wished to proceed on his own plan of acceleration, without respect to the formal program, but taking examinations as fast as he could advance from class to class. This was a poser for Witherspoon; he would have to refer the unusual request to the trustees. In a fortnight Mulligan was informed that usage of the college forbade such an expeditious scheme; Witherspoon was sorry, for he was sure Alexander would do honor to any seminary that educated him.

So Hercules offered his protégé to King's, in spite of the strictures Livingston had visited upon it for "tincturing the minds of the students" with slavish sentiments with which they would betimes govern the community. If Alexander had thrown in his lot with Princeton he might have become a citizen of New Jersey. In public life he would have been of the circle of Livingston, Boudinot, Witherspoon, Stockton, Abraham Clark, Paterson, and other excellent Jerseymen. But New York was a better base for his future operations and influence, for New York's resources were greater and its geographical situation was superior for a champion of national unity. The small state across the river had its company of patriots, but so did New York—James Duane, Philip Schuyler, Alexander McDougall, R. R. Livingston, Egbert Benson, John Lamb, James Kent, and more. As a New Yorker, Hamilton did not lose the support of his first friends of New Jersey.

Though there is conflict in the recollections, set down many years later, of those who knew Alexander as a student, he probably entered King's College in the autumn of 1773 as a special student, then was fully matriculated in 1774, perhaps in the sophomore class. Hamilton had objected in advance to the aristocratic and conservative character of King's, but he and President Cooper, eighteen years his senior, actually had much in common. Each had good looks, facility in expression, a liking for elegance of dress and manner.

Hamilton's friend and roommate at King's recalled that Hamilton originally intended to become a physician, and therefore regularly attended the anatomical lectures of Dr. Samuel Clossy. Hugh Knox, Alexander's patron on St. Croix, was a medical man as well as a minister, and young Edward Stevens, Alexander's boyhood companion, then at King's, intended to study medicine in Edinburgh University. But Hamilton soon abandoned "the Science of Physic" for the fields of political economy, politics, and law. In his second year at King's he studied mathematics as a private pupil with Professor Robert Harpur, who tutored many outside of the classroom. A surviving exercise book of Samuel Bayard, a student who was in Harpur's charge at the same time as Alexander, shows a rapid progress from principles to applications in discount, partners' shares, exchange of currencies, and surveying.

President Cooper had rules for the sake of rules, but Hamilton does not appear in the "Book of Misdemeanours," though half of his classmates do. They ran afoul of the college discipline. Thus one Moncrieffe was restricted to the campus but broke through confinement, for which further disobedience he was to "make public Acknowledgments, in the Chapel and to translate N°s 255, 256, of the Spectator into Latin." He was locked in for these exercises, but friends broke down his door; he loosed himself forever and disappeared from the records. Hamilton was still religiously devoted, which made prayers morning and evening and church twice on Sunday congenial. He got down on his knees even after he entered the army, but thereafter no more is heard of his spiritual observance until near his death.

Hamilton, Troup, Stevens, Nicolls, and other close friends formed a weekly club for improvement in writing and debating. Alexander's performances were especially remembered; he read there parts of his political pieces which became celebrated. Some young men of the town joined this society, among them Nicholas Fish, who had left his studies at Princeton to read law with John Morin Scott in New York. Fish and others later joined the collegians in military drill.

The library of King's was the largest Hamilton had met. While many of the volumes, often given by their authors, were theological treatises or sectarian tracts, numbers of others were suited to Hamilton's purpose. Hutchinson's *History of Massachusetts-Bay* (Boston, 1764) and *A New and General Biographical Dictionary* (London, 1761–62, 11 volumes) survived the pillage and destruction of the Revolution. It is safe to say that works referred to or quoted in the pamphlets Hamilton wrote while he was in King's were in the college library. Such were Grotius, Puffendorf, Locke, Montesquieu, Berlamqui, Blackstone, Postlethwayt, Hume, Lex Mercatoria, recent Parliamentary debates and acts, colonial charters, acts of the General Assembly of New York, the Pennsylvania Farmer, Johnson's dictionary, and an account of the wars of Charles XII and Peter the Great.

Several intimates spoke of Hamilton contributing political pieces to the New York newspapers while he was a student in King's. John Jay in December 1775 had been without Holt's *New York Journal* for three months, so inquired of McDougall whether Hamilton was still writing in that sheet. As the volunteered letters and essays were regularly signed only with a pen name, it is not possible to identify Hamilton's arguments.

The New York colony was not as forward in revolutionary propaganda and acts as were New England, Virginia, and South Carolina. The close ties of its port with Britain, its exposed position, its varied population, and its undeveloped local government were reasons. New York was catching up when, after the Boston Tea Party, the conservative standing Committee of 51 nominated five delegates to the Continental Congress which was to assemble in Philadelphia in September 1774. The militant minority put up a slate of Isaac Low, James Duane, Philip Livingston, John Morin Scott, and Alexander McDougall, but Scott and McDougall, the most vehement protesters, were voted down, and John Alsop and John Jay were chosen instead. The regular committee appointed noon on

July 7 at the City Hall as the time and place for the convening of freeholders to consider the nominees.

But the Sons of Liberty and other Whiggish citizens huddled, and they issued handbills calling for a popular meeting in "the Fields" (now City Hall Park) at six o'clock in the afternoon of July 6, the day before that of the smaller, official conclave. This would attract masses of mechanics who would gather after work to the vicinity of the liberty pole. The "great meeting in the Fields" fetched Alexander Hamilton into American public life. A neighbor encountered Alexander walking under the trees of Batteau Street (now Dey Street, and treeless), talking to himself in an undertone. Struck by the collegian's conversation, the citizen urged him to mount the platform that afternoon. Alexander did not consent, but he listened in the crowd as McDougall, the chairman, castigated "vile arts used by the enemies of America."

At an opportune moment Alexander sprang up beside the chairman. At first he faltered for words, and some called out that he should stand down, but quickly his self-possession returned. He held the audience while he reinforced the resolves that denounced the act closing the port of Boston, cried out against unconstitutional parliamentary taxes, and called for an embargo on imports from and exports to Britain until grievances were redressed. He directed New York delegates to the coming Congress to support these objects. Hamilton's volunteer outburst won him the friendship of older champions such as McDougall, Lamb, Willett, and others with whom he was connected afterward.

Within six months our collegian was publishing replies to the loyalist pamphlets of the "Westchester Farmer" (Samuel Seabury). His elders did not suspect the author of these cogent rebuttals of the practiced polemicist who was twice Alexander's age. His anonymous pamphlets were attributed to patriots long in the public eye, men such as John Jay. In *Free Thoughts, on the Proceedings of the Continental Congress,* Seabury addressed himself to New York. He aimed to produce division in all quarters. He warned farmers against the certainty that, once imports were restricted, merchants would exact unconscionable profits. The West Indies would supply themselves with flour, lumber, and horses from elsewhere. Congress had betrayed the colonies. Farmers should rely on their own New York General Assembly and eschew the *ad hoc* congress and its committees. "Will you submit to them . . . ? . . . by him that made me, I will not—No, if I must be enslaved, let it be by a King at least, and not by a parcel of upstart lawless Committee-men. If I must be devoured, let me be devoured by the jaws of a lion, and not *gnawed* to death by rats and vermin."

Hamilton replied with his *Full Vindication . . . of Congress,* in which he promised to detect the Farmer in all of his artifices. The Congress was protecting the lives and properties of the colonists, assured to them by the British constitution and by their own charters. Further petitions, urged by the Farmer, would be fruitless. Withholding trade was the alternative to armed resistance. If the mother country dared to stop our whole trade, manufactures would "take root among us" and "pave the way . . . to the . . . grandeur and glory of America." His knowledge of the West Indies enabled him to deny that those islands had the capacity to feed themselves and to state that they could not be supplied from Canada. This first pamphlet was not Hamilton's best, for he exaggerated in parts, reducing his effectiveness, and his banter was heavy-handed.

Seabury (who, incidentally, was not a farmer at all) answered with renewed spirit in his *View of the Controversy.* Ironically, he took four positions which Hamilton himself later espoused. Congress enjoyed no immunity against criticism. General concerns could not be confided to the individual colonies, but came under the jurisdiction of Parliament. Responsibility to govern entailed the right to tax. Lastly, it was mistaken to argue that Parliament would take a pound as readily as a penny; confidence must be reposed in the integrity and wisdom of government. Hamilton had merited these corrections. Seabury also forecast trade rivalries between the colonies should Parliament's regulation be withdrawn. For the rest, the Farmer went astray. He scouted the notion that colonists could manufacture their own clothing. He made out that Hamilton was hostile to the West Indies.

Hamilton's *Farmer Refuted* closed the controversy with Seabury. Hamilton dropped the debater's retort for sober reasoning. He had applied himself to the subject of natural law, on which his ideas, Seabury charged, were superficial. Hamilton believed, with Blackstone, that morality was before law, not, as Hobbes claimed, defined by human government. Accepting Seabury's admonition, he avowed his attachment to civil rights. He confined sovereignty over the colonies to the crown; as the colonies were outside of the realm, Parliament could not control them. However, he erred in saying there was no need of general laws for all the colonies; perhaps he did not know of the incentives to the abortive Albany Plan of 1754.

Hamilton did better in his perception of the resources of America and of the development they would undergo. Self-interest was the cement of society, as Adam Smith was soon to declare, but young Hamilton would have government direct selfish means to useful social ends.

Having crossed verbal swords with the Tory Seabury, Hamilton promptly protected the person of the Tory president of King's College, Myles Cooper. Cooper and several other prominent New York men who had given offense to patriots had been menaced in a newspaper publication signed "Three Millions." The threat was that Americans would no longer be content with hanging villains in effigy, and the obnoxious gentry were advised to "Fly for your lives."

In May 1775, at a late hour of night, a mob of hundreds broke down the college gate. They made for the college building where Dr. Cooper lodged, with the intention of tarring and feathering him or doing him greater harm. Hamilton and his friend Troup ran ahead, and Hamilton mounted the stoop and harangued the rioters. They must not bring "disgrace . . . on the cause of liberty . . . of which they avowed themselves to be the champions." The short delay gave Dr. Cooper time to escape by the back way. Another of his students accompanied him to the banks of the Hudson and so he worked around to the house of a friend. Soon he took refuge on *Kingfisher*, a warship, and sailed for England.

Foiled in the descent upon Cooper, the mob assailed the home and shop of the Tory printer, James Rivington, in Hanover Square. He, too, fled to *Kingfisher*, and there remained for some days before venturing to return to his house. A second attack six months later stopped his paper, and he went to England. Captain Isaac Sears of the Sons of Liberty came down with mounted men from Connecticut to punish Tories whom New Yorkers had let off too lightly. Samuel Seabury, Hamilton's pamphleteering antagonist, was arrested at Westchester and sent back to New Haven and prison. The troopers lined up in front of Rivington's shop with bayonets fixed while a detachment rifled his types. As the raiders withdrew they were cheered by citizens near the Coffee House.

Hamilton, in a long letter, protested to John Jay, who was sitting in the Continental Congress. He pointed out that one colony should not presume to discipline another. "The same state of the passions which fits the multitude . . . for opposition to tyranny and oppression . . . naturally leads them to a contempt . . . of all authority." Hamilton regretted whatever hampered total colonial resistance. Suspicions between New England and New York were rife; New York loyalists would be bolstered if they could complain of intervention from Connecticut. The letter failed to resent the offense to freedom of the press as such.

Lieutenant Governor Colden had retired to his country retreat on Long Island because, he informed Lord Dartmouth, the colonial secretary, "When Congresses and Committees had taken the entire direction of the Government, it was extremely disagreeable to Me to remain as Spectator of the . . . confusions in Town, when I had it not in my Power to prevent." And, he added, "The Spirit of arming, and military Parade still runs high in the City[.] Several companies are . . . well armed and cloathed in uniform."

One of the uniformed companies was that joined by Hamilton, Troup, Fish, and numbers of their friends. They drilled every morning in St. George's churchyard under Major Edward Fleming, who had been adjutant of a British regiment. The volunteers wore short green coats and round leather caps with metal plates proclaiming their prowess, but whether the plates read "Hearts of Oak," "Bold Foresters," or "Corsicans" is uncertain. Hamilton's companions remembered that he was always present, zealous in practice, and "became exceedingly expert in the manual exercise." Nor was this all play-acting. The Provincial Congress ordered the guns hauled from Fort George to a place of safety in the town. On August 23, 1775, near midnight, Hamilton's company, as part of Colonel John Lasher's battalion, and artillerymen under Captain John Lamb began removing the cannon. The garrison of the fort had been transferred to *Asia,* man-of-war, but Captain Vanderput had sent a boat to lie near the Battery to report. Some guns had been dragged off when a musket was fired from the boat as a signal to *Asia.* The American militia, thinking that the fire was directed at them, discharged their pieces and killed one man in the retreating barge.

Thereat *Asia* sent single shots and then a broadside at the Battery. Some balls went wild, one crashing through the top story of Fraunces' Tavern. Hamilton eagerly seized a drag-rope from the hands of Hercules Mulligan, as though he were more competent than his giant friend. All twenty-one of the mounted nine-pounders were successfully got off.

Hamilton now went from volunteer service to regular military duty. When the Provincial Congress, in January 1776, required that an artillery company be raised for defense of the colony, Hamilton sought the influence of McDougall to procure the command. The acquaintance they had formed at the mass meeting in the Fields eighteen months earlier had ripened. John Jay, in the Congress, put forward McDougall's request that Hamilton be appointed captain of the artillery company. In hopes of this opportunity, Hamilton had been studying gunnery, and Captain Stephen Badlam gave his certificate that he had examined Hamilton and found him qualified; thereupon his appointment was ordered, March 14, 1776.

Hamilton was recruiting his men when his New Jersey patron, Elias Boudinot, besought Lord Stirling,* then in command in New York City, to take the young captain on as aide-de-camp. Stirling, who had doubtless known Alexander at Elizabethtown, was agreeable, but Hamilton, though appreciative of the offer, declined in favor of retaining his field command. This was probably fortunate, because when he did take a staff position it was with General Washington, and that led on to his action in the siege of Yorktown.

The Province of New York, unlike the Continental Congress, did not furnish uniforms to those enlisting in its units. Captain Hamilton, to spur his recruiting, used either his second and last remittance from St. Croix or his credit to equip his men, and was reimbursed by deductions from the soldiers' pay. Alsop and Hunt delivered seventy-five pairs of buckskin breeches between March and July 1776. As the price rose from 36 to 48 shillings each in the interval, Hamilton had old breeches repaired. The young captain paid 64s. for his own breeches and, similarly, demanded superior shoes for himself. (Through his life he followed Polonius's direction, "Costly thy

* William Alexander's claim to the title was disallowed by the House of Lords, but was accorded to him in America. He was a neighbor of Boudinot's in New Jersey.

habit as thy purse can buy.") He was no less insistent that
enlisted men should have complete uniforms in which they
could take pride. His artillerymen wore blue coats with buff
cuffs and facings, like those of Captain Lamb's continental
company.

His first assignment, as soon as his company was of sufficient strength, was to guard the colony records, relieving
continental troops who served at greater charge, and he welcomed it. However, he respectfully complained to the Provincial Congress of the difference between the wages of his men
and those of the continentals; this was against his company's
articles, and it was hard for him "to get a single recruit" while
Captain Bauman enlisted at the higher scale. Could he be allowed the small "actual expenses" of sending recruiting
officers into the country? Also, if his men could have the frock
given other troops as a bounty they could save their uniforms
while on fatigue. His requests were granted. By October 1776
his company numbered sixty-eight officers and men. Their
names were predominantly English, with some Irish, Scottish,
and Dutch. Many could not write their names; they made their
marks in the pay book. Over the weeks a few deserted, a few
were confined to the guard house.

All troops in New York City were laboring on the defenses
from sun to sun. This exhausting work left little time or inclination for drill, but testimony is that captain Hamilton contrived to train his company to be a model of performance. Nor
could he permit discrimination in rations, a third less than the
remainder of the army received. In his application to the New
York Congress for correction he enclosed the standard "rates
of rations."

Captain Hamilton set a precedent by persuading the New
York Congress to promote from the ranks to fill vacancies in
the officer corps. He recommended that Thomas Thompson,
the first sergeant, be made a lieutenant; he "has discharged
his duty in the present station with uncommon fidelity . . .

and expertness . . . and his advancement will be a great encouragement . . . to my company in particular, and will be an animating example to all men of merit to whose knowledge it comes." After some inquiry, the Provincial Congress ordered the promotion and published in the newspapers the rule it had adopted. Thompson's deserts were confirmed by further advancement; he was killed leading his men in a charge in the battle of Springfield.

Hamilton's artillery was one of Lasher's Independent Companies, which, early in March 1776, began constructing the principal fort of the city's defenses. It was on Bayard's Hill (at the intersection of what are now Canal and Mulberry Streets), an irregular heptagonal earthwork. In mid-May General Washington thanked the fatigue parties "for their masterly manner of executing the work." This redoubt overlooked the city, which then had 4000 houses and 25,000 population and was limited to the southern tip of Manhattan, below Chambers Street. The redoubt mounted twelve six-pounders and was manned by two commissioned officers, four noncommissioned, and twenty privates.

It was on Bayard's Hill that Hamilton was stationed during the battle of Long Island, August 27–29. He had no active part in the disastrous defeat which, in the sequel, lost to the Americans for the remainder of the war all of the territory reaching up to White Plains. After their victory on Long Island, General Howe and his brother the Admiral waited a fortnight before assailing Manhattan. General Nathanael Greene was for abandoning Manhattan and burning the town to deprive the enemy of a most advantageous base. Congress was opposed, and Washington distributed his troops so as to delay British possession of the island. Hamilton's artillery company was among the 5000 men kept on lower Manhattan; 9000 were at Kingsbridge, at the northern extremity, and 6000 were in the space between.

The shameful scamper of American militia at Kip's Bay the

morning of September 15 was the prelude to complete withdrawal. As soon as the British landed Washington galloped
down from Harlem, but in spite of furious efforts he could not
stop the panic rout. This necessitated evacuation of lower
Manhattan. General Israel Putnam, in command, was making
for what is now the upper West Side. Colonel Henry Knox
prepared to follow when he found his own troops, and others,
cut off. He entered Fort Bunker (Bayard's) Hill, Hamilton with
him, resolved to make a desperate stand. However, Major
Aaron Burr, Putnam's aide, came by and told that the way was
open to the Bloomingdale Road. In a march of eight miles in
rain, dragging the guns, all escaped to Harlem Heights by
nightfall. Exhausted, they could only drop down behind the
entrenchments.

Though the Americans had disgraced themselves at Kip's
Bay, they behaved well in the little battle of Harlem Heights.
A chance encounter of patrols was enlarged into a fight in
which the king's troops were driven smartly up the slope to
the crest where Columbia University now stands. As British
reinforcements were coming up, Washington let well enough
alone and withdrew his men. There is no reason to suppose
that Hamilton's company was in this sharp, brief exchange,
though it has been said that at Harlem he first came to the attention of the Commander in Chief, who praised the efficiency
of his men in throwing up earthworks. That may have happened, but the story that Washington invited the young captain to his marquée and marked him as eligible for the headquarters staff is probably not true. Hamilton's swift discharges
at the battle of Trenton would be more apt to take Washington's eye.

On October 9 enemy frigates broke through obstructions in
the Hudson, and three days later a fleet landed Howe's troops
on Throgs Neck, in Westchester. Thus menaced before and
behind, Washington moved his army northward, to the vicinity of White Plains. No contemporary account puts Hamilton's

artillery in the battle on Chatterton's Hill there. This is just as well for his reputation, as the one gun ordered to play on the enemy ascending the slope was poorly served; after two discharges the artillerymen fled.

On November 10–11, Hamilton and his company marched with the main army to Peekskill, preparatory to crossing into New Jersey. General Charles Lee was left in command at North Castle (now North White Plains), General William Heath guarded the Highlands, and Washington would try to prevent the enemy from reaching Philadelphia.

The history of failure and retreat in New York was capped by the unconditional surrender of Fort Washington, on the east bank of the Hudson near the northern end of Manhattan island. The Commander in Chief's judgment told him that this stronghold and its companion, Fort Lee, on the Palisades to the west, were useless, since the enemy had demonstrated their capacity to ascend the river. But General Nathanael Greene, commanding at Lee, and Colonel Magaw at Fort Washington, insisted that those places could be held, and Washington, in fatigue of mind, allowed himself to be persuaded to their optimism. He was wrong. The British took 2850 soldiers prisoner and captured all the cannon, arms, ammunition, and supplies. American dejection at this defeat was deepened when a few days later Lord Cornwallis crossed the river and descended on Fort Lee. Washington dashed there from Hackensack in time to lead out the garrison, but large stores of provisions, tents, and entrenching tools were left to the enemy. These supplies were sadly missed in the retreat of Washington's army across New Jersey.

This was as dreary an episode as the Americans endured. Washington's force, only 3000 men, dwindled by the day as enlistments expired and discouraged troops deserted outright. Governor Livingston appealed to Jerseymen to take up arms in their defense, but they took General Howe's British protections instead. With Cornwallis's army pursuing, Washington

directed General Charles Lee to cross to New Jersey with reinforcements desperately needed. Lee then gave evidence of the
defection that marked his conduct thenceforth. He made every
excuse for disobeying Washington's order. He finally started
off, at a snail's pace, and he himself was captured at Basking
Ridge, while yet a distance from his superior. General
John Sullivan hurried Lee's contingent forward, but they
were too late for Washington's immediate need.

Washington had just crossed the Raritan into New Brunswick when Cornwallis's army appeared on the bluffs on the
opposite side of the stream. Captain Hamilton posted his two
field pieces on high ground and kept up a fusillade while the
Americans proceeded to Princeton. Hamilton then joined the
retreat. This was when his absorption struck "a veteran officer" who "noticed a youth, a mere stripling, small, slender,
almost delicate in frame, marching . . . with a cocked hat
pulled down over his eyes, apparently lost in thought, with
his hand resting on a cannon, and every now and then patting
it, as if it were a favorite horse or a pet plaything."

Hamilton was under fire on the Raritan, but greater danger
and exploit awaited him at Trenton. A fortnight earlier Washington had confided that, unless a new army was recruited, "I
think the game will be pretty well up." Fortunately, his force
had been increased on the west side of the Delaware; Sullivan
had arrived with Lee's troops, General Gates had added a
smaller number, and Philadelphia had furnished recruits.
General Howe had posted a few regiments of Hessians at
Trenton, on the east bank of the Delaware, but they were unsupported and in an exposed position. Washington determined to reverse the American train of defeats and pluck up
the sinking spirits of the country by making a surprise attack
on the Trenton garrison on Christmas night, 1776. Those of
Washington's critics who thought him lacking in initiative had
to make exception of that stroke. The place where the army

passed over the river is called to this day "Washington's Crossing." Floating cakes of ice would have overset the heavily laden boats but for the skill of Colonel Glover's Marblehead watermen. After brief halt at McKonkey's ferry house, the men endured the punishment of a nine-mile march through snow and stinging sleet to Trenton. They covered the locks of their muskets with their coat lapels to keep them dry. The column marched three miles, then divided at Birmingham. Hamilton's battery, with those of Forrest and Bauman, took the upper, or Scotch, road under General Greene; the right wing, under General Sullivan, with other batteries, paralleled them on the river road.

Delay of the attack—it was broad day when the Americans approached the town—did not prevent the surprise. Only when the Hessian pickets were driven in from their posts was Colonel Johan Rall alerted to tumble his troops out of their quarters and form them for the defense. The Hessians responded with spirit, but they were trapped in the narrow streets and beset by musket fire from the buildings. Soon Hamilton planted his battery on the high ground at the head of King Street and Captain Thomas Forrest similarly commanded the length of Queen Street. The enemy, in close ranks, were torn to pieces. Colonel Rall fell from his horse with mortal wounds. Some escaped toward Bordentown; the remainder who had not been killed or wounded were surrounded and captured. Washington returned across the Delaware with 900 prisoners after a tour of duty lasting thirty-six hours.

In spite of the prospect of having a depleted force when the enlistments of most of the continentals expired on December 31, Washington determined to strike another blow in New Jersey. Colonel Cadwalader had already occupied key positions east of the river. The continentals, for a bounty of $10 per man, agreed to extend their service for six weeks. This was in response to the Commander in Chief's appeal, which was reinforced by the oratory of Quartermaster General Thomas Mifflin. Congress gave Washington autocratic power to raise troops and commandeer supplies for six months.

Lord Cornwallis arrived at Trenton with 8000 troops, but he delayed attack on the Americans, who lay in a perilous position between Assunpink creek and the river. A council of war hit on a stratagem to extricate Washington's army. This was to leave campfires blazing with a few men to be seen passing backward and forward before them to deceive the enemy. At one o'clock in the morning of January 3 the artillery was hitched and the troops fell in for a silent detour of the British. The way was by a new woods road toward Princeton.

When the sun rose over the frosted fields, Lieutenant Colonel Mawhood, leading his men toward Trenton, was astonished to see the American army before him. The British triumphed in the opening minutes of the battle. General Hugh Mercer fell with multiple wounds, and his column broke and ran; their flight demoralized Cadwalader's militia, coming to the support. It is not known whether Hamilton's were the "two pieces of artillery [which] stood their ground and were served with great skill and bravery." Then Washington exposed himself in a murderous fire to rally his men and put the enemy to rout.

The action continued briefly in the village of Princeton, where British soldiers retreated into the college building, Nassau Hall. The story is that Hamilton's battery opened on the structure and one of his cannonballs passed through the portrait of George II hanging in the college chapel. The party in the building, variously reported as numbering between sixty and two hundred, surrendered.

General Washington had hoped to push on to New Brunswick, destroy the British stores, capture the military chest of £70,000, and put an end to the war. He believed that with six or eight hundred fresh troops this would have been possible.

As it was, his men were too fatigued for the extra march against the enemy. British troops were in pursuit from Maidenhead (now Lawrenceville), so the American officers decided to turn off for winter quarters at Morristown.

Chapter 3

DELICATE MISSION

Hamilton's reading at Morristown, New Jersey, in January and February of 1777, and perhaps later, he noted in blank pages at the back of the paybook of his artillery company. Some material he condensed; occasionally he took down a quotation or recorded his own reflections on a point. A surprising amount of the information he gathered then was to reappear, variously modified, in his own, later public writings and policies. Hamilton's ideas on national economy are closely linked with the corresponding articles in Malachy Postlethwayt's *Universal Dictionary of Trade and Commerce,* of which four editions had appeared in the quarter-century before Hamilton used the work.

Postlethwayt's two folio volumes reflected basically mercantilist principles of a managed economy, but with revisions drawn from the freer thinking which was already current in France and which soon found full expression in Adam Smith's *Wealth of Nations.* For example, Postlethwayt made goods rather than gold the object of statecraft. He desired a favorable balance of trade, but the ample supply of money thus obtained he valued not for its own sake, but because it would quicken internal commerce, which should be free of controls. Lively domestic competition would lower costs and reduce the rate of interest. Postlethwayt's recommendation of a combination of limitation and liberty became Hamilton's own method.

Plutarch's *Lives* furnished Hamilton with political models. Here the mixture was that of authority on the one hand and popular preference on the other. Thus he approved of Lycurgus' senate in the Spartan state: ". . . the Senate was to the commonwealth what the ballast is to a ship and preserved the whole in a just equilibrium. For they always adhered to the Kings so far as to oppose a democracy and on the other side assisted the people to prevent tyranny." Hamilton quoted from Demosthenes' words, which were to animate him: "As a general marches at the head of his troops, so ought wise politicians . . . to march at the head of affairs; . . . they ought not to want the *event*, to know what measures to take; but the measures which they have taken, ought to produce the *event*."

This interval of reading in the winter at Morristown was interrupted when Hamilton was invited by General Washington to join his staff as aide-de-camp with the rank of lieutenant colonel. His appointment was announced in general orders on March 1, 1777, though by that date he had probably been serving in that capacity for several weeks already. His New York artillery company was taken into continental service. It is not known whether the choice originated with Washington or was by recommendation of one of his officers. General Nathanael Greene, in the days before the battle of Long Island, had admired the drill of an artillery company and had had the young captain as his guest at dinner; he thus began a friendship which brought Hamilton to the Commander in Chief's attention. Service with Washington at headquarters during four years of the war determined Hamilton's later career.

The young artillerist, educated, well reputed, and of graceful manners, must have been peculiarly welcome to Washington,

who was short-handed at the time. Lieutenant Colonel George
Baylor had been chief aide until he was commissioned to command a cavalry regiment. Lieutenant Colonel Robert Hanson
Harrison had been absent from headquarters due to illness.
The exemplary Tench Tilghman was present, but Washington
was writing some letters in his own hand. He required an aide
who could "comprehend at one view the diversity of matter,
which comes before me, so as to afford the ready assistance
which every man in my situation must stand more or less in
need of." And, again, Washington said, "At present my time
is so taken up at my desk, that I am obliged to neglect many
other essential parts of my duty; it is absolutely necessary . . .
for me to have persons that can think for me, as well as execute orders."

Others of the thirty-two staff officers who, first or last, were
in Washington's military family possessed these qualities, certainly Harrison, the "old secretary," did. But Alexander
Hamilton, even before he became the General's "principal
confidential aide," contributed in a special degree. With those
less practiced in correspondence, Washington would outline
the letter he wished written and his helper would put the
points in proper words. With Hamilton, a word was sufficient.
Washington read and often corrected or amended letters and
documents prepared for his signature, those of Hamilton with
the rest, but Hamilton's drafts required little change. Washington and his gifted assistant thought so much alike that
Hamilton's composition was frequently indistinguishable
from that of his superior. Hamilton became Washington's
ready reliance particularly in moments of pressure. If a messenger with dispatches was expected late at night the General
would not sleep. He threw himself on the couch in his office,
with his cloak for covering, while his faithful body servant,
Billy, snored near by. When the courier arrived and his packet
was scanned, the General would rouse Billy with the direction,

"Call Colonel Hamilton." Then the two would work out replies.

At headquarters, in daily, almost hourly communication with the Commander in Chief, Hamilton was at the patriot center of the war. His assignments were varied and responsible. He gathered information of the whereabouts and strength of the enemy by interrogating prisoners and deserters, though Washington alone received news from his spies. Hamilton prepared reports and, as proxy for the General, conducted correspondence. This might be as much diplomatic as military, with subordinate commanders, Congress, governors, and legislatures. Hamilton was "riding aide" as well as "writing aide," for he conveyed orders on the battlefield and served as the General's representative in missions and conferences.

The Arnold tavern on the west side of the village green was headquarters that first winter in Morristown. Doubtless there, as in others of Washington's temporary abodes during the war, the aides had a communal bedroom and another room fitted with tables for their long hours of writing. The General preferred that his aides have no other commitments or distractions. "Aides-de-Camp," he said, "are persons in whom entire confidence must be placed, and it requires men of abilities to execute the duties with propriety and dispatch. . . . I give in to no kind of amusement myself, and consequently those about me can have none, but are confined from morning till eve, hearing and answering the applications and letters. . . . If these gentlemen had the same relaxation from duty as other officers have in their common routine, there would not be so much in it. But, to have the mind always upon the stretch, scarce ever unbent, with no hours for recreation, makes a material odds."

Actually the life of his aides was not without relief. In winter quarters the General always had fellow officers to dine with him and at these gatherings Hamilton often presided with animation. When wives of the higher officers came to camp, as was always signaled by the arrival of Martha Washington, they would bring their daughters, young ladies who enlivened occasional dances. The aides would accompany the General and some of the ladies on afternoon rides. The aides assisted in entertaining distinguished visitors; then reviews and parades broke the routine. Especially while Sir William Howe was the British commander, war was a seasonal affair, and the stay in winter quarters was protracted well into spring because the roads in "mud time" were impassable for artillery. Congenial neighborhood families contributed to headquarters through social exchanges, and they alleviated the duties of preparing for the coming campaign. Hamilton did his serious courting during the second stay at Morristown.

The trials of the war in every department were automatically transmitted to headquarters and there must be dealt with. Disordered finances, the problems of supply and recruiting, the omissions of Congress and the states, jealousies in the officer corps, the sufferings of the soldiers for want of food, shelter, and medical care, all were anxieties that fell on the Commander in Chief. Hamilton was the intimate witness to these troubles; they documented his efforts to achieve governmental reform in future years. Only those who shared his experience of the war could have the same commitment to reaping its rewards. Of all the founding fathers, the military veterans had an added measure of emotional ardor.

Soon after Hamilton joined the staff, he was engaged by a standing committee of the New York legislature to send semiweekly letters with news from headquarters. This correspondence continued, with interruptions, until September, when the British were about to take Philadelphia. The New Yorkers were anxious because their chief city was the enemy base, and the state trembled in the face of Burgoyne's invasion from Canada. Hamilton's letters were mainly directed to Gouverneur Morris and Robert R. Livingston, who sent him apprehensive queries. Hamilton cautioned them: his information must not be taken as reporting the views of the Commander in Chief. His first care was to quiet the terrors at Burgoyne's approach. Hamilton foretold that the invasion would be stopped by a competent force from several quarters. Nor would General Howe move up the Hudson to join Burgoyne. Philadelphia was Howe's object, though Hamilton discounted the military advantage of the capture of the capital if it happened.

He defended Washington against a current criticism. "I know the comments that people will make," he said, "on our Fabian conduct. It will be imputed to cowardice, or to weakness. But . . . it proceeds from the truest policy. The liberties of America are an infinite stake. We should not . . . put it upon . . . a single cast of the die. The loss of one general engagement may effectually ruin us." He also made a characteristic comment on the newly adopted constitution of New York. The governor, he thought, would have more qualifications for vigor if he were elected not by "the people at large," but by "the deliberative wisdom of a select assembly."

As General Howe's campaign was manifestly against Philadelphia, Washington moved to Wilmington. Hamilton was with him on a reconnoiter. From low hills in Delaware they saw the landing of Howe's troops, after his slow voyage from New York, at the head of Chesapeake bay. The efforts of the Americans to block the enemy's march to the capital failed. Howe repeated at the Battle of Brandywine his strategy on Long Island. General Knyphausen was posted to make the Americans believe the attack would come at Chadd's Ford, while Howe and Cornwallis crossed the stream higher up and enveloped Washington's right wing. The British victory, on September 11, 1777, led on to their entry into Philadelphia September 27.

As the enemy closed in, Hamilton was ordered with a party of horse under Captain Henry Lee to destroy flour stored in mills along the Schuylkill, which lay in their path. This was accomplished only minutes before a British detachment galloped upon them. Hamilton and four of the men with him sprang into a barge under volleys that killed one of his companions and wounded another. Directly upon landing, Hamilton dispatched a note to President John Hancock: "If Congress have not yet left Philadelphia, they ought to do it immediately without fail; for the enemy have the means of throwing a party this night into the city." A few hours later he repeated his warning.

Congress at once acted on plans to remove to Lancaster. Actually, the British were slower in their advance than Hamilton thought they would be, which allowed a valuable interval in which supplies of food and clothing in Philadelphia could be retrieved before the enemy arrived. Washington assigned Hamilton to this errand, the aide writing his own instructions. Using Washington's emergency powers, he was to impress blankets, shoes, horses from the citizens. Despite Hamilton's exhortations, the people yielded up little, but he did get all of the public stores off safely.

After British troops entered Philadelphia, Howe stationed his main army north of the city, at Germantown. Washington resolved on another battle. The Americans' approach, in four widely separated columns, was hampered by fog, but the attack was succeeding—until a fatal decision turned victory to defeat. Several companies of the British took refuge in the stone mansion of Benjamin Chew, and from its upper windows they fired on the Americans advancing to the front of the battle, half a mile to the south. When Washington and his aides came up they found Brigadier Henry Knox there. He was determined to subdue this impromptu fort before passing on. It was against the book rules of war to leave an enemy stronghold in your rear. Hamilton and Pickering protested against the delay. The house should be sealed off while the army pressed forward. General Washington was persuaded by

Knox, but Knox's six-pound cannonballs simply bounced off the solid masonry. An American with a flag, demanding surrender, was killed, and Hamilton's friend John Laurens was wounded in his attempt to set the place on fire. The noise of the cannonade attracted other American forces from the attack. The British took the turnabout as retreat, pursued, and a disastrous rout resulted.

Two weeks after Washington's second defeat in Pennsylvania, General Horatio Gates triumphed in New York by compelling the surrender of Burgoyne's army at Saratoga. Adulation poured in upon Gates, especially from New England, which had shuddered at Burgoyne's advance. Congratulations to Gates tended to draw the contrast between his success and Washington's failure. Gates owed his command of the northern army not to Washington, but to Congress. When General Schuyler was displaced because of New England dissatisfaction, Washington preferred that Congress, having interfered, should name Schuyler's successor. Gates was the New England favorite. He did not so much as notify Washington of Burgoyne's surrender, but left the Commander in Chief to learn of that momentous event by other means.

This was the situation at the end of October 1777, when Washington held a council of war at his temporary camp at Whitpain, near Philadelphia. Five major generals and ten brigadiers advised that if the enemy were to be dislodged from the capital a substantial portion of Gates's army would have to be drawn to that of Washington. An aide should be sent to Gates to procure the reinforcement. Washington chose Hamilton for the delicate task. Washington's instructions charged, "you are chiefly to . . . point out, in the clearest and fullest manner, to General Gates, the absolute necessity . . . for his detaching a very considerable part of the army at present under his command, to the reinforcement of this." However, Hamilton was vested with discretion, for the instructions continued, "If . . . you should find that [General Gates] intends, in consequence

of his Success, to employ the troops under his command upon
some expedition, by the prosecution of which the common
cause will be more benefited than by their being sent down to
reinforce this army, it is not my wish to give interruption to
the plan." The young aide was to judge whether a design of
Gates took precedence or was to be overridden as trivial. In effect, he was to decide whether the war was to be prosecuted in
the north or in the region of Philadelphia.

Hamilton started off on October 30, and he rode sixty miles
a day to cover the 250 miles to Albany. Half way along he met
Colonel Daniel Morgan with his corps of riflemen, already on
their march to join Washington. At Fishkill, Hamilton, in
Washington's name, ordered General Israel Putnam to send
down most of his continentals, keeping 1600 militia. At Albany he found Gates inflexible. Washington wanted all three
of Gates's brigades, but the most Hamilton could secure was
one of them. Gates protested that General Clinton might come
up from New York and capture Albany, "the finest arsenal in
America." Also, how could Gates retake Ticonderoga if he
were left as bare of troops as Hamilton proposed?

The young deputy wrote Washington of his perplexity. "I
found myself infinitely embarrassed, and was at a loss how to
act. I felt the importance of strengthening you as much as possible, but . . . I found insuperable inconveniences in acting
diametrically opposite to the opinion of a gentleman whose
successes have raised him to the highest importance." If Gates
were disputed, he had influence in Congress that might serve
to countermand Washington's orders.

When Hamilton learned that Patterson's brigade was the
one Gates proposed to send, he objected. He told Gates that it
was "by far the weakest of the three now here, and does not
consist of more than about six hundred rank and file fit for
duty." The two hundred miltitia with it could not be counted
because their enlistment would expire before they could reach
Washington. The aide therefore felt "under the necessity of

desiring, by virtue of my orders" from General Washington, that Glover's brigade be substituted for Patterson's, and "if agreeable to you, you will give orders accordingly." Hamilton talked with Gates further, and to such good effect that the reluctant conqueror of Burgoyne agreed to send Glover's brigade along with Patterson's. In the draft letter Gates wrote to Washington he crossed out passages which showed his resentment of Hamilton's insistence and of Washington's action in giving "Dictatorial power, to one Aid de Camp sent to an Army 300 Miles distant." Actually, it was soon plain that Gates needed few troops at Albany. He sent cannon and muskets to safety farther inland, and believed that the British were on the point of evacuating Ticonderoga.

As Hamilton returned down the river, he felt satisfied in knowing that Patterson's brigade was following in boats that he had mustered and that Glover's was marching on the east bank. But at New Windsor and Fishkill he met obstacles which he reported to General Washington. Israel Putnam had paid not the least attention to orders given in Washington's name. The brigades of Learned and Poor refused to march because they had not been paid for six or eight months. Poor's men had mutinied, a captain had killed a soldier and was himself shot. Putnam held Warner's militia at Peekskill "to aid in an expedition against New-York, . . . at this time the hobby-horse with General Putnam." (Hamilton further called Putnam's project "a suicidal parade against New York".)

Governor George Clinton came to Hamilton's help. He loaned him five or six thousand dollars for the men's pay, and they started along. He told Washington he wished Putnam was recalled from his command, and that Governor Clinton would accept it. Every part of Putnam's conduct "gives general disgust." Hamilton, acting for the Commander in Chief, had ordered Putnam to send Washington all of his continentals and to keep the militia.

Hamilton's anxious exertions took their toll. He came down

with "fever and violent rheumatic pains" at New Windsor. With slight improvement, he got up to cross the river and hurry down Glover's troops, and he had a relapse. Governor Clinton, alarmed by his condition as he lay at Peekskill, summoned Dr. John Jones of Bellemont. The doctor was himself ill; he sent directions for treatment that did no good. Clinton, and the doctor when he arrived days later, thought Hamilton was "drawing nigh his last." He was cold as high as his knees. Then suddenly the fever abated and he was on the way to recovery. He must have been edgy, because Colonel Hugh Hughes, a friend of Gates, reported that he "is out of Danger unless it be from his own sweet Temper." A minor irritation was word that Poor's brigade, having been mollified with money, was detained because "they were under an operation for the itch."

By mid-November the aide could inform Washington that his reinforcements were on the move from the Hudson. After so many vexations, Washington's letter in reply was welcome: "I approve entirely all the steps you have taken; and have only to wish, that the exertions of those you have had to deal with, had kept pace with your zeal." Unfortunately, the relief was too late. General Howe had been strengthened by troops from New York. The American forts on the Delaware River had been battered down, thus permitting the British to bring up supplies by water. Gates should have flinched at Washington's message. As Howe's reinforcement arrived before "ours from the northward, it was out of my power to afford adequate relief to Fort Mifflin, which fell after a most gallant defence of seven Weeks." The other works were lost as a consequence. Washington's army was about to withdraw to Valley Forge. An officer wrote to Gates, "We are ill Cloathed, the Winter is on, to Hutt near the Enemy will be as arduous as dangerous."

The forecast of Washington that Gates needed few troops at Albany after Burgoyne's surrender was borne out. Gates himself informed the President of Congress that the enemy had evacuated Ticonderoga, abandoned all posts on the Hudson short of Manhattan, and retired to Canada. Soon General Gates, recently so insistent on protecting Albany, came to York, Pennsylvania, as president of the new board of war. Congress praised his peculiar fitness for the office, on which "the safety & Interest of the United States eminently depend." Gates's friends could feel that he had been elevated above Washington.

But General Gates rode too high. Enjoying the worship shown him, he was willing to accept slurs on the Commander in Chief. Gates's adjutant. Colonel James Wilkinson, on his leisurely way to Congress to announce Burgoyne's surrender officially, spent a convivial evening at Reading with the staff of Lord Stirling. He told Major William McWilliams, Stirling's aide, of an extract in a letter Gates had received from General Thomas Conway. He reported that Conway had said, "Heaven has been determined to save your Country; or a weak General and bad Councellors would have ruind it." Lord Stirling, thinking it his duty to detect "such wicked duplicity of conduct," passed the remark on to Washington. Washington, in the briefest of letters, confronted Conway with the slight. This was a principal incident in the so-called "Conway Cabal," the exposure of which Gates, at one point, tried to blame on Hamilton. Conway was an Irish soldier of fortune who had served in the French army before fighting bravely in the colonies' cause. He was boastful and egotistical, and Washington thought him a marplot, but he took less part than some others did in the disparagement of the Commander in Chief. Gates himself, John Adams, James Lovell of Massachusetts, Dr. Benjamin Rush, and General Mifflin were of the group extremely critical of Washington's leadership, if, indeed, they did not positively wish to see Gates given supreme command in his stead.

Mifflin, who had been at Reading when Wilkinson's tongue was wagging, warned Gates that trouble impended. Conway's thrust at Washington "should not have been entrusted to any of your Family," for the injurious quotation had been conveyed to headquarters, and Washington had taxed Conway with it. Some of Gates's best friends (for that read Mifflin himself) might suffer. Evidently, from what happened later, Gates did not notice that Mifflin attributed the disclosure to Wilkinson, Gates's adjutant.

Gates, tipped off by Mifflin, begged Conway "to let me know which of the latters was copied off. It is of the greatest importance, that I should detect the person who has been guilty of that act of infidelity." However, Gates did not wait, but fixed his censure on Hamilton. As soon as Wilkinson returned to Albany, Gates exploded to him, "I have had a spy in my camp since you left me!" According to Wilkinson, Gates continued, "Colonel Hamilton had been sent up to him by General Washington; and would you believe it, he purloined the copy of a letter out of that closet. . . . Colonel Hamilton was left alone an hour in this room, during which time, he took Conway's letter out of that closet and copied it, and the copy has been furnished to Washington."

The guilty Wilkinson tried to shift the blame to Gates's aide, Robert Troup. Troup and Hamilton were fast friends from college days, and they had been much in each other's company when Hamilton visited Albany. Wasn't it probable that Troup had revealed the contents of Conway's letter to Hamilton, who then reported it to Washington? No, Gates insisted, Hamilton was the villain. Gates would compel Washington to admit it, and both Hamilton and Washington would be disgraced.

"I conjure your excellency," Gates wrote to Washington, "to give me all the assistance you can, in tracing out the author of the infidelity which put extracts from General Conway's letters to me into your hands. . . . It is . . . *in your* . . . *power* to do me and the United States a very important service, by detecting a wretch who may . . . capitally injure the *very operations*

under your immediate direction." Gates added that he was sending a copy of his letter to the President of Congress.

In his reply, Washington ignored the insinuations against
Hamilton. He told Gates that it was what Wilkinson, Gates's
own confidant, had babbled at Reading which had reached
him via Stirling, "from motives of friendship." Then Washington reprimanded Gates. Until he had learned that Gates
was searching for an offender, he had supposed Gates had
meant to warn him against "a dangerous incendiary . . .
Genl. Conway. But, in this, as in other matters of late, I have
found myself mistaken."

Gates now protested that the paragraph quoted to Washington was "spurious . . . a wicked forgery." Conway's letter
said nothing of a weak general or bad counselors. Gates no
longer suspected Hamilton; instead, he urged that the faithless
Wilkinson be punished. Washington's long reply was severe
reading for Gates. Why had Gates admitted Conway's stric-
ture, and later denied that it existed? If Conway's letters were
innocent of reflections on the Commander in Chief why had
Gates not produced them? In view of Gates's disclaimers,
Washington was willing to bury their correspondence in silence, "and as far as future events will permit, oblivion."

For Gates's hard words Wilkinson challenged him to a duel,
and, he said, he also would have the blood of Stirling. Gates
offered a tearful explanation; Stirling offered scorn.

Governor George Clinton's help in extracting troops from
Gates to reinforce Washington may have prompted Hamilton's
confidential letter to him amidst the miseries of Valley Forge
(February 13, 1778). Hamilton laid much of the suffering from
cold, hunger, and disease to the "degeneracy of representation
in the great council of America." Though Congress contained
able members, "Folly, caprice, a want of foresight, comprehension, and dignity" described the body as a whole. From
his vantage at headquarters he had reason to know that "Their

conduct, with respect to the army . . . is feeble, indecisive, and improvident—insomuch that we are reduced to a more terrible situation than you can conceive. . . . At this very day there are complaints from the whole line of having been three or four days without provisions." The preference of capable men for leadership in their own states sacrificed "the common interests of the Confederacy." He was glad that New York had sent Duane, Morris, and Duer, but he wished that Jay, R. R. Livingston, and Schuyler were there also. Viewing the defects of congressional management of the war, Hamilton was soon urging that administration of the great public departments be entrusted to single, responsible men.

In spite of twice being given emergency powers, Washington, leading a citizen army in a democratic revolution, was obliged to defer to Congress. Dictatorship, military and political, was abhorrent to everyone, most of all to the Commander in Chief. Washington repeatedly remonstrated against neglect of the army by Congress and by the states. In the dreadful winter of Valley Forge, America was at the end of its first wind and had not got its second.

As spring opened, the shad began to run in the Schuylkill, and horsemen entered the stream and drove them by thousands into nets. The camp went on a fish binge. This was a cheerful portent that things were mending. The surrender of Burgoyne at Saratoga had persuaded France to become America's outright ally, with troops and fleets as well as money and supplies. The camp's economy was suddenly improved when Nathanael Greene took over the duties of Quartermaster General and Jeremiah Wadsworth became Commissary General. Baron Steuben's training converted the dispirited troops into a disciplined fighting force.

Even before Steuben had arrived at Valley Forge at the end of February 1778, Washington had planned reorganization of the army. Ideas submitted in writing by the general officers, and Washington's own design, were worked up by Hamilton into a cogent report. The Commander in Chief gave it to the committee of Congress that was visiting camp. To stop the wholesale resignations of officers, and to animate them to be examples to all ranks, the promise of a pension on retirement was essential. An annual draft of troops, with a small bounty for reenlistment only, was recommended. Weak regiments should be merged. The cavalry arm should be expanded, the Inspector General's functions extended. The service of supply must be reformed. The troops must be paid regularly. Washington's report concluded with the warning that unless remedies for errors of omission and commission were applied at once, "the most alarming . . . consequences" would follow.

Conway had been named Inspector General by Congress, but he had made little progress in his duties, none at Valley Forge. Steuben was heaven-sent. No foreign officer who ever came to the American army under false pretences rendered such genuine services. Benjamin Franklin, then in Paris, had written the letter of introduction, claiming that Steuben had been a lieutenant general in Europe, this to give him a favorable reception by Congress and General Washington. Steuben acquiesced in the fraud, and his air of importance justified the deception. Actually, he had never held rank higher than a captaincy, but he had been a member of the staff school of Frederick the Great and was expert in military exercises. He offered himself as a volunteer, without particular rank or command. He was prepared for any role Washington would assign him.

Washington talked with the Baron, and he thought he would be useful as inspector and trainer of troops at Valley Forge. At first the appointment was provisional, as the American scene was new to Steuben and he could not speak English. Washington deputed Hamilton and John Laurens, both of whom spoke French, as Steuben did, to acquaint him with principal officers and the situation of the camp. He was liked by the Americans and learned rapidly. Soon Conway resigned and Steuben was made Major General and Inspector General.

A perfectionist in Europe, in America he wisely undertook only essential improvements. He has come down in history as "Washington's drillmaster," but he was more than that, for he accomplished important economies in management throughout the army.

The ravages of casualties, desertions, illness, and furloughs, with no recruits coming in, had destroyed uniformity in military units. Steuben observed that "the words company, regiment, brigade, and division . . . did not convey any idea upon which to form a calculation. . . . They were so unequal in their number that it would have been impossible to execute any maneuvers. Sometimes a regiment was stronger than a brigade. I have seen a regiment consisting of thirty men and a company of one corporal. . . . With regard to . . . military discipline, I may safely say no such thing existed."

The Baron was proud, but he was also adaptable. Washington ordered a hundred chosen men to be added to his guard, these to be Steuben's first pupils. Steuben did not leave their instruction to his subordinates, but placed himself before one squad after another to demonstrate the manual of arms and simple evolutions. With the help of these men and his subinspectors—Hamilton's old teacher Francis Barber was one—he enlarged his class, first to a platoon, then to a company; finally he embraced the whole force. He wrote out every day's instructions in the progressive course. Hamilton, Laurens, and others translated the Baron's directions into English, to be copied for all units of the army. Later these were published as *Regulations for the Order and Discipline of the Troops of the United States*, which became the basis of IDR (Infantry Drill Regulations), which are used to the present day. Steuben's instruction was early proved at the battle of Monmouth, where General Charles Lee's retreating soldiers obeyed orders to turn and attack.

A special bond developed between Hamilton and Steuben, even though the Baron was twice Hamilton's age. Steuben needed Hamilton's friendly personal supervision, for he was as prodigal in his private finances as he was economical in his management for the public. One of Hamilton's special services at headquarters was speaking with the numerous French officers in their own tongue. Foremost in this company, and close to Hamilton, was Lafayette, though the Marquis rapidly learned his own brand of English.

Chapter 4

MONMOUTH, MORRISTOWN, AND MARRIAGE

In June 1778 Sir William Howe was being relieved of command in favor of Sir Henry Clinton, who had come to Philadelphia to take over. His officers, the sportive John André prominent among them, gave Howe an elaborate farewell party, the "Meschianza." As soon as it was plain that the British were evacuating the American capital (which they did on June 17) and would march across New Jersey to New York, Washington's army prepared to break camp at Valley Forge. Hamilton for Washington drew up a statement to be presented to a council of general officers. After comparing the strengths of American and enemy forces, it listed queries concerning the course of action to be followed. The army with Washington numbered between 11,000 and 12,000 of all ranks fit for duty. Besides these, Maxwell's brigade of 1300, and Dickinson's militia, 800, were already in New Jersey. Clinton's army was estimated at 10,000, superior in cavalry but at a disadvantage because it was retreating with impedimenta, including 1500 wagons, carriages of loyalists fleeing Philadelphia, and a flock of camp followers.

The crucial point on which opinions were required was, "In case . . . this army . . . overtake the enemy on their march, will it be prudent . . . to make an attack upon them, and ought it to be a partial or a general one?" Three were against hazarding a full-scale engagement. They were Charles Lee, who, after capture and mild imprisonment, had been exchanged; Steuben; and the chief engineer, DuPortail. Wayne, Cadwalader, Lafayette, and Greene were, in different degrees, in favor of bringing on a battle.

On June 18 General Lee led the first contingent across the Delaware river at Coryell's Ferry (from New Hope, Pa., to Lambertville, N.J.). Washington, in immediate command of the main body, left Valley Forge next day, Hamilton with him, and the entire American force was in New Jersey by the twenty-third. From the first day of march the weather was so "excessive hot" that "Some of the soldiers die suddenly." The enemy also lost men from sunstroke and exhaustion, especially the Hessians because of their heavy clothing and packs.

At Hopewell, a few miles northwest of Princeton, the army rested a day while Washington, for the second time, put to his general officers the question whether the enemy should continue to be harassed or whether the Americans should strike an all-out blow. Clinton's columns were creeping forward, twenty-five miles to the south. When again would the Americans have such a chance to pounce on the foe, now vulnerable because retreating and encumbered? As Burgoyne's army had been captured entire, only Clinton's remained to be destroyed and the war would be won. On the other hand, French help was promised, and D'Estaing's fleet was already on the coast. Did prudence dictate waiting until combined forces would make the result certain?

Hamilton, present at the council to record the decision, missed not a word as one after another answered Washington's queries. General Charles Lee argued that the enemy should be allowed to cross New Jersey unhampered. Equal numbers of Americans could not match trained European soldiers in pitched battle. Wait patiently for French assistance. Knox, Stirling, and others would not give the British free passage; 1500 troops should be advanced to add to the detachments already galling Clinton's left flank and rear, while the main army was watchful of events. This was the opinion of the council, signed by all but Wayne, who wanted to bring on a stand-up fight.

Hamilton was indignant. Writing to his friend Boudinot, he declared the conclusion of the council "would have done honor to the most honorable society of midwives, and to them only. The purport was, that we should keep at a comfortable distance from the enemy, and keep up a vain parade of annoying them by detachment." Some years later he further stigmatized the formal vote that "decreed an undisturbed passage to an enemy . . . disheartened by retreat, dispirited by desertion, broken by fatigue, retiring through woods, defiles, and morasses in which his discipline was useless, in the face of an army superior in numbers, elated by pursuit and ardent to signalize their courage." Lafayette and Greene had gone along reluctantly with the majority, and after the council broke up they, along with Wayne, wrote individually to the Commander in Chief, urging him to disregard the timid advice.

In accordance with the majority recommendation, Hamilton penned Washington's order sending Brigadier General Charles Scott with 1500 troops to worry the enemy as Colonel Daniel Morgan and General Dickinson were already doing. Small parties of foot under General Cadwalader and of horse under Lieutenant Colonel Anthony White would be joining them.

Next day (June 25), at Kingston, Washington made his own decision. He saw that Clinton was going the shortest way to the sea, via Monmouth Court House, and would escape him unless prompt action were taken. He ordered Lafayette forward with 1000 troops under Wayne. He should take command of all the detachments near the enemy, some 4000 total, whom he was empowered to commit in an attack. Washington had felt obliged to get Lee to yield his claim, as senior major general, to command the advanced force. Lee agreed, remarking disdainfully that the business was more proper for a young volunteering general (Lafayette). Hamilton described the farcical vacillations that followed. "Some of [Lee's] friends having blamed him for [resigning the command], and Lord Stirling having shown a disposition to interpose his claim, General Lee . . . inconsistently reasserted his pretensions. The matter was a second time accommodated, General Lee and Lord Stirling agreed to let the marquis command. General Lee, a little time after, recanted again and became very importunate. The general [Washington] . . . grew tired of such fickle behavior, and ordered the marquis to proceed." There was one more about-face. When Lee saw that a third of the army was to be led by the Frenchman, he reversed himself again and demanded the honor. As matters turned out, Washington would have done well to confirm his choice of the spirited Lafayette. However, he finally put Lee, with additional brigades, in command of the whole forward corps, but with the instruction that Lee should aid any design formed by Lafayette as his subordinate.

Hamilton was delighted to be detailed to his friend Lafayette as liaison officer. He was in the saddle for the better part of a day and night giving information of the whereabouts of the enemy and of the movements of the American units. The reports which got back to Washington made the General fear that Lafayette and Hamilton, in their enthusiasm, might precipitate action prematurely before the main army could come up, but in fact they did not need his caution on this head. On June 26 Hamilton dispatched to Washington his report that the enemy had encamped with his van beyond Monmouth Court House (now Freehold). Also of importance, he had learned that Clinton had placed his baggage in front, his best troops in the rear, then a guard of 1000 men a quarter-mile behind the main body.

Washington ordered a concentration at English Town, six miles from Monmouth. General Lee marched at five o'clock in the morning of June 28, 1778, and he came up with the enemy at about eight o'clock. The battlefield of Monmouth is a rectangle, roughly two and a half miles by one mile. It lies east and west, with the village on the flat at the eastern end and the Tennent Church dominating an amphetheater of hills on the west. Three "ravines" (actually, marshy depressions) cut the field roughly north and south. Artillery could cross two of these depressions only by a narrow bridge over the western one and a causeway over the middle one. The easternmost marsh lay to the north of Monmouth Court House and was avoided by both sides in the minor fighting that took place at that end of the field. Today the marshes are dried up and the woods that bordered the plain have been cut.

Hamilton was sent by General Washington from English Town toward Monmouth to reconnoiter. He found Lee some distance west of the Court House, his troops in confusion. He urged Lee to order Lafayette to attack the left flank. This done, Hamilton returned to Washington to report. He met the General advancing at the head of the main army, a short distance west of the Tennent Church. Hamilton told him that Lee would soon engage. He recommended that the right wing (Greene) and the left (Stirling) move to support Lee.

No sooner had the order been given than all expectations were reversed. Washington and his aides were met by a fifer who told of a retreat. The General was incredulous, having heard little firing. But when he got the same report from others, he sent aides forward to discover the truth. The officers they met did not know the cause of the backward movement. Colonel Ogden exclaimed, "By God! They are flying from a shadow." The aides galloped back to tell Washington that enemy light infantry and grenadiers were pursuing out of the woods and would be upon him in fifteen minutes.

Washington met Lee with angry words a short distance east of the church. Hamilton described the emergency: "the General rode forward and found the troops retiring in the greatest disorder and the enemy pressing upon their rear. . . . He instantly took measures for checking the enemy's advance, then rode back and formed his own men on the high ground, Stirling on the left, Greene on the right, himself and Lafayette in the center." Hamilton continued, "America owes a great deal to General Washington for this day's work; a general rout, dismay, and disgrace would have attended the whole army in any other hands but his. By his own good sense and fortitude he turned the fate of the day. Other officers have great merit in performing their parts well, but he directed the whole with the skill of a Masterworkman . . . he brought order out of confusion, animated the troops and led them to success."

Hamilton did not speak of his own action on the field; he was posting troops to protect American artillery in danger of capture, and he was incapacitated when his horse was wounded and fell. A fellow aide wrote that Hamilton "was incessant in his endeavours during . . . the whole day—in reconnoitering the enemy and in rallying and charging." American artillery and thrusts of infantry, especially under Wayne, drove enemy dragoons, grenadiers, and guards under Cornwallis back over the ground of Lee's retreat. Darkness closed the longest and hottest day of battle (thermometer at 96°). Washington and his troops lay on the field they had won, intending to renew the fight next morning. But Clinton stole away in the night and was not pursued. Monmouth was a drawn battle, though it demonstrated that the Americans, trained by Steuben and capably led, could repel the best soldiers of Europe.

Hamilton testified twice at Lee's court-martial, principally that the night before the battle he had dispatched to Lee, at

Washington's order, a letter directing him to attack. Lee should give time for the main army to come up for a general engagement. In the hurry of preparation no copy of the letter had been kept, but Hamilton stressed that Lee had been similarly ordered by Washington orally. Lee's position was that, in command on the field, he was bound to use his own discretion under conditions which the Commander in Chief could not foresee. He insisted that by prudent retreat in the face of superior force he had saved his portion of the American army. There were other exchanges, including attempts made by Lee to discredit Hamilton's word. The court-martial found Lee guilty of disobedience in not attacking, of making an unnecessary retreat, and of disrespect to the Commander in Chief. He was suspended for a year and later Congress dismissed him.

Not until many years later was it known that Lee, while a prisoner, had offered General Howe a campaign plan by which the colonies would be defeated. If this had been revealed after Lee returned to the American army he undoubtedly would have been tried and hanged for treason.

Hamilton's friend John Laurens, as an aide of Washington, conceived himself entitled to challenge Lee to a duel for his expressions abusing the Commander in Chief. Hamilton was second to Laurens; General Lee's second was his aide, Major Evan Edwards. The combatants, supplied with two pistols each, approached each other, firing as they pleased. Lee was wounded, but he protested that he wanted to renew the fight. The seconds overruled him, and they published a statement that the demands of honor had been met. Other duels with Lee threatened, but they were averted. He died in 1782, unbefriended by all but a few.

Hamilton's skill with the written word was frequently availed upon by General Washington when he had to meet an embarrassing situation. Not that Washington himself lacked gifts of expression; the fact was that the two collaborated on ticklish occasions. In August 1778 plans for a combined attack on the British in Rhode Island were forfeited when Count D'Estaing, having encountered a storm, insisted on taking his fleet from Newport to Boston for repairs. Washington warned that enemy reinforcements were on the way, and General John Sullivan saved his army by a skillful retreat. Washington foresaw American resentment of the French ally. He wrote, in Hamilton's phrases, "Should the expedition fail, thro' the abandonment of the French fleet, the [American] Officers . . . will be apt to complain loudly. But prudence dictates that we should put the best face upon the matter and, to the World, attribute the removal to Boston, to necessity."

Unfortunately, this caution did not reach Sullivan in time to bridle his Irish ire. In general orders he stated that he hoped "the event will prove America able to procure that by her own arms, which her allies refuse to assist her in obtaining." Lafayette, on the Rhode Island scene, and acting as the French always did when they were offended, regretted Sullivan's indiscretion, and others also wrote Washington in alarm. How could Sullivan be reprimanded, as French umbrage required, while America was admiring Sullivan's feat of extricating his army when left in the lurch? Washington employed Hamilton to deliver the soft impeachment. "The disagreement between the army under your command and the fleet," it ran, "has given me . . . singular uneasiness. The continent at large is concerned in our cordiality. . . . In our confuct towards [the French] we should remember that they are a people . . . very strict in military etiquette and apt to take fire where others scarcely seem warmed. Permit me to recommend in the most particular manner, the cultivation of harmony."

As in other instances, Hamilton was called on to write in his own name what should not appear over the signature of the Commander in Chief. In a semi-public letter to Boudinot in Congress, he stigmatized Sullivan's remark as "the summit of folly" and "an absurdity without parallel." On recommendation of Lafayette he went on to praise the valor of the French

officer, Major Louis Tousard, who had lost an arm in his attack
on an enemy cannon on Rhode Island. The French were mollified because this letter issued from American headquarters to
Congress. Hamilton also wrote for Washington a soothing
message to Count D'Estaing. The Count probably knew Hamilton's part in the peacemaking, for he complimented the
aide whose "talents and . . . personal qualities have secured
for him for ever my esteem, my confidence, my friendship."

Alexander Hamilton was usually candid, ready to have his
sentiments known even though they were unpopular or accu-
satory of others. He offended in the autumn of 1778, when he
wrote three letters of "Publius" in Holt's *New-York Journal*
which pilloried Samuel Chase of Maryland. As a member of
Congress, Chase had known of the secret plan to secure flour
for the French fleet, and he had passed on his information to
confederates who meant to reap a great profit by cornering the
article. Hamilton's attack on Chase was too virulent to have
been made without identifying himself. In fact, his language
was so extravagant that he almost discredited his censure;
thus, "were I inclined to make a satire upon the species [hu-
manity] I would attempt a faithful picture of your heart. It is
hard to conceive . . . one of more finished depravity." A
friend of Chase's besought James McHenry to reveal the author of the assault, but Hamilton maintained that his pieces
were in the public interest. In spite of formal exculpation, he
believed Chase guilty; if he were persuaded otherwise, he
would "make . . . the most explicit . . . retribution."

These letters contain Hamilton's definition of an honorable
legislator or other person in public life. A member of Congress
"is to be regarded not only as a legislator, but as a founder of
an empire. A man of virtue and ability, dignified with so
precious a trust, would rejoice that fortune . . . placed him in
circumstances, so favorable for promoting human happiness.
. . . To form useful alliances abroad—to establish a wise government at home—to improve the internal resources and fi-

nances of the nation—would be the generous objects of his care. . . . Anxious for the permanent power and prosperity of the state, he would labor to perpetuate the union and harmony of the several parts."

Hamilton was pleased when General Washington, offsetting the recent reproof, named Sullivan to lead a punitive expedition against the Iroquois. Hamilton had been with Washington for six weeks of conferences with a committee of Congress; the subjects on which the aide prepared queries included plans for the campaign of 1779. It was proposed, in summary, that the main body of the army should "lye quiet in some favourable position for confining . . . the enemy in their present posts (adopting at the same time the best means in our power to scourge the Indians and prevent their depredations) in order to save expences, avoid New Emissions, recruit our finances, and give a proper tone to our Money for more vigorous measures hereafter." The official wording conveyed the low state of the country, in materials and morale, which made it desirable to undertake only limited military operations in the near future. Meantime, resources could be recruited to utilize French aid, when available, to drive the enemy from the continent.

Hamilton, for Washington, rejected a more ambitious program proposed by Gouverneur Morris, who was a member of the conference committee. His reasons were less reserved than those Morris had presented to Congress. "The rapid decay of our currency," Hamilton wrote, "the extinction of public spirit, the increasing rapacity of the times, the want of harmony in our councils, the declining zeal of the people, the . . . distresses of the officers of the army . . . are symptoms . . . of a most alarming nature." Considering this exhaustion, it was best to replenish the army by resolving "to pacify party differences, to give fresh vigor to the springs of government, to inspire the people with confidence, and above all, to restore the credit of our currency."

Punishment of the Indians on the long-suffering frontiers of Pennsylvania and New York was an eligible interim project. It would occupy attention, keep up spirits at home and credit abroad. Using detachments, it would not drain supplies. Because of economy it would not be possible to attack the British posts, chiefly Niagara, from which the Indians were led and munitioned. However, if the Indian country were devastated and the tribes compelled to burden the forts, that would be next best to conquest.

The command of the expedition was first offered to Horatio Gates, who declined it with the ungracious implication that Washington proposed to him the only service to which his age made him unequal. Sullivan relished the opportunity; he wanted to fight in cooperation with General James Clinton. Hamilton penned Washington's instructions for the unequal contest. Thereafter the cruel sweep of the Indians' towns and fields was no part of Hamilton's story. There had been grievous faults on both sides, but this was the first in the long series of national actions to dispossess the original inhabitants of the continent.

Shortly afterward, Hamilton participated with his friend John Laurens in a more humane project. Both young men had grown up in slave societies; Hamilton's West Indies were similar to the coastal strip of South Carolina of Laurens's youth. Both were then detached, for education, to areas of freer thought—Hamilton to New York, Laurens to Geneva and London. Laurens wrote his father, who was then the President of Congress, "we have sunk the African[s] and their descendants below the standard of humanity, and almost render'd them incapable of that blessing which equal Heaven bestow's upon us all." It would be necessary to bring slaves to freedom by "shades and degrees." He was going to South Carolina to try to repel the second, this time successful, British invasion (1780). In the current shortage of troops, what more suitable than to enlist slaves and give freedom to those who survived the war? Washington's tentative reaction was unfavorable, but on his way Laurens would seek the approval of Congress.

Hamilton gave Laurens a letter to President John Jay. It was intended to persuade Congress to take several battalions of slaves, if enlisted, into continental pay. The need was pressing, as Savannah and Augusta had both fallen and Charleston was surely threatened. "I have frequently heard it objected to the scheme of embodying negroes," Hamilton observed, "that they are too stupid to make soldiers. This is so far from . . . a valid objection, that I think their want of cultivation (for their natural faculties are as good as ours), joined to [their] habit of subordination . . . will enable them sooner to become soldiers than our white inhabitants. Let officers be men of sense and sentiment and the nearer the soldiers approach to machines, perhaps the better."

Habitual contempt for Negroes made men "fancy many things that are founded neither in reason nor experience," and the clutch at valuable property "will furnish a thousand arguments to show the . . . pernicious tendency" of a measure that sacrificed selfish interest. (It was proposed to require owners to contribute slaves in proportion to the numbers they possessed). He added what Washington well knew, that the enemy would arm slaves if the Americans did not do it, giving them "their freedom with their swords." The Americans should use this method to animate the courage of those enrolled and open the door to emancipation of those who remained.

Congress recommended that South Carolina and Georgia should raise 3000 Negro troops under white officers; the continent would recompense masters for the slaves thus serving and freed at the war's end. However, in spite of making repeated efforts in the legislature, of which he was a member, Laurens met with no success in South Carolina.

Army officers in that day were especially jealous of their honor, apt to "find quarrel in a straw" and invoke the *code duello*. Though Hamilton had acted as John Laurens's second in the duel with General Lee, a year thereafter he was involved in a serious controversy, and at that time he expressed his aversion to the practice. The occasion was a report "Colonel Hamilton . . . had declared in a public coffee house in Philadelphia, that it was high time for the people to rise, join General Washington, and turn Congress out of doors." It was added that the report was highly credible because "Mr. Hamilton could be no ways interested in the defence of this country", presumably as he was not native-born, and therefore would give rein to his great ambition.

This came to Hamilton in a letter from Lieutenant Colonel John Brooks of Massachusetts, who said he had it from Francis Dana, delegate in Congress from his state. Hamilton immediately pursued the canard, because it was damaging both to him and to the Commander in Chief. He asked his friend Colonel David Henley in Boston to deliver his letter demanding of Dana whether he uttered the reproach, if so, on whose authority, and threatening a duel if Dana did not clear himself. Dana replied that he had repeated what he heard from the Reverend William Gordon of Jamaica Plain. Dana accepted Hamilton's denial of having made such a statement.

As Gordon himself explained, "In consequence of my connections thro the Northern States & down to Philadelphia, with persons, in & out of Congress, in civil & military life, I have had opportunities of seeing & receiving a variety of letters & of knowing many secrets." He used his chain of communications to garner materials for the history he was writing of the American Revolution. He protested—too much—to Washington that he hid in his own bosom whatever was injurious to the country.

Of course Hamilton at once required Gordon to disclose the authority on which his story was founded, with a caution against "the least hesitation or reserve." Gordon already knew the contents of Hamilton's correspondence with Brooks and

Dana. In his patronizing reply to Hamilton's query—he wished him "more conversant with the world"—he wrote that he believed Hamilton had said what was reported. He would reveal his informer if Hamilton would promise on his honor that he would "neither give nor accept, cause to be given nor accepted a challenge upon the occasion, nor engage in any rencounter that may produce a duel."

Hamilton's answer made it necessary for Gordon to give up his author or invite the conclusion that he himself had fabricated the tale. For Hamilton disavowed any intention toward a duel; instead, he would confront his accuser in the presence of witnesses who would be able to testify that he was innocent and injured, and his accuser was "a contemptible defamer." Colonel Henley, who transmitted Gordon's letters, believed Gordon was "the cause of this mischievous and false report," and he gave Hamilton independent evidence of Gordon's bad character. Hamilton charged Gordon; "you are yourself the author of the calumny; such I . . . shall represent you. . . . I only lament that respect to myself obliges me to confine the expression of my contempt to words."

In May of 1780 Lafayette returned from France with the glorious news that King Louis XVI was sending fighting forces to help the Americans—6000 troops under Rochambeau and a fleet commanded by Destouches. The irony was that America was painfully unprepared to cooperate with the promised reinforcements. Hamilton wrote, for Washington, to governors and members of Congress pleading for recruits and supplies. To "bring out the resources of the Country with vigor and decision" Congress must send to headquarters at Morristown a small committee empowered to give authority to requirements of the Commander in Chief. General Philip Schuyler was Washington's first choice for the committee. Hamilton, as in other instances, wrote his private letter urging for the Commander in Chief a control which Washington himself would not ask. The letter was to James Duane: "For God's sake, my dear sir, engage Congress to adopt it. . . . We have not a moment to lose. . . . The fate of America is perhaps suspended on the issue; if we are found unprepared, it must disgrace us . . . defeating the good intentions of our allies, and losing the happiest opportunity we ever have had to save ourselves." Duane assured him that the committee sent to camp would act for Congress in civil matters and never "interfere in the exercise of [Washington's] free Judgement" in military operations.

These exhortations were sharpened by the exhaustion of the army at Morristown. Governor Trumbull should bestir Connecticut: Washington told him that "we are reduced to . . . extremity for want to meat. On several days . . . the Troops have been entirely destitute of any" after having suffered "at a half, a quarter, and Eighth allowance." A mutiny of hungry, unpaid Connecticut regiments had been quelled the night before, but barely. The states must respond to the entreaty of the committee of Congress. Hamilton, for Washington, pictured the emergency: "The Country exhausted; The people dispirited; the . . . reputation of these States in Europe sunk; Our friends chagrined and discouraged; our Enemies deriving new credit; new confidence, new resources." Washington, in Hamilton's words, was peculiarly candid with his former aide, President Joseph Reed of Pennsylvania. "All our . . . operations are at a stand and unless a system very different . . . be immediately adopted throughout the states our affairs must soon become desperate beyond the possibility of recovery. . . . Indeed I have almost ceased to hope. The country . . . is in such a state of insensibility . . . to its interests, that I dare not flatter myself with any change for the better." If the call to the states did not produce men and materials, "I shall consider our lethargy as incurable" and would sacrifice "public good and even self preservation." Pennsylvania was "full of flour. . . . Either Pennsylvania must give us all the aid we ask of her, or we can undertake nothing." This plea was not disappointed; Washington got the aid.

It was evident to many, to none more than to Washington and Hamilton, that, besides immediate aid, a renovation of the government of the union was highly desirable if the war were to be won. A meeting of representatives of New Hampshire, Massachusetts, and Connecticut in August 1780 was the most recent of several conferences of states seeking economic and political reforms. The proposal was that Congress should be given power in national affairs to which the particular states were not competent. Washington devoutly hoped that this recommendation would be carried into effect.

Hamilton supported the effort with a letter on his own to James Duane in September 1780. This, and others of his writings shortly after, gave foretaste of policies he would advocate a decade later in the Constitutional Convention and in the Treasury. Details of his remedies altered in the interval, but essential features of his program remained the same. The costly omissions in public life which he experienced at headquarters during the war pointed to the corrections for which he continued to beg.

"The fundamental defect is a want of power in Congress." Congress, in the beginning, when it was simply *de facto*, had exercised the highest sovereignty. It should have continued to use "discretionary powers, limited only by the object for which they were given; in the present case the independence and freedom of America." The Confederation was "neither fit for war nor peace." Only a union framed to compel "the obedience of the respective members" would serve. The army would be weak and distracted, "a mob . . . ripening for a dissolution," so long as it was dependent for support on the willingness of the separate states. Congress must have independent, permanent revenues. Hamilton called for a constitutional convention "to conclude finally upon . . . a solid co-

ercive union." Congress, a legislative body, should not try to
play the executive. Capable individuals should administer the
great departments, say, General Schuyler in the war office,
McDougall in marine, Robert Morris in finance. The army, "an
essential cement of the union," should be recruited for the war
and be paid by Congress. The confronting emergency required
a foreign loan; taxes in money and in kind; and a national
bank, combining public and private credit, which would issue
a reliable currency. Hamilton anticipated his *Federalist* papers
when he urged that these reforms should be induced "by sensible and popular writings."

The winter and spring of 1780 at Morristown headquarters
were by no means all anxiety for Alexander Hamilton. Indeed,
the crisis which brought General Philip Schuyler to that place
as a member of the committee from Congress much promoted
the aide's happiness. Before the Schuylers arrived their two
elder daughters, Angelica (Mrs. John Barker Church), and Elizabeth came on a visit to their aunt, Mrs. John Cochran, wife of
the surgeon-general of the Middle Department. Until then
Hamilton had been attentive to Cornelia Lott and one Polly
(last name unknown), girls of the neighborhood. He would
have been quite willing to leave Morristown had John Laurens
succeeded in having him sent by Congress as secretary to the
American minister at Versailles, but more to his liking was a
field command in the South, for which he applied. From this
he was dissuaded, evidently by Washington.

In his first mention of Elizabeth Schuyler he wrote of a party
which she and Catharine Livingston were to attend. He seems
to have recruited Tench Tilghman, his fellow-aide, to drive
their sleigh in the event that he would be unable to be of the
party.

However, the acquaintance of Elizabeth and Alexander ripened fast to mutual attraction. In February he was writing to
her sister Margarita that Elizabeth "has found out the secret of

interesting me in every thing that concerns her. . . . She is
most unmercifully handsome and so perverse that she has
none of those pretty affectations which are the prerogatives of
beauty." He acknowledged he had been compelled to "surrender at discretion. . . . It is essential to the . . . tranquillity of
the army . . . either that she be immediately removed from
our neighbourhood, or that some other nymph qualified to
maintain an equal sway come into it." And Tilghman remarked, "Hamilton is a gone man."

Tilghman had described Elizabeth five years before: "A
Brunette with the most good natured lively dark eyes . . .
which threw a beam of good temper . . . over her whole
Countenance." The Marquis de Chastellux, visiting the
Schuylers while the newlywed Hamiltons were there, spoke of
Elizabeth's "mild agreeable countenance." Hamilton's own
least impassioned description of her was given to John
Laurens six months before Hamilton's marriage. "I give up my
liberty to Miss Schuyler. She is a good natured girl who I am
sure will never play the termagant; though not a genius she
has good sense enough to be agreeable, and though not a
beauty, she has fine black eyes—is rather handsome and has
every other requisite of the exterior to make a lover happy.
And believe me, I am lover in earnest, though I do not speak
of the perfections of my Mistress in the enthusiasm of Chivalry." Several months later he wrote to Elizabeth herself: "I
love you more and more every hour. The sweet softness and
delicacy of your mind and manners, the elevation of your sentiments, the real goodness of your heart—its tenderness to
me—the beauties of your face and person—your unpretending
good sense and that innocent simplicity and frankness which
pervade your actions, all these . . . place you in my estima-
tion above all the rest of your sex."

He told her, "You engross my thoughts too entirely. . . .
You not only employ my mind all day, but you intrude on my
sleep. I meet you in every dream." Still, he had an eye to the

practicalities of their lives together. As with nearly all young women then, Elizabeth had little formal education. He charged her to employ "all your leisure in reading. Nature has been very kind to you, do not neglect to cultivate her gifts and to enable yourself to make the distinguished figure in all respects to which you are entitled to aspire. You excel most of your sex in all the amiable qualities, endeavor to excel them equally in the splendid ones. You can do it if you please, and I shall take pride in it,—It will be a fund too to diversify our enjoyment . . . and fill all our moments to advantage." He wanted her not to miss the opportunity to visit Philadelphia.

Amid his rhapsodies, he paid her the compliment of commenting to her on public events. The defeat of Gates at Camden and his subsequent scamper filled out the picture she had of Gates as rival of her father in the northern command and the accuser of Hamilton himself in the Conway Cabal. Hamilton also wrote for her what became a classic account of Arnold's treason. Surely, she had full knowledge of her lover's disappointed application to Washington to be given a field command, and of abortive efforts made by his friends to have him appointed to a mission to France and, later, be chosen Adjutant General.

Midway of their engagement, Hamilton asked, "Do you soberly relish the pleasure of being a poor man's wife? . . . I cannot . . . forbear entreating you to realize our union on the dark side and satisfy . . . your self, how far your affection for me can make you happy in a privation of those elegancies to which you have been accustomed." If she could not contemplate bitter with sweet, "we are playing a comedy of all in the wrong, and you should correct the mistake before we begin to act the tragedy of the unhappy couple."

The scene of Hamilton's courtship, aside from dances and outings, was the Cochrans' comfortable frame house, still standing near the Ford Mansion, which was Washington's headquarters. Here Alexander and Elizabeth became engaged in March 1780, and immediately thereafter General and Mrs. Schuyler gave their consent to the marriage. General Schuyler wrote: "You cannot my dear Sir be more happy in the connection you have made with my family than I am. Until the child of a parent has made a judicious choice his heart is in continual anxiety; but this anxiety was removed the moment I discovered on whom she had placed her affections. . . . I shall therefore only entreat you to consider me as one who wishes in every way to promote your happiness, and I shall." In proper terms, Hamilton thanked Mrs. Schuyler for her confidence in him. Before the Schuylers came from Philadelphia Hamilton was accepted in the household, and thereafter his intimacy with Elizabeth's parents must have included discussions of Washington's business with the Committee of Cooperation, since Hamilton was often the go-between.

The story is told that on one occasion Hamilton, after an evening with Elizabeth and her family returned to headquarters without the password—his infatuation had driven it from his mind. The sentry refused to let him enter until Mrs. Ford's little son came to his rescue. General Washington had given the boy the password to permit him to play in the village. Seeing Hamilton in a quandary, he whispered to him the secret syllables.

The impatient engaged couple wished to be married at Morristown, but the Schuylers objected: they should wait and have their wedding in the family mansion in Albany. Angelica and Church had eloped, a proceeding which her parents found indecorous, and the Schuylers did not propose to be deprived of a home ceremony in Elizabeth's case. (This was their due, for as it turned out, both of Elizabeth's younger sisters made runaway marriages, albeit to eligible husbands and under auspices of friends of the family). The marriage took place in Albany, in the Schuyler's drawing room, on December 14, 1780. James McHenry of Washington's staff was best man, and the next day he wrote an ode celebrating the occasion. The bride was twenty-three, the groom just under twenty-six. They spent their honeymoon in the Schuyler home, then repaired to headquarters at New Windsor, New York, where General and Mrs. Washington welcomed them.

Suspicious chroniclers have supposed that Alexander Hamilton married Elizabeth Schuyler less for love than to further his ambitions. Born out of wedlock and propertyless, he certainly found that alliance with an old and wealthy family brought him social position and material prospects. But the evidence is all the other way. It was a love match. He urged Elizabeth to back out of her engagement if she could not be content with comparative poverty. He was never dependent on the Schuylers financially, though he and Elizabeth received family presents and unfailing hospitality at Albany. General Schuyler had admired Hamilton's talents and devotion as aide at headquarters long before there was any notion of the young officer becoming his son-in-law. The assumption of one critic that Alexander concealed from the Schuylers his illegitimacy is false. This is sufficiently plain in General Schuyler's acknowledgment of Hamilton's show of "delicacy" in asking for Elizabeth's hand, and, anyhow, Hamilton's history was surely known to his sponsors, who were Schuyler's close friends. If more is needed to dismiss the charge of deception it is found in the desire of the Schuylers to place value upon the merits of an individual. Hamilton had achieved the enviable position of confidential aide to the Commander in Chief.

Hamilton was far from being an unworthy conniver in his marriage. Nor was General Schuyler, though Arthur Lee sourly remarked (October 1780) that "Schuyler . . . may give his daughter to Hamilton to gain a sway over Washington or be in the military plot with him to surrender America back to great Britain. . . ."

The above conjectures are not worth noting, except that they were uttered. The marriage of Alexander and Elizabeth lasted twenty-four years, and it was happy and fruitful. Elizabeth, in her long widowhood of fifty years, devoted herself to preserving his memory. Her loyalty rose superior to his conjugal lapse (see below), which did not interrupt his affection for his wife. Loyal, sincere, and unselfish, she was the right helpmeet for a man of genius. Her religious devotion was a grateful ingredient in the storms and sorrows they suffered together. Hamilton's filial relationship to Philip Schuyler was perfectly fortunate in the private and public spheres. Their political principles were the same, and the influence of either would not have gone so far without the other.

During their engagement Elizabeth made her visits away from Morristown at times when Hamilton was absent from headquarters on errands for Washington. Much of the month of March 1780 he spent at Amboy, New Jersey, as one of the commissioners sent by Washington to settle with the enemy a general cartel for the exchange of prisoners. Hamilton and his friend Lieutenant Colonel Edward Carrington were juniors under Major General Arthur St. Clair, and Major General William Phillips and two lieutenant colonels were commissioners from Sir Henry Clinton. The meetings, as Washington expected, came to nothing, as did other similar attempts. The British commissioners were not empowered by their superior to treat with the Americans on a national basis, authorized by Congress. If they had done so they would have been recognizing the sovereignty of the United States, which the British, putting down rebellious colonies, consistently refused to do. General Phillips and his associates were limited to arranging an agreement between the Commanders in Chief. This the Americans regarded as "inadmissible, delusive and impracticable," as whatever Sir Henry Clinton pledged might be violated by his successor. Nor did informal talks looking to an inclusive exchange of prisoners make any progress. Both sides professed the desire to end the sufferings of captives, but the fact was that a standing system for freeing prisoners would have been more advantageous to the British than to the American army. This was because the soldiers received back by the British were in fit condition, while the Americans to be released had been ill treated in their confinement by the enemy. Furthermore, the British, aside from loyalist volunteers, had to recruit from across the Atlantic, while the Americans had the native population on which to draw. Throughout the war exchanges of prisoners were partial and local.

More disappointing, not to say distressing, was the aftermath of Hamilton's journey with Washington to Hartford to confer with the French officers.

Chapter 5

VICTORIOUS AT YORKTOWN

The all-important business of General Washington was to concert with General Rochambeau and Admiral DeTernay plans for what proved to be the final campaign of the war, and Hamilton frequently wrote the preparatory letters. The Commander in Chief, Lafayette, Knox, Hamilton, McHenry, and other aides took horse at headquarters in Bergen County, New Jersey, September 17, 1780, for Hartford. At dinner that night at the home of Joshua Hett Smith, convenient to the Hudson crossing by King's Ferry, General Benedict Arnold was a guest. Pleading that the wound he had suffered at Saratoga disabled him from field command of the left wing of the army to which he was appointed, Arnold had prevailed on Washington to place him in charge of the fortress of West Point and its dependencies. In that post Arnold had used the confidential services of Smith, as had General Robert Howe before him. Smith was reputed to be a firm patriot, though his brother William was Chief Justice under the British at New York.

Arnold affected to inquire of Washington whether he should

comply with a request of the British Colonel Beverley Robinson, who had written that day from the sloop of war *Vulture* off Teller's (now Croton) Point. Robinson's business was said to be about his house across the river from West Point, which Arnold used as his headquarters. Washington said no, Robinson must pursue his property affairs with the civil government. As later developed, Washington's refusal to allow the use of a flag compelled Arnold to the secret tryst which led to disclosure of his treasonable action.

At Hartford, Washington's conclusion with the French allies was tentative. The American commander emphasized that "of all the enterprises which may be undertaken, the most important and decisive is the reduction of New York, which is the center and focus of all the British forces." That object required a naval superiority. The hope was that the Count De Guichen would arrive with his fleet from the West Indies in October to block the mouth of the Hudson. If that did not happen, then "an expedition should be made against the enemy in the Southern states," where Cornwallis was overrunning the Carolinas and Virginia.

On their return, the American officers spent the night at Fishkill. They started before breakfast for Arnold's headquarters and an inspection of the defenses at West Point. Hamilton remained with Washington and his generals, who turned off to visit redoubts on the east bank of the river, while McHenry and other aides posted ahead to give notice that the party would soon arrive at the Robinson house for breakfast. When they got there, Lieutenant Colonel Richard Varick and Major David Franks, Arnold's aides, told them that Arnold had been suddenly called to West Point but would promptly return.

After breakfast, Washington, Lafayette, and Knox were rowed across to West Point. Hamilton, at the Robinson house, was writing a letter to his fiancée. He was interrupted by "Mrs. Arnold's unhappy situation [which] called us all to her assistance. . . . Raving distracted," she complained of hot irons on her head, accused Varick of ordering her infant killed, and begged for the child's life. She seemed all the wilder because she was in her nightclothes, her hair streaming. Hamilton, Varick, Dr. Eustis all assured her that Arnold would soon return, to which she cried, "No, no, he is gone forever!"

If Arnold's aides already suspected that he had gone to the enemy, they did not share their fears with Hamilton. Arnold's sudden departure, his barge pointed downriver, his wife's distress, the report of a spy taken on the American lines, all were ominous. Not until later did Hamilton know the story. Arnold had been seated at breakfast when an officer brought him letters. He had showed no alarm, but had soon gone up to Mrs. Arnold's room. Two minutes later Washington's servant had announced that the General was at hand. Franks had informed Arnold, who "came down in great confusion . . . ordering a horse to be saddled, mounted him and told me to inform his Excellency that he was gone over to West Point . . ." The message that had put Arnold to precipitate flight had come from Lieutenant Colonel John Jameson, commanding the outpost of North Castle (now North White Plains). Jameson told that a southbound traveler, "John Anderson," had been captured with incriminating papers which had been dispatched to Washington. Arnold had seen only a moment for escape. Actually, Jameson's courier with the fatal papers had missed the General on the road; he did not reach the Robinson house until Washington had gone over to West Point. Hamilton had kept the packet unopened for the General's return.

Washington arrived mid-afternoon, disturbed that he had not found Arnold at West Point, where all preparation for defense had been neglected. The packet from Jameson left no doubt of the reasons. It contained a pass for "John Anderson" in Arnold's hand; a plan of the fortifications at West Point, with directions for an attack against them; a return of garrison, ordnance, and stores; and a copy of the minutes of Washing-

ton's recent council of war. These had been found in the stocking feet of the traveler captured by militiamen at Tarrytown.
The clincher was a letter from the prisoner, Major John André,
Adjutant General of the British army. Admitting that he had
come ashore from *Vulture* seeking military intelligence, he protested that he had gone within the American lines and donned
civilian clothing against his will. He begged to be exculpated
"from an imputation of having assumed a mean character for
treacherous purposes." He did not need to name Arnold to fix
the identity of his fellow-conspirator.

Hamilton and McHenry galloped the dozen miles to Verplanck's Point to try to intercept Arnold on his way to *Vulture*.
Hamilton could only confess that they arrived "much too late."
Indeed, he sent back to Washington a letter from the traitor on
the vessel, who brazenly protested that he sought to serve the
colonies by bringing them back to their right allegiance. Enclosed was Arnold's letter to his wife, which Washington delivered to her unopened.

Being nearer than Washington to the army on the west side
of the Hudson, Hamilton alerted General Greene to start a
brigade toward King's Ferry, for the enemy might attack West
Point that night in spite of discovery of the plot. He would try
to find Colonel Jonathan Meigs, whose corps was on the east
side of the river, and hurry him to strengthen the garrison at
West Point. Hamilton himself would prepare the defenses at
Verplanck's. He hoped General Washington would approve
his emergency measures.

Dinner at the Robinson house that afternoon, in spite of the
plentiful table, was one of the most melancholy of the war.
Washington had been taken to the bedside of the frantic Peggy
and assured her that she would not be harmed. At the meal,
her delirious ravings still ringing in his ears, he alone behaved as though there had been no shocking betrayal.

Hamilton was intensely occupied that night. He worked
until past two o'clock next morning, preparing against a possi-

ble stroke by the British. The orders to Greene were amplified,
Wayne, at Haverstraw, was to march his brigade to West
Point. Directions to Colonel Nathaniel Wade, now commanding at West Point, were more particular. Hamilton, for Washington, informed Governor George Clinton of the plot, and,
what was harder, in the final minutes of their vigil, he disclosed the mischief to General Rochambeau. Hamilton added
lines to his letter to Elizabeth Schuyler. His tenderness for her
was reflected in his conpassion for the distressed Peggy Arnold. "Her sufferings were so eloquent that I wished myself
her brother, to have a right to become her defender." Both he
and General Washington believed, as Arnold had declared,
that she was innocent in the treason. In this they were deceived, for she had been privy to the negotiations from the
first and had transmitted some of the guilty messages. It was
noted afterward that she had delayed her mad scene long
enough to give Arnold a head start toward *Vulture*.

Meantime, André was to be lodged under close watch at
West Point. Lieutenant Colonel Gouvion had hastened to Fishkill to arrest Joshua Hett Smith, Arnold's go-between, and
bring him to the Robinson house for examination. This was
directed next morning, September 26, by Washington in the
presence of his officers. Robert Hanson Harrison took notes,
which Hamilton summarized in his own testimony at Smith's
court-martial later. Hamilton and others referred to Smith's
"confession," which was rather his story as conductor of
André before and after André's interview with Arnold. In
spite of chills and a night ride to the angry summons—
Washington had "expressed himself with some warmth"—the
bewigged squire was collected under the questioning. He had
served commanders at West Point, first Robert Howe, then Arnold, as intermediary with spies. Arnold had furnished him a
boat and Smith had engaged two of his tenants, the Cahoon
brothers, to row him to *Vulture* the night of September 21 to
bring off, as he believed, Colonel Beverley Robinson. Robin-

son was to give Arnold military information in return for help
in regaining his estate. Smith's passenger was not Robinson,
but "John Anderson," whom Smith had taken to a spot near
Haverstraw, where Anderson had met Arnold in a copse of fir
trees. At morning light the weary rowers had refused to return
Anderson to the warship, so he had been lodged at Smith's
house till the next evening. Arnold had told Smith that Anderson was a mere merchant who had borrowed a red coat out of
vanity. Smith had then furnished Anderson with a civilian
cloak and hat, had seen him that night across King's Ferry,
and had accompanied him for a distance toward New York.
Smith protested that he knew nothing of what had passed between Arnold and Anderson. Because of Arnold's high office
and distinguished reputation, Smith could not suspect him of
any evil design.

Smith appealed to Hamilton to confirm that in New York
Smith bore the character of a patriot. Hamilton replied that
Smith's "intemperate zeal" in the Whig cause made his sincerity questionable, but he admitted that suspicion was fed by
the toryism of his brother rather than by any political actions
of his own. Washington concluded from the preliminary inquiry that Smith "had a considerable share in this business,"
in fact had "confessed facts sufficient to establish his guilt."
Smith was tried by court-martial, September 30, 1780; he was
charged with complicity in Arnold's plot. He was acquitted
October 26 for lack of evidence. He was then arrested by New
York authorities and imprisoned at Goshen; but he escaped in
May 1781, went to New York City and was there maintained
by the British.

Major André was transferred from West Point to Tappan,
New York, where he was confined in the village tavern
("Stone House," yet standing) near Washington's headquarters. Hamilton penned Washington's letter, dated September 29, to the board of general officers ordering André's court-
martial. André's frank confession was in itself sufficient to

produce the verdict that he "ought to be considered as a Spy, . . . and . . . agreeable to the Law and usage of Nations . . . ought to suffer Death." Hamilton had solicitude for André, and he visited him several times. He recorded that the prisoner "united a peculiar elegance of mind and manners, and the advantages of a pleasing person. His sentiments were elevated, and inspired esteem. His elocution was handsome; his address easy, polite, and insinuating." Hamilton drew the doomed man's thanks for what services he could render; he took to Washington André's request to be allowed to write to Sir Henry Clinton, exculpating his General from blame for his fate.

Moreover, Hamilton supported André's entreaty that he be shot and not suffer the shame "to die on the Gibbet." The refusal of the plea was not told to André, to spare his feelings as long as possible. Hamilton thought that compliance with the request would not have had "an ill effect . . . some people are only sensible to motives of policy, and . . . from a narrow disposition, mistake it."

Whether Hamilton, in a disguised hand, with the signature "A B," urged Sir Henry Clinton to save André by surrendering Arnold is disputed. "Though an enemy his virtues and accomplishments are admired. Perhaps he might be released for General Arnold, delivered up without restriction or condition, which is the prevailing wish. Arnold appears to have been the guilty author of the mischief; and ought more properly to be the victim, as there is great reason to believe he meditated a double treachery, and had arranged . . . that if discovered in the first instance, he might have it in his power to sacrifice Major André to his own safety." A postscript warned, "No time is to be lost." The letter is dated Tappan, September 30, 1780. It is likely that it reached Clinton by the hand of Lieutenant General James Robertson, who came to Dobbs Ferry on October 1 to plead with General Greene, representing the American army, to spare André. While these two conferred,

Hamilton walked with Murray, Robertson's aide, and slipped to him the note. Sir Henry Clinton endorsed the missive "Hamilton. W[ashington's] aid de camp, received after A['s] death."

Phrases in the letter are like those Hamilton used to his friend John Laurens. Also, Washington had authorized a proposal to Clinton to give up Arnold for André, to which the scornful answer was that a deserter was never surrendered. One paper by Hamilton in a disguised hand (in connection with the Reynolds affair, below) is known. Against Hamilton's authorship is his statement that he refused to propose the exchange to André because he would neither offend André's honor nor involve himself in "the impropriety of the measure." Actually, André rejected the suggestion, which was made to him by another officer. Hamilton declared, "The moment he had been guilty of so much frailty, I should have ceased to esteem him." Lastly, Hamilton would never have composed the senseless introduction, reciting what Sir Henry Clinton too well knew.

The story of Arnold's treason was told by Hamilton in a long letter (probably written October 11, 1780) to Lieutenant Colonel John Laurens, a copy of which he sent to Elizabeth Schuyler. His execration of Arnold is in contrast to his pity for André. The doings which came under Hamilton's eye are certainly accurately related, though there are unconscious errors in what he learned afterward. He was mistaken in supposing that Arnold had been in correspondence with the British for three months; the correspondence had gone on for eighteen. For completeness he described the execution of André, though he did not witness it, as General Washington and his staff stayed away.

General Washington's worries made him edgy at times, though if any man was self-controlled and considerate of others it was he. As for Hamilton, after his first months as aide he had a cumulative itch for an assignment more militarily active than service at headquarters, most of which was paperwork. In the autumn of 1780 he and his close friends Lafayette, Laurens, and Greene had projects for employing him elsewhere, but they were disappointed. Hamilton readily acquiesced in Washington's preference for Brigadier General Edward Hand for Adjutant General and was glad to see John Laurens chosen by Congress for a special mission to France. However, the failure of two prior applications to Washington to release him for field command left him intent on another try. Lafayette, who was always hatching new adventures, was his coadjutor in plans for an attack on New York in which Hamilton would command light troops. Congress, at Washington's urging, had commissioned aides for line duty. Washington had approved the scheme, but then it was suddenly abandoned.

The relative quiet of winter headquarters at New Windsor sharpened Hamilton's frustration. He and the Commander in Chief had worked until midnight of February 15, 1781 on dispatches to be got off early next morning to the French allies at Newport. The new day brought another pressing order with which Hamilton was hurrying down the stairs when he passed General Washington ascending. Washington directed his aide to join him in his room above. Hamilton quickly delivered his papers to Tilghman, and as he was returning he was buttonholed by Lafayette. After an impatient minute's exchange, Hamilton quit Lafayette abruptly. Instead of finding Washington in his room as usual, he stood at the head of the stairs, in Hamilton's account, "accosting me in a very angry tone, 'Col. Hamilton (said he), you have kept me waiting . . . these ten minutes. I must tell you Sir you treat me with disrespect.' I replied without petulancy, but with decision 'I am not conscious of it Sir, but since you have thought it necessary to tell me so, we part.' 'Very well Sir (said he) if it be your choice' or something to this effect and we separated. I sincerely believe my absence which gave so much umbrage did not last two minutes."

Hamilton was nursing his resentment when, within the hour, "Tilghman came to me in the Generals name assuring me of his great confidence in my abilities, integrity usefulness &c and of his desire in a candid conversation to heal a difference which could not have happened but in a moment of passion. I requested Mr. Tilghman to tell him, that I had taken my resolution in a manner not to be revoked." He begged to be excused from an interview, but promised not to quit headquarters until other aides returned and said that, meantime, they should behave toward each other as though nothing had happened. Washington was thankful for his continuing assistance, and there the matter stood.

Hamilton a few days later described the contretemps in a long, self-justifying letter to his father-in-law, General Schuyler. He did not want Schuyler's friendship with Washington to suffer from his own defection, which had long been premeditated if ever an unpleasantness should occur. Public knowledge of friction between them would probably have ill results, so some plausible ground should be ascribed for their break. Hamilton added that he could not think of quitting the army during the war. He was balancing between reentering the artillery and seeking a command in the light infantry for the coming campaign.

Hamilton comes off badly in the incident, and his behavior is not helped by his description of it. General Washington did all in his power to heal the breach. He generously assured Hamilton of his confidence in the fine qualities of his aide and offered, in a frank conversation, to repair the spat. Hamilton was abler than his fellow aides, but had he been older, as was Harrison, or self-abnegating, as was Tilghman, he would have answered Washington differently. His brilliance did not save him from the unwisdom of youth, false pride, and vanity. He took pleasure in imagining that by refusing to be reconciled he had subjected the Commander in Chief to humiliation! He declared what Schuyler abundantly knew, that "The General is a very honest man. His competitors have slender abilities and less integrity. His popularity has often been essential to the safety of America, and is still of great importance to it." However, "for three years past I have felt no friendship for him and have professed none."

In underrating Washington and denying his attachment he was alike at fault. In his cross mood he did himself an injustice. His support of the General spoke a different language, and less than a year before he had signed himself to his superior "affectionately." Schuyler hoped he would choose to remain in the post "which you have . . . filled so beneficially to the public, and with such extensive reputation." But Hamilton was envious of the aides who had left the headquarters staff for field service, such as Baylor, Fitzgerald, Webb, Laurens, and Scammell, for they took satisfaction in their exploits and usually gained advancement in rank and seniority. Their options pleased Hamilton more than the constancy of Tench Tilghman, who, after brief field experience, came to Washington as volunteer at headquarters, there remained throughout the war, and stood by the side of the Commander in Chief when he resigned his commission. It was a matter of temperament. Hamilton felt that the war would be over at end of the next campaign; if he was again to show bravery in battle he must at once down pen and seize sword. He was now married, which doubtless put a new value on the character he should bear in civil life. On the other hand, as Schuyler suggested, he was uniquely valuable at headquarters, while others, such as his companions in the assault at Yorktown, would have led an attack with the same spirit.

All in all, it was probably fortunate that Hamilton had his return to field command, though the occasion of his quitting Washington's staff was to be regretted. He did not cease to

urge reforms in military and political establishments, the need
of which he had learned as Washington's aide. His influence
as a statesman was helped by his experience in combat. It gave
him a closer tie with field officers who were afterward, in large
numbers, prominent in government. Lastly, and chiefly, the
coolness between him and Washington was soon ended; their
collaboration was resumed, and it became one of a closeness
and consequence which neither could have foreseen.

Mrs. Hamilton, as hostess at New Windsor, behaved as
though nothing untoward had occurred. She served tea "with
much grace" to Washington, Knox, and the aides, the special
guest being Baron von Closen, who had brought dispatches
from Newport. Hamilton, as always, was in the General's
party on the visit to the French commanders early in March
1781. Von Closen was along, but doubtless Hamilton found
use for his ability to translate and interpret. Newport was illu-
minated in welcome to the Commander in Chief. Hamilton, as
often before, penned the General's grateful acknowledgment.
The American officers accompanied their hosts to see the fleet
of Destouches, with 1100 troops of Rochambeau's force, sail
for the Chesapeake. Earlier, a smaller naval detachment under
De Tilly had been unable to menace Benedict Arnold, now in
British service, in his fortified post at Portsmouth, Virginia. It
was hoped that the larger fleet, with its land force, would cooperate with Lafayette and Steuben to capture Arnold, who
otherwise would add to the ravages of Cornwallis in the
southern states.

Hamilton did not return with Washington to New Windsor,
but joined Elizabeth at her parents' home at Albany. A few
weeks later he was back at headquarters; numbers of his letters for the General reported difficulty in finding commands
for deserving officers, Lafayette included, and these gave Hamilton gloomy foretaste of what he himself must encounter.
About the middle of April 1781 Betsy, down from Albany,
joined him in their first independent home, the DePeyster

house, on what is now Denning's Point on the east bank of the Hudson opposite New Windsor. (The building, much altered from its original Dutch style, and, sadly, surrounded by railroad and industries, stood until 1953. It was a gracious dwelling.) The Hamiltons occupied it for less than three months. For ten days, however, Hamilton appears to have gone back and forth from the house to headquarters at New Windsor; his letters, for Washington and himself, are dated from there.

Hamilton, never idle, when he was out of the General's family and had not yet returned to the army at Dobbs Ferry took the interval to write some of his notable early papers. He had his hand in, for he had recently prepared a letter for John Laurens to take to France, where he sought monetary and military help for a final effort of the Americans to expel the enemy. Hamilton used the high diplomacy of entire frankness. Unless his country received fresh aid, resistance was finished, and all that France had furnished in the past would be forfeited. On the other hand, once the war was won, America would develop her vast latent resources and repay her debts within a short period. His optimism contrasted with the apprehensions of French and British economists of the day. Whereas they, in old countries, had been impressed by the lessons of diminishing returns in production, Hamilton, in a youthful society on the edge of a continent of untapped riches, foresaw ever ampler material rewards. In order to give Hamilton's plea to the French court the authenticity of his own autograph, Washington copied the letter delivered to Laurens.

At the same time, Hamilton did not omit to plump for renewed energies at home. His urgent recommendations were expressed in his letter to Robert Morris, amounting to an essay. As the great departments of government should no longer suffer from the fumbling of committees of Congress, but be entrusted to able individuals, he begged Morris to accept the office of public Financier, to which he had been named.

Hamilton asked Quartermaster General Pickering to furnish
him with works on economics which would help him prepare
his argument. (How Pickering could produce writings by
Richard Price, David Hume, Malachy Postlethwayt, and others
when he could not summon up food and clothing for the army
is a mystery.) Hamilton outlined the organization of a national
bank which would "increase public and private credit. The
former gives power to the state . . . and the latter . . . ex-
tends the operations of commerce among individuals. Industry
is increased, commodities are multiplied, agriculture and
manufactures flourish, and herein consists the true wealth and
prosperity of the state."

Morris was thankful for Hamilton's volunteered "performance" and would benefit from it; the letter soon led to active
cooperation between the two men.

At DePeyster's Point Hamilton commenced and probably
completed the series of five papers entitled "The Continentalist," which were published at intervals over the period of a
year in *The New-York Packet*. (Incidentally, they were signed
"A B," the same initials put to the secret letter to Sir Henry
Clinton asking for the swap of Arnold for André, which may
be a point favoring Hamilton's authorship of the latter.) The
thrust of these pieces, which depicted the low state into which
the country had fallen, was that it was necessary to strengthen
the central government. To render the coming military campaign decisive, "we ought . . . to ENLARGE THE POWERS OF
CONGRESS. Every plan of which, this is not the foundation, will
be illusory. The separate exertions of the states will never suffice. Nothing but . . . exertion of the resources of the whole,
under the direction of a Common Council with power . . . to
give efficacy to their resolutions, can preserve us from being a
CONQUERED PEOPLE now, or can make us a HAPPY PEOPLE
hereafter." The papers were not hortatory only, for he listed
economic means of national health. Later he did not approve

of land and head taxes; a sinking fund which he suggested in "The Continentalist" became his characteristic policy.

General Washington drew his former aide back to headquarters to help compose an embarrassing apology to Count Rochambeau. Washington had criticized the French allies for not sending to the Chesapeake the larger fleet and ground force of Destouches in the first place, as he had urged, instead of the naval detachment which was powerless to dislodge Arnold. The American commander's complaint was set out in a private letter to his kinsman and Mount Vernon manager, Lund Washington, but by bad luck that mail was captured by the British and Washington's strictures were paraded in Rivington's *Gazette*. Lafayette, naturally eager to promote unbroken harmony with the French, was upset by the disclosure, and he reported that Congress was buzzing with the indiscretion. Rochambeau wrote Washington in restrained protest. He and the naval commanders at Newport wished to obey Washington's orders to the letter, but in this instance the orders had not arrived in time to prevent the error. Rochambeau charitably suggested that perhaps the published letter was a forgery.

Washington and Hamilton collaborated in the reply. They pointed out the fact that no such censure had been addressed to any public body. Washington's fault-finding had been expressed to his relative only. However, there was nothing for it but to admit that Rivington had not changed one sour comment of Washington's; the letter too well suited the Tory's purpose as it stood. Washington sincerely regretted the indiscretion and hoped it would not disturb cordial relations with the French allies, of whose conduct he had the fullest appreciation. Rochambeau replied that on his part there would be no interruption of mutual confidence.

When he was about to leave Washington's staff, Hamilton inquired of General Greene whether there was anything worth while he could do in the southern army, and he added, "You know I shall hate to be nominally a soldier." Shortly after that he wrote to General Washington in the same vein. Having applied several times before and been refused, he evidently preferred a letter to a personal interview. He explained that he now had a commission permitting him an assignment in the line, but since he belonged to no regiment he could command only in a specially formed light corps. He believed that, knowing his desire to serve the country, field officers would not oppose his appointment.

General Washington answered the same day. He wrote that he was embarrassed to be unable to hold out a prospect of granting his former aide's wish. Other staff officers had recently been given commands, and the line officers who had trained the troops and had expected to lead them in battle had objected strongly. Hamilton's merits could not be disputed, and the Commander in Chief could order as he chose, but "it will not do to push that right too far . . . in a service like ours—and at a time so critical as the present." He trusted that Hamilton would not impute his refusal to any other cause, meaning their friction back in the winter.

Hamilton's disappointment was keen, but he waited a few days before making his considered reply. He did not mean to be importunate or to press for any favor which the General thought not for the good of the cause. However, he explained why his case differed from those of officers whose preferment had provoked protest. He had not given up hope of seeing action.

He escorted his wife, now three months pregnant, to the Schuyler home at Albany; then, on July 8, he reported to Washington's camp near Debbs Ferry. There the Americans had been joined by the French from Rhode Island. Hamilton evidently felt that being on the scene might produce results. However, when nothing was said of a command for him, he wrote to Washington, enclosing his commission. The General promptly sent Tilghman to him, urging that he should not resign and promising that something close to his wishes would be offered. Hamilton accepted this assurance, and at the same time he begged his wife to believe that the dangers he would meet would be less than she feared. By polite invitation he quartered with General Benjamin Lincoln at Kings Bridge, where he was cordially received by friends in both armies.

Three weeks later general orders announced that Lieutenant Colonel Hamilton would command the light companies of the first and second New York regiments, together with the two companies of York levies under Captains Sackett and Williams. Nicholas Fish would be major of the battalion, which when formed would join the advanced corps under command of Colonel Scammel. This was precisely to Hamilton's liking. He set about equipping his troops with necessities. He needed from Quartermaster Pickering tents for the field officers and camp kettles and pails for the men. Tilghman thought the Continent could not furnish the militia with shoes, so Hamilton applied directly to General Washington, explaining that the state did not supply them and the men had spent their bounties.

The demonstrations of the combined armies before New York were just that—only demonstrations. The enemy on Manhattan island was too strong to be attacked. In the meantime, the military situation in the South was parlous. Lafayette, commanding in Virginia, had written Hamilton toward the end of May, "I have . . . so many difficulties to Combat, so many Ennemies to deal with that I am just that much of a general as will make me an Historian of misfortunes and nail my name upon the ruins of what good folks are pleased to Call the army of Virginia, . . . We have 900 Continentals, their Infantry is near five to one; their Cavalry ten to one our Militia are not numerous, come without arms, and are not used to war. . . . The . . . great disproportion of forces gave the Ennemy such advantages that I durst not venture out ant listen to my fondness for enterprise." Two months later

Hamilton himself wrote of "the enemy making an alarming progress in the southern states, lately in complete possession of two of them, though now in part rescued by the genius and exertions of a General [Nathanael Greene] without an army, a force under Cornwallis still formidable in Virginia."

Washington wrote in his diary on August 1 that, lacking troops for an attack on New York, "I turned my views . . . to an operation to the Southward." By the middle of that month he had learned from Lafayette that Cornwallis was fortifying himself at Yorktown, Virginia. Hamilton prepared his wife gradually for news that he was going to the southern scene of war. To allay her alarm he said what in fact the American command feared, that "ten to one . . . our views will be disappointed, by Cornwallis retiring to South Carolina by land." Anyhow, all would be over by late October, then he would speed home to her.

On the eve of marching, Hamilton got an increase in his corps of two companies with appropriate officers formed by the Connecticut line. All crossed Kings Ferry August 20 and were at Haverstraw that evening. General Schuyler wrote later from Albany, "My Dear daughter is in good health but was so sensibly affected by your removal to the southward that I apprehended consequences; she is now at ease." From Hamilton's letters to his wife we can follow his course. Five days after crossing Kings Ferry he left the Hudson, going first to Springfield, then on to Brunswick, Trenton, and the Delaware. Washington took every pains to encourage Sir Henry Clinton's spies to report that the allied attack was to be against New York by way of Staten Island. Why would Washington trundle along thirty flatboats on carriages unless it was to cross the Kill van Kull? And why were large bake ovens constructed at Chatham, New Jersey, unless that place was to be a base for assailing Mahattan? Clinton's fears kept him snug and allowed free passage of the American and French armies to Trenton and beyond, where they were out of the British reach. The deception of the enemy may have been helped by a ruse employed by Hamilton at headquarters some months earlier. An American spy was found to be in pay of the British, and he was allowed to see a map marked as for a naval and land attack on New York. The double agent, to be sure, asked Hamilton what was to be the destination of the army. Hamilton gave a double twist to his answer; knowing that the truth would be most misleading, he replied, "We are going to Virginia."

General Washington was entered on the greatest concentration of military and naval forces of his career, from divergent quarters and chancy in the timing, for all were to converge on Yorktown at once. His anxieties were correspondingly acute. As Hamilton had been so long in on headquarters secrets, he probably knew the hopes and fears of the Commander in Chief. Would Admiral Barras with his squadron from Newport reach the Chesapeake with provisions and heavy ordnance to unite with the larger fleet of Admiral De Grasse, which was promised to arrive from the West Indies with an army of 3000 men? Or would Barras be destroyed by the twenty warships of British Admirals Graves and Hood, which had put out from Sandy Hook? Washington was mightily relieved when he met an express near Chester who reported that De Grasse was within the Virginia capes with twenty-eight ships of the line. His army would be debarked at Jamestown to reinforce that of Lafayette. Hamilton, at Head of Elk (Elkton, Maryland), promptly wrote his wife that he had news that made victory certain.

Boats were gathered at the top of the Chesapeake, but there were only enough to take half the armies. As the light corps would be the first needed on the Virginia peninsula, Hamilton embarked with his battalion on September 7, 1781. The craft were inferior, and the voyage was maddeningly slow. Five days later word came that De Grasse had left the Chesapeake to battle a British fleet, and so could not protect the flotilla of troops; therefore the vessels bearing Hamilton's contingent were ordered to safety at Annapolis. After this interruption they rounded into the James River and quickly were ashore at Williamsburg, the concentration point for all land forces. There Hamilton was reunited with Lafayette and with his old teacher at Elizabethtown, Lieutenant Colonel Francis Barber, who had campaigned with the Marquis. Also he met John Laurens, back from his successful visit to France, for which Hamilton had helped prepare. Laurens was now on Washington's staff, and he wrote for the general a beseeching letter to De Grasse. That old sea dog, having been victorious over the British fleet of Graves and Hood, now proposed to sail from his station at the mouth of the York River to chase off the small squadron of Admiral Digby. The armies were about to encircle Cornwallis on the land side, and if De Grasse left the river it would be open for the entrance of a fleet from New York to rescue the besieged Cornwallis. De Grasse relented, and he continued to give the indispensable sea blockade.

Hamilton's battalion, now in Hazen's brigade, marched the dozen miles to Yorktown on September 28 and took post in the great semicircle of allied troops a mile from the enemy's outer defenses. Cornwallis would never have dug in at Yorktown except for the promise of his superior, General Sir Henry Clinton at New York, to relieve or evacuate his force of some 7500 if it were menaced. Cornwallis, on a cliff bulging into the river, was partially protected by ravines and marshes, but a gap of open ground half a mile wide formed the obvious allied approach. This would have to be by siege tactics, connecting trenches with redoubts and batteries at intervals.

The bombardment of Yorktown began on October 9 from the outer parallel (trench) 600 yards from the enemy defenses. Progress on the inner parallel, at half the distance, was stopped by enfilading fire from two British advanced redoubts, known as numbers 9 and 10. On October 14 the Americans turned their fire on them, damaging the abatis of felled trees and the embankments fraised with jutting sharpened stakes. By late afternoon the engineers thought the destruction sufficient to permit the storming of these menacing forts that night. Lafayette was placed in over-all command of the American attack on No. 10, on the brow of the cliff. Rochambeau named the officers who led the French assault on the larger fort, No. 9.

Lafayette assigned the honor of leading the American battalions of light troops to his aide, Lieutenant Colonel Gimat, who had served with him through the Virginia campaign. This was a stunning blow to Hamilton, for during his years of noncombatant duty he had yearned for such a chance of derring-do. He instantly pressed his claim on Lafayette. He was senior to Gimat, and besides, he was officer of the day. Lafayette and Hamilton took the question to General Washington. Probably Hamilton's plea was brief as it was ardent, for the Commander in Chief knew the whole story back of his former aide's entreaty. Soon Hamilton broke from the tent and embraced Major Nicholas Fish, exclaiming "We have it! We have it!" Lafayette contented Gimat by giving him leadership of the storm on the right.

In full darkness, on signal of six cannon fired in rapid succession from the French batteries, both storming parties sprang from the nearest trenches. Hamilton commanded his men to advance with unloaded muskets, relying on the bayonet only. They rushed upon the work under furious fire from above, not waiting for the sappers and miners to remove the obstructions. Hamilton was first over the parapet and into the fort. Lieutenant Colonel Laurens had circled and came in from the rear, Fish from the left side. Francis Barber led the supporting column. "The redoubt," Hamilton later reported to Lafayette, "was in the same moment enveloped and carried in every part." He gave high praise to all of his companions.

The French were similarly victorious in their storm of No. 9. Hamilton had nine killed and thirty-one wounded, including numbers of the officers. The enemy casualties were far fewer;

twenty were captured. The losses at No. 9 were similar in
proportion to the larger forces engaged. "Few cases," Washington pronounced, "have exhibited stronger proofs of In-
trepidity, coolness and firmness than were shown upon this
occasion."

Hamilton got off a brief letter to his wife telling of the success of his command and assuring her that, in the unlikely
event of another storm, it would not fall to his lot to lead it.
Washington informed General Greene that capture of the
enemy redoubts "will prove of almost infinite importance in
our Approaches." These forts were taken into the close parallel
and their guns were turned on the inner defenses of Yorktown. Lord Cornwallis reported to Sir Henry Clinton, in a letter that had gone only a few miles when its prediction came
true, "we shall soon be exposed to an assault in ruined works,
in a bad position, and with weakened numbers." Two days
more passed, and his lordship asked General Washington for
terms of surrender. He signed, and Washington, Rochambeau,
and Barras—De Grasse was detained by illness—put their
names to the capitulation in the redoubt which Hamilton's
troops had captured. This was October 19, 1781. The battle
proved to be all but the end of the fighting war.

Hamilton waited only for the surrender ceremony before
hastening to his wife at Albany; "Indeed," said Schuyler, "he
tyred his horses . . . and was obliged to hire others to come
on from Red Hook."

Chapter 6

CONGRESS AND CAMP

Yorktown saw the end of Hamilton's service in the Revolutionary army. The stresses of the war as revealed at military headquarters informed his future actions in public life. The emergency government had been unable to summon the resources of the country, and once peace was declared, a competent structure for the new nation had to be achieved. In this task none was more eagerly creative than Alexander Hamilton. He is known to most for his success, as our first Secretary of the Treasury, in restoring public credit and launching the economy on a prosperous course, but although his accomplishments as fiscal manager were of high order, they came as the second phase of his program. As prerequisite, the distracted political framework of the Confederation had to be discarded and replaced by a constitution that would permit stability and progress. Hamilton was a first-rate national economist, but, more than that, he was a statesman, a political organizer.

Hamilton's efforts for the Constitution, before and after the convention of 1787, take precedence of his Treasury policies, in importance as well as in time. He disagreed fundamentally with Adam Smith's laissez-faire philosophy. The reasons for his emphasis on cooperation rather than on competition, on social collaboration instead of on individual acquisitiveness, are not far to seek. The great Scottish founder of the "classical" school of political economy was prescribing for Britain, which was due to throw off the shackles of over-regulation. Hamilton's therapy, by contrast, was designed for an infant country in need of public planning. Smith dismissed mercantilism (government management of commerce and industry), which had run its course in Europe; Hamilton embraced essential features of mercantilism as the means of national economic development. Both men were right, for in social policy all is relative to time and place.

The notion that Alexander Hamilton was the proponent— even the progenitor—of American private capitalism is mistaken. True, in his insistence on cohesion he valued elements in the society which were active and knew their own interest. He patronized moneyed men—merchants, manufacturers, bankers—because they could advance his program for the common benefit. His program was not framed for the special advantage of capitalists; to him they were a precious nucleus, not a cynosure. Since he promoted business it has become too common to think of him as special pleader for economic privilege. The fact is that he used investors and enterprisers—he did not make himself their servant. The picture of Hamilton the aristocrat against Jefferson the democrat is false. Hamilton was solicitous of the well-being of all of the people. Historians who ought to know better have said that Hamilton's motive springs were personal glory and power. It seems not to have occurred to them that his passion was unselfish, that he strove for the welfare of the entire community. The rights of man were Jefferson's noble ideal. Hamilton wished to clothe those rights with material benefits and social responsibilities. Advocates who belong in the pantheon are not promoters of class interest, but apostles of the *summum bonum*.

Jefferson—ruralist, student, scientist, colleague of the French *philosophes*—stressed individual endowments and initiative. His thought tended toward dispersal, toward centrifugal forces in society. Hamilton was urban, collectivist, impressed by the importance of centripetal motion or magnetic pull. In practical terms, the distinction was between states' rights and central control. Of course these two were leaders of "factions" (political parties) which embraced others of similar views and in some cases hardly inferior faculties. Madison, Patrick Henry, Richard Henry Lee, William Branch Giles, and John Taylor of Caroline belonged in Jefferson's camp, while Hamilton's associates included Timothy Pickering, George Cabot, Fisher Ames, Rufus King, Henry Knox. The two men were not heroes *sans peur et sans reproche*. They were sons of Adam. Jefferson's ideal of the rights of man stands in shocking contrast to his possession of large numbers of slaves on whose labor he lived; he sold slaves, sometimes secretly and at a distance from their home plantations. He was capable of conscious deception. Hamilton, while more frank than Jefferson, in his ardor became too confidential with British representatives—official and unofficial—entertained the project of a filibuster in Latin America, and, toward the end, confused Federalism with Christianity. Hamilton and Jefferson quarreled to a degree dangerous to the nation which they both loved. These were their human failings, without which the story of their services would be dull.

In April 1782 Hamilton applied to the Supreme Court of New York for a six months' extension of the time before which he should be obliged to take his examination for admission to the bar. He said he fell into the class of those who "had directed their studies to the profession of the Law" before the war, but whose preparation was interrupted by military ser-

vice. This is the first we hear of his having pitched on a legal
career while still in college. He might have become a doctor—
witness his early attendance on anatomy lectures. His religious
devotion as a youth might have pointed him toward the
church. But both caduceus and cloth, if they had ever attracted
him, faded from his mind. His patriot pamphlets had taken
him into constitutional history and works on international
law; his involvement in the colonies' cause must have shown
him his aptitude for public life. The fact that he needed an extension of time beyond that which others received indicates
that, quick study though he was, he had not commenced a
course of legal reading before the war. He simply put himself
in the group excused from serving a three-year legal clerkship.

He was never afterward closely allied with either medicine
or the ministry, particularly not with the latter. He was associated with men of business and through his brother-in-law
Church or his old sponsors the Crugers, might have entered
commerce, though trade was disordered at the time. His
choice of the law for his career was exactly right for him and
for his place in his country's history. His older friends—Elias
Boudinot, William Livingston, James Duane, and others—
were eminent lawyers who may have inclined him in their direction.

Officers took their leave from the Revolutionary army at
will. In Albany in the winter of 1781–82, Hamilton foresaw
little military activity; he preferred not to ask for a new assignment. He would answer the call to duty if needed, and he
asked to be allowed to retain his rank while forgoing any
emolument from his commission. He said he would like some
day to travel abroad, and military rank would help to introduce him. (Actually, he never left the American continent).

He wrote to Lafayette in early November 1782, "I have been
employed for the last ten months in rocking the cradle"—his
first child, Philip, was born in January of that year—"and
studying the art of fleecing my neighbours. I am now a Grave

Counsellor at law." His friend Robert Troup, who was also studying law at Albany, was admitted to the bar in April. He was invited to live with the Hamiltons, and he assisted Alexander in his reading. Troup recorded that Hamilton, as was his habit, walked to and fro with his book long enough to have traversed the continent! James Duane invited Hamilton to use his law library, which was an important contribution. Hamilton knew that he would be confronted at the start with the use of legal forms, so while he was studying he prepared for himself a manual, "Practical Proceedings in the Supreme Court of the State of New York." The only known copy is in another hand and was surely used by students of a later day. Hamilton's handbook covers rules of the court and steps in a variety of pleadings; it deals only incidentally with substantive law. In his handbook Hamilton was breaking ground, for there was no prior work on the subject. He used English sources, modifying their authority as they applied in New York. His task was complicated because practice in New York was in flux during the Revolution. An expert estimate of Hamilton's manual of practice calls it admirable for its industry and early date of compositions, but still "student work." *

Hamilton was deep in his law books when, on May 2, 1782, Robert Morris, the Financier, invited him to be Receiver of Continental Revenue for New York. Morris had accepted his post on condition that he be able to name his own subordinates, a provision which Hamilton had urged; this excused Morris from relying on the loan commissioners, whose attachment was apt to be to the states. Hamilton was grateful for Morris's confidence, but he declined the appointment because the compensation was too small and he was unwilling to be diverted from his preparation for his bar examination. Morris came back with the promise of increased pay and the opinion that his duties as Receiver need not interfere with his studies.

* See Julius Goebel, Jr. (ed.), *The Law Practice of Alexander Hamilton*, vol. 1, pp. 37ff. (New York, Columbia University Press, 1964).

Thereat Hamilton accepted, but with the frank declaration that under the circumstances prevailing in New York he could not earn his salary. "The whole system (if it may be so called) of taxation in this state is radically vicious, burthensome to the people and unproductive to government. As the matter now stands there seems to be little for a Continental Receiver to do. The whole business appears to be thrown into the hands of the County treasurers, nor do I find that there is any appropriation made of any part of the taxes collected to Continental purposes, or any provision to authorize payment to the officer you appoint." This wholly negative situation left him only one way to be useful. He could work with the legislature to rouse a response to Morris's applications. "In popular assemblies much may sometimes be brought about by personal discussions, by entering into details and combating objections as they rise." He would undertake this lobbying if Morris approved. Meantime, he would inform himself on Morris's instructions and make necessary inquiries in New York. As soon as he had taken his bar examination he would hasten to Philadelphia for a personal interview.

Hamilton received his commission from the Financier July 13, 1782, and posted to Poughkeepsie for the special meeting of the legislature. It was called to provide Congress with war revenue, but so had the previous special session been, and it had produced nothing. Hamilton would try to squeeze blood from the turnip. To extract even a little, "mountains of prejudice . . . are to be levelled." For adequate results, the tax system of the state would have had to be renovated.

This association of the two chief figures in early American public finance had commenced with Hamilton's volunteer letter to Morris the year before. A promising apprentice never had a better master. Morris was fully appreciative of the extraordinary initiative which Hamilton showed. Here was a subordinate who not only anticipated his principal's wishes, but devised means of his own. Morris and Hamilton agreed on almost all points, though the older man was able to teach the younger here and there. Particularly, Morris insisted that his own notes (drafts on his agent Swanwick) should remain of large denominations, going into the hands of merchants and others who would know their value. If they were of lower denominations they would share in the depreciation of paper money generally. Thus Morris curbed Hamilton's constant preference for a lively circulation.

After making diligent researches into the financial machinery of New York, Hamilton reported to Morris its deficiencies of plan and operation. Favoritism in tax assessment and negligence in collection were principal complaints. Due to enemy occupation and other causes, "the efficient property, strength and force of the state will consist of little more than four counties" out of fourteen. He estimated that New York could furnish £40,000 to the Financier if the revenue system were reformed, otherwise Morris could expect only a third of that sum. Hamilton had pressed for the act to raise £18,000 in specie, bank notes, and Morris's notes destined for the Financier's order. Also he had procured a recess committee with which he would cooperate to devise an improved system of taxation.

The account which Hamilton gave Morris of the finances of New York bespoke his thoroughness and judgment, qualities which he manifested on a far larger scale a decade later when he was Secretary of the Treasury. Also he furnished Morris with a confidential picture of New York politicians from governor down, so that the Financier might know what to expect from legislators and administrators.

Hamilton had by this time (July 1782) been admitted to practice as an attorney in the Supreme Court of New York, and thus was able to devote himself fully to the Financier's business. What he urged on the committee of the legislature is embodied in his plan for specific taxation. The object was to eliminate the abuses of loose quotas and arbitrary assessments, and to make collection efficient. He proposed taxes on lands, houses, and luxury possessions; excises on salt and tobacco; polls of servants; stamps for legal documents; and import duties. Except for the last he sought to classify and graduate the taxes to correspond with ability to pay. The committee would not agree to his recommendation of an excise on distilled liquors; he had to be content with tavern licenses, differing in amount according to the kinds of liquors sold. When this scheme was put to the committee the result was disappointing, as Hamilton had feared it would be. Some members had special interests to protect, others offered objections generally. The committee did agree to an actual valuation of lands, with a tax of so much in the pound.

Hamilton's habit always was to meet the immediate problem as best he could, but at the same time to urge fundamental remedies. He reported to Robert Morris a significant action of the New York legislature on which he and his father-in-law, Philip Schuyler, collaborated. They were both in Poughkeepsie at the time, Schuyler in the Senate, Hamilton on Morris's business. Joint resolutions (Hamilton was probably the author), passed on July 20, 1782, proposed "to Congress to recommend, and to each State to adopt the Measure of assembling a general Convention of the States, specially authorized to revise and amend the Confederation, reserving a Right to the respective legislatures, to ratify their Determinations." This was the first call of a public body for a constitutional convention, it anticipated by four years the similar call—again, Hamilton's work—of the Annapolis Commercial Convention. The New York resolutions recited the perilous posture of the country from continued British hostilities and from the need to bolster public credit. The argument echoed what was appearing in the last of Hamilton's "Continentalist" papers, that he realized the insufficiency of "partial Deliberations of the States, separately; but that it is essential to the common Welfare, that there should be . . . a Conference of the Whole."

Hamilton had been moved by the objections which he heard in New York: "What avails it for one State to make [reforms or exertions] without the concert of the others?" Hamilton was in Congress and on committees which considered the proposal. After more than a year it was postponed—the problem was whether the states would furnish Congress with an independent revenue—and that was the end of the project of a constitutional convention for the time being.

Two months later Hamilton and Schuyler collaborated in a proposal for conventions of a different sort; these would be meetings of the public creditors of New York and, they hoped, of all the states. A similar move had been made in Philadelphia in June. Schuyler presided at the meeting held in Albany on September 25, 1782, which adopted an "Address to the Public Creditors of the State of New York." That address bears every evidence of Hamilton's composition. It was a calm review of the depleted state of the public finances, and it concluded that the only remaining resource was further loans from individuals. Such would not be forthcoming unless funds were pledged to pay the interest on old and new borrowings. Hamilton's future funding system was succinctly described. If the public securities obtained value they would be negotiable and would serve as the means of enlivening the economy. Incidentally, as with Hamilton's call issued by the Annapolis convention, a definite day for the New York meeting at Poughkeepsie was named, November 19, 1782. Apparently, no meeting was held.

As agent for Robert Morris, and otherwise, Hamilton had made a good impression on the New York legislature, for on July 22, 1782, he was elected a delegate to the Continental Congress for a term of one year, beginning the first Monday in November. Hamilton was the only new delegate, the others (James Duane, William Floyd, John Morin Scott, Ezra L'Hommedieu) being re-elected. When Hamilton was proposed by the Assembly, Schuyler withdrew his nomination by the Senate. Schuyler had forecast, a year earlier, that the New York legislature would send Hamilton to Congress.

Hamilton took his seat November 25, and on that day he ended his engagement as Continental Receiver. He turned over his remaining small cash receipts and his records to Dr. Thomas Tillotson, who was Morris's choice as Hamilton's successor.

On hearing the news of Hamilton's election to Congress, his intimate friend John Laurens, who remained in the army in South Carolina, wrote him. Laurens was delighted that Hamilton was in public life. He "should fill only the first offices of the Republic," perhaps being sent to Paris as a peace commissioner. Laurens himself found military service languid. He begged Hamilton for "the *consolation* of your letters." Hamilton replied, "Peace made, My Dear friend, a new scene opens. The object then will be to make our independence a blessing. To do this we must secure our *union* on solid foundations; an herculean task and to effect which mountains of prejudice must be levelled! It requires all the virtue and all the abilities of the Country. Quit your sword my friend, put on the *toga*, come to Congress, We know each others sentiments, our views are the same; we have fought side by side to make America free, let us hand in hand struggle to make her happy."

Laurens probably never received this promising invitation, for a fortnight after it was written he was killed in what General Greene called "a paltry little skirmish" with an enemy foraging party on the Combahee River. Hamilton felt the "deepest affliction" at his personal loss and grieved that America could not have the services of a patriot of "so many excellent qualities." Hamilton and Laurens would have been a good pair in the national adventures ahead, for they were companionable as well as in agreement. The combination of middle states and deep South would have been fortunate. Of course Hamilton had able coadjutors, but most of them were older than he, and, in many instances, they were men with whom he did not share army experience. Madison was the most intimate of his collaborators in the stage of adoption of the Constitution, and no one could have substituted for his knowledge and expositor's skill. From Hamilton's standpoint, enduring Madison's later change of views and allegiance was like having an arm become palsied, though others in Congress came manfully to his assistance. In fact, it was desirable that the Federalists not determine policy without meeting stout opposition, and in this respect, Madison's joining the Antis was a national advantage.

In the army Hamilton had been an observer of the shortcomings of Congress. As Continental Receiver for New York he had learned in detail the financial faults of his own state. Now, as a member of Congress, he tried to correct the defects of which he had complained. Actually, only one of the confronting problems was solved—the discharge of the army with a little pay in hand and the promise of full satisfaction later—but that was more the work of Robert Morris than of the legislators. Peace loomed, but, ironically, that pleasing prospect relaxed exertion. Delay was more attractive than action. This procrastination was the fault of the states more than of the Congress. However, attendance on the legislative body was thin, often it was difficult to summon enough votes to pass important measures, and usually not more than twenty members were present. A few of first-rate capacity—Oliver Ellsworth of Connecticut, Madison of Virginia, James Wilson of Pennsylvania, John Rutledge of South Carolina—were available for longer or shorter stays during Hamilton's tenure (November 1782 to July 1783), and Elias Boudinott was President. These were supplemented by others of excellent intent, men such as Nathaniel Gorham of Massachusetts. Thomas Fitz-Simons and Richard Peters of Pennsylvania, Ralph Izard of

South Carolina, and Hugh Williamson of North Carolina. But the political machine, now lacking war urgency, could only fumble and fail.

Certain competent scholars have offered a more favorable view of the accomplishments of the Confederation Congress, but all of their ingenuity is required to show positive gains. Anyone who reads the journals must be thankful that military victory did not drive the country into political calamity and credit collapse.

Hamilton's main effort in this session was to persuade Rhode Island to approve the 5 per cent import duty which would permit Congress to pay the war debts. This would have been far short of conferring the independence of action which Congress required, for the revenue was for the one purpose and for a limited period, but even this partial relief was stubbornly refused by Rhode Island, as it had been since passage of the resolution almost two years earlier (February 1781). An evil accompaniment of failure of the impost was the threat of states to divert funds from Congress to the payment of creditors within their own borders, which would have withdrawn from the central authority both material and moral support.

Besides Rhode Island, only Georgia was a holdout, but her assent was not necessary because of British occupation. Hamilton, Rutledge, and Madison drafted a resolution (December 6, 1782) calling on the states to pay their requisitions and providing for a deputation to visit the Rhode Island legislature to urge approval of the impost. The Rhode Island delagates voted with the rest in favor of the payment of requisitions, but they wanted no deputation sent to their state. That same day the assertive David Howell of Rhode Island was exposed as the author of a newspaper piece which falsely made the credit of the United States appear flourishing, so that no import duty was needed. He had also betrayed secrets of Congress and barely escaped censure by name in the journal.

Five days later a letter was read on the floor. It was from the speaker of the lower house of Rhode Island to the President of Congress, and it gave the reasons why the impost would not be allowed. It would bear hard on Rhode Island, a commercial state. The federal collectors would be unknown and unaccountable to Rhode Island and contrary to her constitution. Relinquishing agreed import duties would reduce the right of the state to raise its quota of taxes in whatever way it chose. Congress, with a fixed revenue, would be able to disregard its constituents. The Rhode Island delegates moved to cancel the visit of the committee to remonstrate, but were defeated. A committee of Hamilton, Madison, and FitzSimons drafted a short letter to Governor William Greene, begging him to call a special session of the legislature, if necessary, to hear the committee from Congress and concur in the impost to save the credit of the country.

A full answer to Rhode Island's objections to the import duty was given by Hamilton for his committee a few days later. His persuasive manner and luminous exposition convinced even the Rhode Island delegates to approve it. Rhode Island, in the light of Hamilton's reply, seemed to be an alien society, unaware of the pressures upon the Confederation. Hamilton patiently spelled out the shifting of an import tax to consumers everywhere, and showed that the federal government must have internal agents if it were to function. The later part of the report was a concise and early statement of Hamilton's funding policy. To attract lenders, "We must pledge an ascertained fund, simple and productive in its nature, general in its principle and at the disposal of a single will." This would pay the interest on the debt, and any surplus would go into a sinking fund dedicated inviolably to discharge of the capital sum. By these means evidences of the debt, instead of being reproaches to the neglect of the nation, would come alive; they would be the basis of private credit. The unserviced debt was a bane; if the interest were paid and redemption of the principal provided, it would be a benefit.

Hamilton's lucid plea was unsuccessful at that time, but a decade later his simple formula of national honesty worked a miracle. Those who, at the inception of the Constitution, speculated on the intentions of the Secretary of the Treasury, had they reverted to this report need have been in no doubt that, to the limit of practicality, he would honor the government's obligations. But the report was buried in the futilities of the old Congress, and it lived on only in Hamilton's unfailing purpose. A reader may feel that particulars of Hamilton's fiscal plans are technical and uncongenial. Later, when he was Secretary of the Treasury, opponents in Congress were to charge that his schemes were deliberately complicated in order to obfuscate the legislators who were coerced to accept what they did not understand. The complaints then were false and any puzzlement now is needless.

The fact is that Hamilton's financial "wizardry" was simple honesty, his triumph was moral. Combined with his integrity was his confidence in the productive capacity of the country, which would permit the discharge of the debt in a score of years. Back in the early 1780's, with the enemy still menacing, creditors clamoring, the army threatening rebellion, and Congress empty-handed, many were too oppressed by the low-hanging clouds to foresee the sunshine of peace and plenty. Hamilton is frequently quoted as despairing of his countrymen, and, indeed, of human nature. Those expressions were temporary reactions from his pervading, intense optimism. In the early American period philosophers commended themselves by professing more than a touch of melancholy, as though lamentation proved a superiority to mundane follies. Hamilton, now and then, did not escape this pose. The doubter of his sincerity in the public behalf does well to recall that he died a sacrifice to his hope of being useful to the community in future.

After Hamilton's report set aside the circumscribed inhibitions of Rhode Island, one of her delegates, Jonathan Arnold, after voting for it, depreciated it as "a very lengthy performance, wherein a State of Public Affairs . . . was laboriously wrought up to the liking of a majority of Congress."

The committee which was to travel to Rhode Island was carefully chosen to represent the three sections of the country; its members were Samuel Osgood of Massachusetts, Thomas Mifflin of Pennsylvania (who was a notable public speaker), and Abner Nash of North Carolina. They departed December 22 with Hamilton's refutation in hand, but had not gone far when Nash mentioned an unofficial report reaching Congress that Virginia had withdrawn her consent to the import duty and that Maryland seemed likely to follow. The deputation turned their horses' heads and returned to Congress to find the backsliding of Virginia—to Madison's embarrassment— was all too true. Thus baffled, Hamilton's committee was bidden to cobble together several sources of revenue for Congress, which they undertook without heart.

While trying to devise income for the government, Hamilton and Floyd had to importune Governor Clinton to forward their state allowances, or they would be penniless. Hamilton said Morris's notes, if they had not long to run, would be as good as specie. He was urging his wife, with their year-old son, to join him as soon as a good snow permitted travel. He had no money to send her for the journey, but suggested that friends along the way would supply her.

About this time Hamilton showed in Congress, as he had done in camp, his friendship for Baron von Steuben. The Baron had petitioned for fulfillment on the part of Congress of his oral agreement when he volunteered for service in the army on his arrival from Europe in 1778. He did not underrate his financial claims, as was known to the legislators, but, on the other hand, he had expertly reorganized and trained the army and, by his oversight of military administration had saved the government much money. Hamilton reported, in effect, that Steuben should be compensated for revenues that he had relinquished in Europe and for his expenses in coming to America; he was owed back salary, and he should be given an income for life. All of this must wait on improvement of the public finances. The Baron was now out of funds and should be given advances to permit him to take the field next campaign. It is probable that Steuben did not expect more than this at the moment, and he must have been pleased with Hamilton's allusions to his distinguished services. But in spite of Hamilton's persistent efforts to have Steuben properly recompensed, the old General endured repeated disappointments from the Confederation.

As though Congress did not have enough worries, the independent State of Vermont, which Congress preferred to call simply the people inhabiting the New Hampshire Grants, expropriated the property of individuals who clung to the sovereignty of New York and sent them complaining to Philadelphia. Hamilton seconded a motion committing Congress to intervene in the district of the Green Mountain Boys unless order was observed and the banished persons were permitted to return to their estates. The mistreatment of landowners whose titles were disputed were minor rumblings. The real fear was that the Vermonters would seriously assist the enemy. Hamilton's participation at this early stage of the controversy is important because several years later he did much to bring Vermont into the Union.

The approaching peace produced a critical problem with the army. Idle and unpaid in the principal encampment at Newburgh, all ranks brooded on what their fate would be when they should be discharged. The officers sent General Alexander McDougall and Colonels Matthias Ogden and John Brooks to Congress with a memorial (January 6, 1783) begging what was due in the present and promised for the future. Here was a poser. It called for a grand committee composed of a member from every state. Robert Morris "informed them explicitly that it was impossible to make any advance of pay in the present state of the finances . . . and imprudent to give any assurances with respect to future pay until certain funds should be previously established." The Financier had over-drawn expected European funds to the extent of 3,500,000 livres.

The grand committee met the officers, and Robert Morris was present, his pockets figuratively turned out. General Mc-Dougall, well knowing the treasury vacuum, subordinated the particular demands to the stern charge that Congress address itself to "the debility and defects in the federal Govt., and the unwillingness of the States to cement & invigorate it."

Hamilton, for a committee made up of himself, Madison, and Rutledge, drafted the reply to the officers. It was bound to be empty, which stirred resentment at Newburgh. The Financier should offer present pay when he was in funds. Arrearages of pay should be settled by the states with their respective lines of the army up to August 1, 1780, and the Financier should contrive settlement since that date. This mere verbiage cried for support. It was resolved "that the troops of the United States in common with all the creditors . . . have an undoubted right to expect . . . security." To that end Congress would at once make efforts to get from the states revenue adequate to funding the whole debt of the United States.

The officers at conclusion of the war could either have half pay for life or full pay for blank years—Hamilton first wrote six—and widows and orphans would be protected. More information was needed before the committee could report on deficiences of rations and clothing.

Hamilton wrote Governor Clinton, "We have now here a deputation from the army, and feel a mortification of a total disability to comply with their just expectations." He believed, however, that their applications "may be turned to a good account," evidently by reinforcing the urgency of other creditors. "Every day proves more & more the insufficiency of the confederation. The proselytes to this opinion are increas-

ing fast," and many sensible men wished for the reorganization of the government recommended by the New York legislature. Congress was pondering how lands might be valued as
the basis of state contributions, though Hamilton did not
prefer that gauge of revenue. He thought the negotiation of
peace, considering "the variety of interests to be conciliated,"
would be "a work of difficulty."

For the next months Congress debated means of getting income, which it hoped would be of a sort to enable funding the
debts. A complication was the requirement of the Articles of
Confederation that states contribute in proportion to the value
of their lands. Hamilton and Madison urged that this was a
bad method, unequal if the states did the valuing, expensive if
undertaken by the central govermnent; it would be better to
find another mode. Early in the controversy Hamilton discredited any funds but such "as wd. extend generally & uniformly
throughout the U.S., and wd. be collected under the authority
of Congs." This revenue would be simpler and more certain
than that "established separately within each State, & might
consist of any objects which were chosen by the States." Federal taxes would be more economical because collectors named
by the states would serve popularity rather than efficiency.
John Rutledge attempted to revive the 5 per cent import duty,
now to pay interest and principal on the foreign debt. This
Hamilton opposed; the domestic creditors, discriminated
against, would be soured, and they would not exert themselves with the state legislatures to furnish a general revenue.

In harmony with his desire for equality in contributions, he
was against a move for the states to value lands and report
results to Congress as the basis for requisitions. If land value
was to be the criterion (which he did not approve) the determination should be made with great care and by agents of the
central government. Defer the valuation until Congress was
financially able to carry it through. He prepared a resolution to
commit Congress to permanent and adequate funds, operating

nation-wide and collected by Congress, but he did not submit it because a similar resolve of Madison was rejected.

The refusal of Congress to reform the finances in spite of the demands of the unpaid camp at Newburgh induced Hamilton to make a dangerous proposal to General Washington. The incident showed the superior judgment of the latter. Hamilton reported that the soldiers believed if they laid down their arms they would not be recompensed. What did Washington think of allowing the army to seek redress with a measure of menace? This would assist Congress to extract funds from the state legislatures. Washington should direct the army's threat, but do so through a confidential subordinate, such as General Knox. A few days later Hamilton told close friends in Congress of his recommendation to Washington. The General's patriotism would be necessary to rule the storm, for an unprincipled leader would excite the army to excesses.

Washington's answer was an unequivocal No. Hamilton's suggestion of letting the soldiers prick the government with bayonets "would . . . be productive of Civil commotions & end in blood. . . . God forbid we should be involved in it." Instead, Hamilton's fears that peace would find the army turned off empty were mistaken. Washington had faith that the disabilities of Congress and reluctance of the states would yield to the demands of justice. This was his expectation in spite of the danger of disaffection in the army again being secretly promoted—by General Horatio Gates was his plain meaning.

Washington added the proposal that Congress adjourn to permit the members personally to urge their constituents to confer more federal authority: "for it is clearly my opinion, unless Congress have powers competent to all *general* purposes, that the distresses we have encountered, the expences we have incurred, and the blood we have spilt in the course of an Eight years war, will avail us nothing."

An unmistakable sign of financial peril was the resolve of

Robert Morris to resign unless suitable plans for revenue were adopted by the end of May. Congress kept his letter secret for a month, and then some members disparaged Morris's administration. Hamilton and Wilson "went into a copious defence & Panegyric of Mr. Morris, the ruin in which his resignation if it sd. take effect wd. involve public credit."

The muttering in the army suddenly became a shriek. On March 10, 1783, the Newburgh encampment was stirred by an anonymous notice to the officers to meet next day for a "last remonstrance" to Congress for inaction on their demands. The call was supported by an address, also anonymous, inciting the officers, if the war continued, to abandon the country, or, if peace were concluded, to use military force to pry funds from Congress. General Washington promptly wrote Hamilton in Congress of the "storm [which] very sudenly arose with unfavourable prognostics." He enclosed the papers that explained the situation. He had countermanded the irregular meeting for March 11 and had appointed March 15 for a calm consideration of what further measures the officers should embrace. This, Washington said, was because "I was obliged . . . to arrest on the spot, the foot that stood wavering on a tremendous precipice, to prevent the Officers from being taken by surprize while the passions were all inflamed, and . . . from plunging themselves into a Gulph of Civil horror from which there might be no receding."

The Commander in Chief's check to the crisis provoked a second address calculated to sustain indignation. The writer declared that America had disdained the officers' cries. "If this, then, be your treatment, while the swords you wear are necessary for the defence of America, what have you to expect from peace, when your voice shall sink, and your strength dissipate by division? . . . If your determination be in any proportion to your wrongs, carry your appeal from the justice to the fears of government." If the war continued they should "retire to some unsettled country" and "mock when [the people's] fear cometh on."

Pending the outcome of the meeting of officers, General Washington begged Hamilton to try to bring Congress to a liquidation of accounts and assurances for the future. Otherwise many of the officers "have no better prospect before them than a Gaol." The imminence of action was dramatically evident in the news sent to Washington that same day by President Boudinot: Captain Joshua Barney had arrived with the preliminary treaty of peace which had been signed by American and British commissioners in Paris on November 30, 1782.

Hamilton was in a stew until he learned that Washington's wisdom and affecting appeal to the self-respect of the officers had turned dire threats into a resolution of confidence in the good intentions of Congress. Long afterward it was revealed that the incendiary addresses had been written by Major John Armstrong, who, not accidentally, was aide to General Gates.

Hamilton believed, rightly, that the provisional treaty meant the end of the war. Lafayette and Franklin soon notified the American authorities that the preliminary treaty between Britain, France, and Spain put an end to hostilities. Immediately (March 24, 1783), Hamilton congratulated General Washington on the happy conclusion of his labors and called him to further service. "It now only remains to make solid establishments within to . . . make our independence truly a blessing. Your Excellency's exertions are as essential to accomplish this end as they have been to establish independence." The work would be difficult, for the seeds of disunion were more numerous than those of union. Salvation depended on "the men who think continentally." Washington, in reply, wrote that he was sure that if we were to improve the peace and become "a great, a respectable, and happy People . . . it must be . . . by other means that State politics, and unreasonable jealousies & prejudices." He declared, feelingly, that to "want of Powers in

Congress may justly be ascribed the prelongation of the War."
It was with these sentiments, often repeated, that Hamilton
and Washington entered on their peacetime collaboration.

The plan finally proposed for funding the debt was a revision of the former import duty, with miscellaneous additions.
Hamilton thought it had not much more chance of acceptance
by the states than a better one, and that it could not serve its
purpose, so he voted against it. He explained his reasons to
Governor Clinton: much of the revenue relied upon was at the
will of the states, the duration of the fund was less than that of
the debt, the collectors were servants of the states. Lacking adequate security, evidences of the debt would not be negotiable, could not supply bank capital, could not quicken commerce. Still, it was the interest of New York to approve the
plan.

Hamilton was on the deputation which persuaded Robert
Morris to remain as Superintendent of Finance longer than he
had wished. Morris had noted in his diary that he yearned
"for nothing so much as to be relieved from this cursed Scene
of Drudgery and Vexation." His reports on the problem of dis-
banding the army, with the Treasury empty, amply justify
Hamilton's testimony that "no man in this country but himself
could have kept the money-machine a going." The Revolution
ended with the private credit of Robert Morris the chief resource of the government. To give the troops, on disband-
ment, three months' pay required Morris to issue his own
notes for half a million dollars. Naturally, he insisted on continuing in office until these notes were redeemed, as he could
not trust his credit to any successor. Overdrawn on problematical loans in Europe, petitioning France for further favors,
getting poor response to requisitions on the states, and auc-
tioning army horses and wagons at low prices, the finances of
the liberated country had reached nadir. Hamilton lamented,
"It will be shocking and indeed an eternal reproach to this
country, if we begin the peaceable enjoyment of our indepen-

dence by a violation of all the principles of honesty & true policy." That we did for seven lean years. Nothing more was needed to spur Hamilton, when Secretary of the Treasury, to construct a dependable, ongoing system for meeting the nation's obligations.

Hamilton, because of his war experience and, particularly, because of his knowledge of army administration, was often the servant of Congress in dealing with military affairs. No occasion was more critical than that when Congress was surrounded by mutinous troops (June 1783). Discontents in the barracks in Philadelphia had already given concern when word was received that eighty soldiers had broken away from their officers at Lancaster, Pennsylvania, and were on their march to Philadelphia to make demands on the state government. Hamilton, as chairman of the committee, with Oliver Ellsworth and Richard Peters, appointed by Congress to deal with the revolt, dispatched Major William Jackson, Assistant Secretary of War, to try to turn back the rebels, but his warnings had no effect. The insurgents reached the city Friday morning, June 20. The 500 men in the barracks were seething for the next twenty-four hours; they even forced some furloughed veterans from Charleston to join in the revolt.

At noon Saturday some three hundred mutineers, under their sergeants only, surrounded the State House (Independence Hall), where the Pennsylvania Council was meeting. President Boudinot summoned Congress in emergency session in the same building. The members had not long been assembled when President John Dickinson of the Pennsylvania Council entered to announce that the Council had received a peremptory demand from the rebels. The Council had been given only twenty minutes to authorize the men to choose commissioned officers to negotiate for them. While bayonets poked through the windows of the Council chamber, the message was read: "You will immediately issue such authority and deliver it to us, or . . . we shall instantly let in these injured soldiers upon you." The Council would take no action while thus menaced.

Congress also sat for three hours within the cordon of armed, often drunken defiants, and heard their body cursed by name. General Arthur St. Clair, commanding the Pennsylvania line, was in the city, attempting to persuade the troops back to their barracks. Congress adjourned, and the delegates, who were not harmed, met again that evening. They resolved to inform the Pennsylvania Council that the authority of the United States had been insulted, that the peace of the capital was endangered, and that order must be restored at once. General Washington was ordered to call in a detachment of continentals from West Point under Major General Robert Howe, but this was subject to countermand if the Pennsylvania government promptly offered protection. The demonstrators around the State House had returned to their quarters, but others held several arsenals, had possession of field pieces, and threatened to rob the bank.

Hamilton and Ellsworth visited President Dickinson, read him the resolves of Congress, and received his promise to call his Council to meet them next morning, Sunday. The Congressmen required "that vigorous measures should be taken to put a stop to the further progress of the evil and to compel submission on the part of the offenders." The Council would not comply until they had consulted officers to determine whether the militia would respond. Hamilton and Ellsworth renewed their mission next day, requesting the answer of the Pennsylvania Council in writing. This was refused, because it was not customary. The oral reply was that "the Militia of the city . . . were not only ill provided for service, but disinclined to act upon the present occasion . . . the Council did not believe any exertions were to be looked for from them, except in case of further outrage and actual violence to person and property. That in such case a respectable body of citizens would arm for the security of their property and of the public peace, but it was to be doubted what measure of outrage would produce this effect; and . . . it was not to be expected merely from a repetition of the insult which had happened."

The Council trusted to negotiation with commissioned officers whom St. Clair allowed the mutineers to appoint. Hamilton and Ellsworth insisted that the excesses had passed the bounds of compromise. The dignity and safety of government required that the mutiny be put down, then the Pennsylvania authorities could be moderate in punishment. (So far from talks with the rebels promising peace, the six commissioned officers representing them were charged by the mutineers "use compulsive measures should they be found necessary—which . . . we will support you in to the . . . utmost of our power. Should you . . . not . . . do all in yours, Death is inevitably your fate.") Hamilton's language to the Council was formal, but he told Governor Clinton, "The conduct of the executive of [Pennsylvania] was to the last degree weak & disgusting."

Next day, Tuesday, brought no improvement, so Hamilton, as he had been empowered to do, recommended to President Boudinot that Congress remove its meetings to Princeton. New Jersey. Boudinot at once issued his proclamation. Hamilton had been reluctant to have Congress leave its capital because such a move would be productive of strained relations with Pennsylvania and Philadelphia and would surely be unfavorably interpreted abroad. He later resented the accusation that he had hastened the exit of Congress from Pennsylvania in order to improve the chance that the permanent seat would be fixed in New York State. Actually President Boudinot saw no impropriety in rallying his brother Elisha to prepare his "Troop of Horse . . . to meet us at Princeton," in the bid for placing the capital in New Jersey. Soon after assembling at Princeton, Hamilton wrote and seconded a motion of Mercer of Virginia that Congress should return to Philadelphia, made safe by Howe's troops, until a permanent location was chosen.

Of course, the fact was that the mutiny caused a seven-year departure from Philadelphia, while Congress wandered to Annapolis, to Trenton, to New York City.

Learning that General Howe's detachment was nearing, the mutineers surrendered, two of their inciters fled to Europe, others were arrested, and the Lancaster column returned to its post. Too late to escape blame, the Pennsylvania Council exacted "dutyfull submission to the offended Majesty of the United States."

The failure of the local government to protect Congress encouraged the later provision of a federal district over which the nation exercises complete control. The contretemps with Pennsylvania undoubtedly strengthened Hamilton in his later plans for a standing army and for a degree of federal power over the militia of the states. Also, a decade afterward, when western counties of Pennsylvania were in insurrection against the excise taxes, Hamilton did not tarry with hope of repression by the state, but asserted federal force.

When Hamilton was about to quit Congress, he congratulated John Jay on "The peace which exceeds in the goodness of its terms, the expectations of the most sanguine." Peace did not come too soon for the "internal embarrassments and exhausted state of the country." The political shortcomings were as bad as the economic. "We have now happily concluded the great work of independence," he wrote, "but much remains to be done to reach the fruits of it. Our prospects are not flattering. Every day proves the inefficacy of the present confederation, yet the common danger being removed, we are receding instead of advancing in a disposition to amend its defects." He echoed the recent testimony of General Washington, that for the want of power in Congress "the resources of the country during the war could not be drawn out." The government "at this moment experience[s] all the mischiefs of a bankrupt and ruined credit. It is to be hoped that when preju-

dice and folly have run themselves out of breath we may return to reason and correct our errors."

To prompt the imperative reforms, Hamilton drew up a full
statement of defects of the Articles of Confederation, which he
intended to become a resolution of Congress for a convention
to amend the constitution. He did not submit his paper because Congress was thin, often lacking the representation of
nine states necessary for important action. He demonstrated a
round dozen of faults in the Articles, "the constitutional imbecility of which," he said elsewhere, "must be apparent to
every man of reflexion." The substantial remedies he listed
corresponded to the changes embodied in the Constitutional
Convention of 1787.

With this he took leave of Congress. He had served with
only one other delegate from New York, William Floyd, since
December 1782. He accompanied Mrs. Philip Schuyler to Albany, on the way, at her wish, passing through New York
City. He was glad to see British evacuation beginning, but
sorry that anti-loyalist statutes threatened to drive out "too
large a number of valuable citizens." Many merchants, "characters of no political importance, each of whom may carry
away eight to ten thousand guineas have . . . lately applied
for shipping to convey them away. Our state will feel for
twenty years at least, the effects of this popular phrenzy." (Actually, it was officially reported that some 29,000 loyalists
sailed from New York in 1782). During Hamilton's chance visit
to New York City, Nicholas Hoffman, a loyalist sufferer, retained him as attorney.

Chapter 7

THE CALL FOR A CONSTITUTIONAL CONVENTION

Nearing the end of his first term in the Continental Congress, Hamilton had applied to Governor Clinton to relieve him by sending a replacement. "Having no further view in public life," he wrote, "I owe it to myself to enter upon the care of my private concerns without delay." While in Albany waiting for the evacuation of New York City, Hamilton worked assiduously on briefs in his first war case, the defense of Nicholas Hoffman against the loss of his estate under the Confiscation Act.

From the beginning Hamilton's practice of the law was not tentative, experimental, or minor, but thorough, skilful, and original. Now twenty-nine, he was one of the notable company of young lawyers whose careers at the bar had been delayed by service in the army. Prominent from the start, he rose rapidly, and, following his return to practice after his tenure at the Treasury, he was the leader of his profession in the state.

Hamilton's performance as lawyer was characteristic of his work habits. All his life he exerted himself to the full; he had no lapses into languor, when his powers lay fallow. He seemed to need no periods of recruitment of his capacities. It was actually a fault that he applied himself unremittingly. More indulgence in recreation, an occasional spell of indolence, might have saved him from faulty judgments in his last years. Not that he ever lost his bearings except temporarily; after unfortunate deviations he would return to his finest perspectives.

Hamilton was involved in more than three-score cases arising under anti-loyalist statutes of New York. These laws were commonly known as the Confiscation Act (October 1779, providing for forfeiture and sale of estates), the Citation Act (July 1782, relieving debtors of loyalists), and the Trespass Act (March 1783, providing for recovery of damages where patriot property was occupied or injured by loyalists). Forty-five of Hamilton's cases concerned the Trespass Act. In the effort to leave the defendant no protection, the legislature had stipulated, first, that judgment in an inferior court—local, informal, and apt to favor the plaintiff—was final, and, second, that no defendant would be permitted to plead any military order of the enemy.

The Confiscation and Citation statutes affected persons of means, but that covering trespass engaged plaintiffs of many degrees of wealth and prominence. Furthermore, the use, abuse, or purchase of patriot property in the power of the enemy cried loud for compensation. Confiscation of loyalist estates was agreeable to patriots, as was the stay of patriots' debts owing to loyalists, but in trespass the shoe was on the other foot. The three statutes, especially the last, brought a harvest of cases to New York lawyers because the southern counties of the state had been in enemy hands from 1776 until the peace, New York City being the main enemy base throughout the war. To defend a loyalist, be he estate owner, creditor, or invader of patriot premises, seemed, especially to poorer plaintiffs, to mark one as himself an enemy. The reputation of being pro-British attached to Hamilton from this cause in the beginning, though his genuine admiration of the British governmental system and his desire to cultivate British trade were better reasons for it.

Rutgers v. Waddington, in which Hamilton was principal counsel for the defendant, was regarded at the time as a test case under the Trespass Act. Moreover, the principles which Hamilton advanced informed his legal advocacy and political tenets afterward. Elizabeth Rutgers had fled the city when the British came in. Her brewhouse and malthouse in the East Ward had been stripped of essential equipment. In September 1778 the British commissary general had assigned the property to the use of Benjamin Waddington and Evelyn Pierrepont, British merchants whose agent was Joseph Waddington. The enemy occupiers spent £700 in replacements and improvements before they could start brewing. They had had the premises rent free until May 1, 1780, when the British commander of the city had ordered them to pay £150 a year in rent for the benefit of the poor. As of May 1, 1783, the British commandant had ordered Waddington to pay rent to the owner's agent, Anthony Rutgers, as the city was soon to be evacuated. Rutgers had postponed naming terms, but finally he had demanded that the tenants pay £1200 back rent and that they leave the fixtures they had installed. This was refused. Then, two days before the British evacuated the city, the brewery burned, with a loss of some £4000 to the occupiers. They nonetheless tried to settle what they owed, but got no response until February 1784, when Rutgers sued in the mayor's court for the rent, £8000.

Hamilton forecast the grounds of his defense of Waddington in his first *Letter from Phocion to the Considerate Citizens of New*

York (January 1784), and he confirmed them in a second letter of Phocion in April. These pieces were searching remonstrances against proposed legislative punishment of loyalists in contravention of common law, the Confederation and state constitutions, the peace treaty, and international law. He conceded that "Nothing is more common than for a free people, in times of heat and violence, to gratify momentary passions, by letting into the government, principles and precedents which afterwards prove fatal to themselves." He reprobated at the start the denial of due process of law in the attempt to "punish whole classes of citizens by general descriptions, without trial and conviction of offences known by laws previously established declaring the offence and prescribing the penalty." (His censure was disregarded by the United States immediately after our entrance into World War II, when citizens of Japanese ancestry were forcibly removed from their homes and confined in "reception centers," which were actually concentration camps.) He refuted the assumption that the state could amerce all loyalists because under the treaty Congress was bound only to *recommend* restitution. Not so, for, as the fifth article of the treaty declared, "There shall be no future confiscations made, nor prosecutions commenced against any person or persons, for, or by reason of the part which he or they may have taken in the present war, and no person shall, on that account, suffer any future loss or damage, either in his person, liberty, or property." A subordinate consideration, not of law but of policy, was that if America broke the treaty with respect to loyalists, the British might refuse to surrender the western posts. His whole argument was against the prevailing jingoism which threatened to precipitate tyrannous actions.

Associated with Hamilton in the defense of Waddington were two young lawyers who shared Hamilton's principles, Brockholdst Livingston and Morgan Lewis. The plaintiff's counsel, slightly senior, were Egbert Benson, Attorney General of New York (and nephew of Mrs. Rutgers), and another man whom Hamilton admired, John Lawrence. The mayor's court, meeting in the City Hall (later Federal Hall), was presided over by James Duane, whose associate judges were Recorder Richard Varick, and aldermen.

Hamilton's argument was that Waddington owed nothing to Mrs. Rutgers because he occupied the property by permission of the military which had gained possession. This was the law of nations, which was a part of the common law, adopted by the New York Constitution of 1777. As for the stipulation in the Trespass Act that a defendant could not plead military authority, the Treaty of Peace, which provided mutual amnesty for wartime acts, was national law and superior to the state statute. The latter should be held null and void. There were difficulties along the way, particularly the questions of whether national exceeded state authority in the last analysis and whether the court could overrule a law of the state. Hamilton chose to stand upon the highest ground.

The opinion of the court was not rendered until August 1784. It was evidently the work of Duane, in which the other judges concurred. He regretted that a case of such consequence should be decided in the mayor's court, which was of limited jurisdiction. The industry and learning of counsel compelled Duane to explore authorities, especially in the law of nations, which no minor magistrate ever before entered upon. The conclusion of the court was that for the period when the merchants had occupied the Rutgers property under license from the commissary general, paying no rent, they owed restitution to Elizabeth. For the time they were tenants under order of the commandant of the city and paid rent as directed, they were not subject to Mrs. Rutgers's demand.

Hamilton's argument for Waddington against Rutgers was more original than that which he presented in the dispute between New York and Massachusetts over western lands in 1785–86. The New York commissioners were disappointed in trying to secure first James Wilson and then Gouverneur Morris as counsel; in 1785 Hamilton and Samuel Jones were engaged. Hamilton's brief owed much to that earlier prepared by James Duane, who was actually the manager of New York's case. The dispute had long slumbered, except for occasional abortive attempts at adjustment. In the absence of an established federal judiciary, the issue was intended to be decided by an *ad hoc* court, but the members who were mutually agreed upon declined to serve, one after another. Therefore, the commissioners of the two states finally met at Hartford, in November 1786, to reach a solution.

Massachusetts claimed the vast area west of the Hudson by virtue of Cabot's discovery along the Atlantic coast and charters which defined Massachusetts as running "from sea to sea." Hamilton, borrowing from Duane, countered for New York that not mere discovery by the English, but settlement and possession by the Dutch, confined Massachusetts well to the east of the Hudson. He buttressed his historical evidence with the reasoning of Vattel, which he had used in the trespass case. Doubtless, in the Hartford discussions Hamilton's brief had the effect of confirming Duane's prior opinions. The result of the negotiation was that Massachusetts retained ownership of the soil in question, while New York kept jurisdiction over the area.

The peaceful compromise between New York and Massachusetts, so different from the violence of the land dispute between Pennsylvania and Connecticut, was important partly because it contributed, through Hamilton among others, to the later settlement of the quarrel over the New Hampshire Grants. In the latter case Hamilton urged that the actual political control of the area justified the claim of Vermont. Hamilton was among the most active in bringing Vermont into the Union as the fourteenth state.

Hamilton took an early part in the establishment of the Bank of New York, though he was not the first to do so. His influence in its formation and conduct was so important that the bank, the earliest to be established in the city, still regards Hamilton as its founder. In 1783 he had been asked by his brother-in-law, Church, and by Church's partner, Jeremiah Wadsworth, both of whom were then in Europe, to organize a bank in New York in which they would be dominant stock-holders. He was spurred to act when, in February 1784, a group led by Chancellor Robert R. Livingston proposed a bank on a plan which Hamilton knew to be mistaken. He wrote Church of the "project for a land bank" of which "the Chancellor with a number of others have . . . petitioned the Legislature for an exclusive charter. . . . I thought it necessary not only with a view to your project, but for the sake of the commercial interests of the state to start an opposition to this scheme; and took occasion to point out its absurdity . . . to some of the most intelligent Merchants, who presently saw the matter in a proper light and began to take measures to defeat the plan."

The error of this enterprise, which, if incorporated, would have had a monopoly of banking in the state, was that two-thirds of its capital was to be subscribed in land security, only one-third in cash. It took some doing to convince the lawmakers against such non-liquid bank assets. "The Chancellor had taken so much pains with the country members"—the chancellor himself was a notable agriculturalist—"that they all began to be persuaded that the land bank was the true Philosophers stone that was to turn all their rocks and trees into gold—and there was great reason to apprehend a majority of the Legislature would have adopted his views." As a counterpoise, "Some of the Merchants . . . set on foot a subscription for a money-bank and called upon me to subscribe." He agreed, thinking he could serve the interests of Church and Wadsworth. The maximum votes for a shareholder had been set at seven before Hamilton came into the planning. In order to give Church "a proper weight in the direction," Hamilton prevailed on a later meeting to allow a vote for every five shares above ten.

The country, still indulging in liberty in all quarters, was apprehensive of any sort of combination, especially in matters of trade or finance. In Philadelphia James Wilson, Pelatiah Webster, and Thomas Paine had been compelled to impress on the legislature the utility of the Bank of North America lest its charter be revoked. Hamilton used his good offices for the Bank of New York. He argued that banks were esteemed in all commercial countries and that by facilitating trade and industry they benefited agriculture and increased land values. They loaned to government and supplied, in their notes, a dependable element in the currency. Much of Hamilton's economic wisdom may be summed up in the one word *credit*, of which well-conducted banks were chief engines. From the time, during the war, when he urged that Robert Morris found a bank, he was always a bank apostle.

The required half of the capital was promptly subscribed, and the Bank of New York was organized. Alexander McDougall was named president and Hamilton a director, along with a dozen whom he knew well. Hamilton would keep his director's seat until Church or Wadsworth returned, then yield to one of them if they chose to be stockholders. They both took shares, and Wadsworth became the second president. It seems probable that Hamilton drew up the bank's constitution; he certainly petitioned the legislature for the charter conferring limited liability on stockholders, provided that all payments and receipts should be in gold or silver coin or bank notes only, and forbade the institution to engage in trade. However, such was the suspicion of banks that the legislature took seven years to incorporate that of New York.

The Chancellor denounced "The endeavour . . . to sow distrusts between the Landed & the commercial interests of this country" which could "only originate in the extremes of ignorance or malice." He accurately described himself as "a mere

speculative man," for he recommended for directors of the
bank men who had retired from "the adventitious spirit that
supports commerce."

The day-to-day manager of the Bank of New York was the
cashier, William Seton, a Scots merchant who had remained in
the city during the occupation, a passive loyalist. Hamilton
understood the principles of banking, but he, like Seton, was
unfamiliar with the details of bank practice. He dispatched
Seton to Philadelphia for brief training in the Bank of North
America. Seton was to discover, among much else, how better
to pay out gold than by weighing it in quantities—this in the
absence of coinage. The success of the Bank of New York in a
city so recently recovered from long enemy occupation illustrated the observation that a country's recuperation from war
is apt to be surprisingly rapid; indeed, in this case the war led
to fresh enterprise.

Hamilton owned only one share in the Bank of New York,
and he remained a director only until 1788. When he became
Secretary of the Treasury he relied on William Seton as a confidential agent, especially during the speculative panic of 1791–
92.

A fully documented life of Alexander Hamilton was briefly
noticed in *The New Yorker* magazine, with the critic's summary estimate of the man: "He was a genius, but he was hard
as nails." Among much evidence that he was not flinty is his
compassion for Negro slaves. He had been well acquainted
with the conditions of slaves in the sugar islands, and that
must have prepared him to make efforts in their behalf in the
United States. Incidentally, the statement sometimes made
that Hamilton himself had Negro blood, or, less flatly, that he
was of dark complexion, is mistaken. Any race that contributed to his makeup would be honored, but his ancestry was
Scots, French, and English. He was of high coloring, with vio-
let blue eyes and reddish brown hair. Unlike some of his contemporaries who talked loudly of freedom, equality, and the

rights of man, he never owned a slave. It is recorded in his expense accounts that he bought a slave woman from Governor
Clinton for his wife—the Schuylers owned slaves—but the circumstances are not known.

Aside from his compassion for the slaves themselves, his
whole economic philosophy rejected the institution. He was
properly solicitous for agriculture, which he believed would
prosper by activity in commerce and industry, but it was the
latter forms of enterprise on which he laid emphasis. He constantly showed his concern for the welfare of wage earners.

He was a founding member (1785) of the New York Society
for Promoting the Manumission of Slaves and Protecting Such
of Them as Have Been or May Be Liberated. At the second
meeting of the society he was named chairman of a committee,
with his friends Troup and White Matlack, to recommend pro-
cedures. The society's work was to begin at home, with counsel to any members of the society who owned slaves. Besides,
all persons who manumitted slaves were urged to register
them with the society, which would thus be "Enabled to detect Attempts to deprive [them] of their Liberty." John Jay was
the first president.

As soon as Lafayette, in Europe, read in a New York newspaper of formation of the society he wrote Hamilton, "As I
ever Have Been partial to my Brethren of that Colour, I wish if
you are one in the Society, you would move . . . for my Being
Admitted on the list." Shortly before Hamilton was elected for
the second time to the New York Assembly he and a number
of other petitioners begged the legislature to end the slave
trade, which the petition called "a commerce . . . repugnant
to humanity, and . . . inconsistent with the liberality and justice which should distinguish a free and enlightened people."

Hamilton's aid to John Laurens in the proposal to enlist
slaves—who should have their freedom with their swords—in
the Revolutionary army has been told. As a result of this bond
and of Hamilton's part in the Manumission Society he had an

affectionate exchange of letters with Henry Laurens. Hamilton told Laurens the story of Frederic, who claimed to have been freed by John Laurens. Frederic was lodged in a New York jail. Henry Laurens wished to have him returned to the Laurens South Carolina plantation where, if he were of good conduct, he would be manumitted. Henry Laurens found that his efforts to abolish importation of slaves offended many: "a whole Country is opposed to me . . . the Number of wretched Slaves, precarious Riches, is our greatest Weakness—but alas! these Southern States are not at this moment in a disposition to be persuaded tho' one should rise from the dead." Laurens had a presentiment of what should result: "God forbid our conversion be too long a Delay, shall be the Effect of a direful Struggle."

A principal defect of the Confederation, of which Hamilton repeatedly complained, was that Congress had no power over commerce, foreign or domestic. Congress could make no trade treaty which the states were not at liberty to modify or annul by imposing their own embargoes or import duties. Competition between the states created jealousy and backbiting. If one state collected duties at its ports and sought to supply its neighbors with foreign wares, then one or more of the other states would welcome imports freely in retaliation. States hindered themselves from securing needed commodities from adjoining districts. Firewood did not enter Manhattan from New Jersey, nor did vegetables from Connecticut, without paying a tariff. Tobacco crossing the Potomac River and Chesapeake Bay between Virginia and Maryland was under the same impediment.

The attempt of Congress in 1781 to recruit independent funds by uniform import taxes had been wrecked by the refusal of Rhode Island to agree. In the spring of 1786 the New York legislature was hesitating for the third session over Congress' renewed appeal of 1783. Hamilton drafted the petition of citizens of New York City which begged the lawmakers not to hold out on "a measure in which the sentiments and wishes of the Union at large appear to unite and by a further delay may render itself responsible for consequences too serious not to affect every considerate man." The frustrating result was that New York consented, but with conditions which Congress could not accept. So the reform was rejected.

The willful disorders in commerce were rendered worse by the economic depression which began about 1785 and hung on until the new Constitution was adopted. New York merchants were special sufferers because, with western posts still in enemy hands, the fur trade was diverted to Montreal, and also because British mercantile creditors were oppressing their New York debtors. The most alarming distress, with violent consequences, was in Massachusetts. Farmers of the western counties, burdened with debt, forcibly prevented the courts from foreclosing on their land. Under Daniel Shays, who had been a brave captain in the Revolution, they formed a spontaneous army which attacked the government arsenal at Springfield. Riots and little battles occurred in towns from Worcester to Sheffield.

James Madison was early active for reform of trade between the states. Lamenting "the present anarchy of our commerces," he believed that "most of our political evils may be traced up to our commercial ones." A proposal in the Virginia legislature in 1784 for a federal convention failed because Patrick Henry was, more than most, opposed to closer union. Madison took another tack: he penned directions for Virginia commissioners Mason and Henderson, who were to meet with Marylanders Chase and Jenifer, on trade across Potomac and Chesapeake. These talks, begun at Alexandria, were speeded to success when Washington sent his coach to bring the conferees to enjoy the hospitality of Mount Vernon. Maryland would enlarge the understanding by enlisting Delaware and Pennsylvania, "who will naturally pay the same compliment to their neighbours."

In mid-March 1786 Governor Clinton submitted to the New
York legislature the invitation of Virginia to send commissioners to a meeting of the states "for the purpose of framing
such regulations of trade as may be judged necessary to promote the general interest." New York almost failed to act, for
only at the end of the session were Robert R. Livingston,
Leonard Gansevoort, Robert C. Livingston, Hamilton, James
Duane, and Egbert Benson appointed. Any three were to
serve. Hamilton promptly engaged to be one, and supposed
that his companions would be the chancelor and either
Gansevoort or R. C. Livingston. As it turned out only Egbert
Benson went with Hamilton to Annapolis. Richard Varick had
arranged a dinner-party sendoff for them at his home on September 1, but Hamilton wished to be with his family on the
eve of departure, and would let Benson, "a prophane bachelor," be Varick's guest.

Hamilton felt better in health for the week's horseback journey via Philadelphia, but begrudged what he expected would
be the fortnight in attendance on the meeting before he could
start home. The meeting was to begin on the first Monday in
September. The Virginia delegates had chosen Annapolis,
avoiding the vicinity of Congress and large commercial towns,
"in order to disarm adversaries of insinuations of influence
from either of these quarters." Maryland, whose capital was
host town, sent no delegates, fearing that commercial discussion was an excuse for introducing political reform.

Commissioners trickled in slowly; it seemed to be the custom to wait until the date for an interstate meeting was past
before delegates set out from distant points. After what was
doubtless impatient waiting, only five states were represented—New York, Virginia, Pennsylvania, Delaware, and
New Jersey. New Hampshire, North Carolina, Massachusetts,
and Rhode Island named delegates, and those of the last two
states actually set out, but none arrived in time. Connecticut,
South Carolina, and Georgia appointed no participants. Also,

New York and Pennsylvania were not officially represented, since the first had only two and the latter only one of the three delegates enjoined for each state.

Finally, no more delegates appearing, troubled discussions were held for three days. Egbert Benson kept notes and acted as chairman of a steering committee. The committee took a fortunate direction. Since too few states were present to enter into commercial comity, the delegates seized on the wider powers which New Jersey had given its commissioners. They might consider how far commercial arrangements "and *other important matters,* might be necessary to the common interest and permanent harmony of the several states." Abraham Clark of Newark called attention to his wide option and it was determined to seize the opportunity to recommend to the states and to Congress the calling of a convention to revise the Articles of Confederation.

It is uncertain whether Hamilton was deputed to draft the address, or whether he volunteered. In any event, the report recited the fatal defects of the existing plan of union. Governor Edmund Randolph of Virginia objected to Hamilton's original statement "as too strong; whereupon Madison said to Hamilton: 'You had better yield to this man, for otherwise all Virginia will be against you.' " Thus the plea "was toned down . . . to suit tender stomachs, and in this . . . milder shape was adopted." Hamilton himself, three years later, may have forgotten some of the inhibitions of colleagues when he recalled what had happened. Since the few states there were unable to proceed with even the commercial assignment, those present "were unanimously of the opinion that some more radical reform was necessary," and "they, with one voice, earnestly recommended" the Philadelphia meeting "with power to revise the confederation at large."

The report, addressed to their own states but sent as well to the other states and to Congress, declared that comprehensive commercial regulations would "require a corresponding adjustment of other parts of the Foederal System." All knew the respects in which the Confederation stood in need of repair. Therefore, it was solicited that "Commissioners . . . meet at Philadelphia on the second Monday in May next, to take into consideration the situation of the United States, to devise such further provisions as shall appear to them necessary to render the constitution of the Foederal Government adequate to the exigencies of the Union." An act for that purpose should be reported to Congress, and when there agreed to, be confirmed by the legislature of every state. Naming a particular date for the Constitutional Convention was a stroke in keeping with the earnestness of the appeal. The ill wind of slim attendance at Annapolis had blown good to the country. States that would not stir themselves to remedy their commercial faults were now to abandon partial measures and harness themselves in a truly national enterprise.

Doubtless Hamilton in his return journey rode as far as Philadelphia with Madison and Tench Coxe, and their conversation may have been preparatory to work they would do together in the next years.

Chapter 8

SHOCKING SPEECH, PERSUASIVE ESSAYS

In the New York Assembly, from January to April, 1787, Hamilton was often concerned to have his state conform to the needs of the Confederation. Distracted as the central government was, and in need of being superseded by a firmer Union, Hamilton tried in every appropriate way to maintain respect for the obligations of Congress. At the outset he deplored the refusal of Governor Clinton to call a special session of the legislature to bring the proposed federal impost into effect. Hamilton had pleaded for the measure when first urged by Congress in 1781 (it was then blocked by Rhode Island and Virginia), had helped frame the renewed request of 1783, and now was sorry to see New York persist in obstruction. He spoke against a motion of Richard Varick which congratulated the Governor on his inaction. Hamilton assailed the complaint of Clinton's supporters that Congress was attempting to dictate to the state legislature. Most of the Assembly voted against him.

As a corollary of cooperation with Congress, Hamilton strove to have New York adhere to the Treaty of Peace by repealing laws which penalized loyalists. This subject recurred in different forms, and Hamilton became ever more ardent in his efforts for correction. He stressed that, from a selfish view, New York should not give the British any excuse for holding the western military posts and thus diverting the valuable fur trade. He finally succeeded in repealing a restrictive part of the Trespass Act.

He exerted himself mightily to have New York acknowledge the independence of Vermont and so pave the way for that state to enter the Confederation. He explored the situation in its every aspect, especially the danger that the Vermonters, if their demands were not respected, would join Canada. The Assembly consented, but the Senate refused.

He worked out a new system of taxation for New York; it was designed to eliminate inequalities and the favoritism of assessors. But he was unable to persuade the legislature. Samuel Jones, a Clinton supporter, made the motion for rejection.

As always, Hamilton insisted on a large and independent electorate. The will of the people, expressed by their chosen representatives, was the very basis of his system of government. This was in spite of the fact that in some districts of New York illiterate voters composed one-half or one-third of the whole. He would not have them, as was proposed, be guided by the inspectors of elections. Rather, let them be solicited by all parties and reach their conclusions as best they could.

With touching compassion as well as practicality, he succeeded in obliterating a cruel feature of a bill concerning murder. It provided that a woman clandestinely delivered of a child which died or was stillborn must within one month thereafter come before the magistrate with at least one witness to prove that the child was not murdered. Failing this appearance, she was to be held guilty of murder. The poor woman was punished enough by her loss of her child, and should not be obliged to suffer doubly by being "compelled . . . to publish her shame to the world." She would probably prefer to run the risk of the law and, if detected, her violation of it would be leniently viewed.

Hamilton acquiesced, temporarily, in a feature of a divorce bill to which the Council of Revision objected. It was that a marriage partner convicted of adultery would not be allowed to remarry. The Council observed that unless such offenders were to be confined in a "cloyster," it was foolish to expect them to live celebate in society. For the sake of the desirable divorce law Hamilton let the penalty on the guilty party pass, with the promise that he would try to correct it later. Under Danish law his mother, divorced by Lavien, had been unable to marry James Hamilton, as doubtless she would have done, thus making her sons legitimate. It should be said here, however, that Hamilton's birth out of wedlock did not hamper his career, in spite of ungenerous sneers of enemies who thereby dishonored themselves.

It was inevitable, after his long advocacy of a constitutional convention to revise the Articles of Confederation, that Hamilton should move in the Assembly (February 1787) that delegates be appointed to meet those from other states according to the call of Congress. The Assembly accepted his proposal that there be five delegates, but consented to the Senate's preference for three. Limiting the number of delegates to three was deliberately designed by the Clinton forces. Schuyler had moved in the Senate for five, but John Haring, a Clinton faithful, succeeded in cutting this to three, the vote being eleven to seven. In choosing delegates in the Assembly, every member voted for Robert Yates (52 votes); Hamilton had the nominations of all but himself, Samuel Jones, and Matthew Patterson (49); John Lansing, Jr., was third (26). Hamilton's nominees, Duane and R. R. Livingston, came fourth and fifth. The Senate chose the same three as the Assembly had (Hamilton, Yates, Lansing). As Yates and Lansing were Clinton stalwarts, this composition of the delegation meant that the vote of the New York majority in the convention would be against strengthening the central government. This intention was evident when a resolve that no changes in the Confederation should be inconsistent with the constitution of New York was defeated by only one vote—that of the presiding officer, Pierre Van Cortlandt. In April Hamilton renewed the effort for five delegates—two in addition to those already appointed. He recommended that Chancellor Livingston, James Duane, Egbert Benson, and John Jay would be desirable choices. He particularly favored Jay, because of Jay's experience in the domestic and foreign affairs of the country. His renewed motion for five delegates was agreed to by the Assembly, but rejected in the Senate. Had the majority of the New York delegation been Hamilton, and, say, Duane and Chancellor Livingston, the state would have exerted a steady influence for an effective Union. We also may guess that Hamilton, acting in the convention with sympathetic colleagues, would not have overreached in his first proposals for reform of the Articles. Being in the minority, he felt under the impulse to counteract the inhibitions of Yates and Lansing. Furthermore, as Yates and Lansing were destined to abandon the convention, for the remainder of its sittings New York had no vote. The fight for ratification of the Constitution in New York, the most strenuous in any state, would have been easier had not the majority delegates denounced the document to the legislature. Five years afterward Hamilton wrote that he "was the only member from the state to which he belonged who signed the constitution, and, it is notorious, against the prevailing weight of . . . official influence . . . and against what would probably be the opinion of a large majority of his fellow-citizens, till better information should correct their first impressions." The final act of the convention listed eleven states as present and assenting, and "Mr. Hamilton from New York."

None of the founding fathers rendered greater service to the Constitution than Alexander Hamilton, but his contributions were before and after the convention rather than in the discussions at Philadelphia. For years he had publicly deplored the anemia of the Confederation, had moved the New York legislature to propose a meeting of the states for its reform, and had penned the successful summons from the Annapolis convention. Then, when the Constitution was on the tapis for approval by the states, he was chief author of the *Federalist* papers, which persuasively explained the benefits to be expected from the new structure of government. He, with the valiant support of colleagues such as James Duane and R. R. Livingston, was the unremitting champion of ratification in the New York convention at Poughkeepsie. Once the Constitution was installed, as Secretary of the Treasury Hamilton gave the national government "not only . . . a strong soul, but *strong organs* by which that soul is to operate." In justifying the first Bank of the United States, he developed the doctrine of implied powers in the Constitution, which inspired the decisions of Chief Justice John Marshall for a generation after Hamilton's death.

This is not to say that Hamilton's magnetic pull for a dominant central authority was not felt in the Constitutional Convention itself. His extreme views, as first expressed, had a nuisance value. The most that could be said for conferring power on Congress and executive had been aired, and others less bold could approach his limits with some impunity. Even while absent from the Convention he publicly defended its program. When he returned he played a conciliatory role and espoused particular features that met agreement. Nobody worked harder to dissuade three members from their refusal to sign the document.

Hamilton was an embarrassing exception to Professor Charles A. Beard's thesis, stated early in the twentieth century, that the makers of the Constitution were pocketbook patriots. Most were possessors of property in public securities, lands, slaves, or merchandise, all of which were threatened by the imbecility of the Confederation. In Beard's view their wealth must be rescued by dismissing the present political house of cards and substituting a firm structure with a competent national authority to ensure union, peace, and solvency. In this endeavor they were selfishly motivated. They were not moral supermen or statesmen of purest wisdom. The Constitution was a partisan plot hatched in secret to serve a class interest.

Within recent decades this charge of a disingenuous design on the part of the framers has been seriously questioned, if not substantially discredited. The particulars of this rerevisionist scholarship need not enter here. It is sufficient to note that men in public life, chosen by the state legislatures to devise reforms in government, had generally acquired private means. They had assisted in financing the Revolution and had invested in the future of the country. This was evident from the fact that they had the leisure to devote time and talents to their critical assignment. As for holding the debates behind closed doors, that was sensible on several counts. Much would be proposed in the Convention only to be discarded, but if it were aired it would provoke controversy and retard progress toward a satisfactory conclusion. Speakers on the floor would be hesitant to express views which they would later modify or abandon. The feasible procedure was to shape an instrument with the benefit of their combined judgment and then present it on its merits. The document was to be submitted to the people of the states for approval or rejection. The fact that within a year it was ratified by nine states and so came into effect as the fundamental law was testimony to its expected utility. The inevitable multiplicity of wanted changes was reduced after an interval to ten desirable amendments.

As for Hamilton, for years, since he had been an impecunious subaltern, he had been urging that additional power over continental affairs be vested in the central government, leaving to the states their local concerns. As a member of the convention he had only the income from his expanding law practice. He had married into a wealthy family, but subsidy was never in his mind nor in that of the Schuylers. Having no property to protect, some have said that he strove for glory. That object may be accepted if it is understood to mean a reputation for service to the community. The same applies to the members of the Convention as a whole. As leaders in the Revolution, which most of them had been, had they not sacrificed for what they believed to be the common interest? Their personal concerns tinctured their advocacies, but they were above all distinguished by their public spirit. Having won independence, were they not committed to preserving it? Does the most suspicious critic allege that Washington, chairman of the Convention and thus chief champion of the Constitution, was meanly inspired?

The Convention had a quorum and began its sessions May 25, 1787. Hamilton nominated Major William Jackson, who had been Assistant Secretary of War, for secretary, and he was elected over William Temple Franklin. The choice was a poor one, for the records were not well kept. Hamilton served on the rules committee. Otherwise for four weeks he sat, merely attentive, taking desultory notes which were as much his own reflections as memoranda of what was being said.

On June 18 he broke his silence with a vengeance in a five-hour speech which startled all of his hearers and drew sympathetic comment from only two or three. His perfect candor threw persuasion to the winds. He explained that he was not offering a scheme for debate, much less adoption. He was giving his own ideas which later he would apply in amendment of the proposals of others. The convention had before it the Virginia plan, which reduced autonomy of the states, and the New Jersey plan, which left state sovereignty virtually untouched. He showed why, in his view, the first was an insufficient reform and the second deserved summary dismissal. The pens of all in the convention who recorded speeches were busy with Hamilton's utterance. A single sentence of those caught by Rufus King spoke the whole: "you must make the national Sovereignty transcendent & entire." And he shocked colleague Yates: "all federal governments are weak and distracted. . . . we must establish a general and national government, completely sovereign, and annihilate the state distinctions; and unless we do this, no good purpose can be answered." That was radical enough, but he went further. As Madison noted, "In his private opinion . . . the British Govt. was the best in the world: and . . . he doubted . . . whether anything short of it would do in America." The new Constitution should approach as closely to monarchy as republican preference would allow. The chief executive should serve for life, be an elective king.

The effect on the convention was as if, after the defeat of Hitler, a responsible statesman had urged fascism for the United States. His explicit cautions evaporated in the telling of his enemies forever afterward. Hamilton now figured as the foe of democracy. His means of capturing stability in society with security of the individual were forgotten. "The voice of the people has been said to be the voice of God," but "It is not true in fact. The people are turbulent and changing. . . ." Their mercurial impulses in the lower house of Congress should be steadied by senators, of the privileged classes, continuing in office during good behavior. The chief executive should have an absolute veto on all national legislation. The general government should appoint executives of the states, now to be mere administrative subdivisions, and those executives in turn would have complete veto power.

In the background of Hamilton's derogation of the states' authority was Shays's insurrection in Massachusetts, to which he referred. There the state had been unable to protect life and property within its own confines. Hamilton believed that popular sentiment, then coinciding with the permissive New Jersey plan, was altering to favor a stronger government and would soon demand more vigor in the central organs than the Virginia plan offered. His plea for decisive power in chief executive, Congress, and a supreme judiciary reflected the political philosophy of Thomas Hobbes, including the right of the people to revolt if those entrusted with highest power failed in their duty. Short of this drastic remedy, the offending executive could be impeached and convicted.

In debate on following days Hamilton gave back to the states some of their functions. In his behavior in the convention it was as though he had descended from his soaring flight, and wanted to use more nearly the common language of the delegates. He did not hold, for instance, with the dogmatism of Gouverneur Morris, who trembled at the ability of states to weaken the Union. Hamilton exclaimed, "What if all the Charters & Constitutions of the States were thrown into the fire, and all their demagogues into the ocean. What would it be to the happiness of America." A week after this high toned speech, Yates had Hamilton saying, "Real liberty is neither found in despotism or the extremes of democracy, but in moderate governments. . . . if we incline too much to democracy, we shall soon shoot into a monarchy."

Though Hamilton's ideal scheme appeared outlandish to most of his fellow delegates, by benefit of his concessions later, much that he recommended was engrafted in the Constitution. A principal innovation of the document was that it empowered the national government to act directly upon the individual citizen, without the mediation of the state. This was an insistence of Hamilton throughout. In justifying unequal representation of the states in the Senate he queried, "as States are a collection of individual men which ought we to respect most, the rights of the people composing them, or of the artificial beings resulting from the composition [?]" Or, as another quoted him, "is it our interest . . . to sacrifice individual rights to the preservation of the rights of an *artificial* being, called states?"

As his views were negatived by his two colleagues, Hamilton left the convention at the end of June for New York, but he was not idle in behalf of a strong constitution. He published a rebuke to Governor Clinton for his public attacks on the Convention as not necessary and bound to have mischievous effect. During the war Hamilton and Clinton had been friends; Clinton had nursed the young officer when he fell ill on his mission to New York and had aided his assignment with money; Hamilton in turn had hoped that Washington would recall Putnam and give that command to Clinton. Certainly, from the time of Clinton's obstruction of the effort to give Congress an independent revenue, he and Hamilton were at odds, and the differences between them deepened. As Jefferson was Hamilton's foil in the national arena, so was Clinton in what pertained to the state. Clinton was the preferable foe, for he fought openly and if he acted through agents they were unmistakably known.

Also in service of the convention Hamilton inquired into a report, circulated by loyalists in Connecticut, that the delegates at Philadelphia wanted to install the second son of George III, Duke of York and secular bishop of Osnaburgh, as King of the United States. Hamilton did not say so, but perhaps he wished to discredit this rumor because his own leanings toward monarchy had already harmed the deliberations.

Having felt that the convention was faltering, and knowing that Washington shared his disappointment, Hamilton wrote

him an encouraging report of popular sentiment he had encountered in New Jersey and New York. The country would
accept an energetic government if the delegates had the
courage and decision to offer one. Washington replied
gratefully. He almost despaired of a favorable issue of the
Convention. "I am sorry you went away. I wish you were
back. The crisis is equally important and alarming, and no opposition . . . should discourage exertions till the signature is
fixed."

While Hamilton was in New York he helped compose a
quarrel between two friends, merchants and public figures. It
was a disagreement which had threatened to end with pistols.
In correspondence with his opposite second, he spoke of the
only excuse for a duel, a "necessary sacrifice to the prejudices
of public opinion." This justification, as he believed it to be,
was to bring him to his death.

He was back in the Convention briefly in mid-August, then
returned early in September and was an active participant to
the conclusion. He was for increasing the number in the
House of Representatives. "He avowed himself a friend to a
vigorous Government [read highly centralized] but would declare at the same time, that he held it essential that the popular
branch of it should be on a broad foundation. He was
seriously of opinion that the House . . . was on so narrow a
scale as to . . . warrant a jealously in the people for their liberties." He gave Madison, for his record, his draft of a constitution which, in contrast to his first speech, approached what
the convention actually adopted. Some thought the Constitution should not be submitted first to the Continental Congress,
for that body was to be abolished and would not commend the
new fundamental law to the states for ratification. Hamilton
insisted that courtesy compelled the risk, if risk there was.

He was more concerned that three members of the convention were refusing to sign the document. Edmund Randolph
and George Mason of Virginia, reversing their previous

stands, and Elbridge Gerry of Massachusetts, who had been equivocal, discovered insuperable objections to attaching their names. Hamilton begged for unanimous approval. "A few characters of consequence," by rejecting the offering to the country, might "do infinite mischief." His plea to the recalcitrant few was peculiarly telling. "No man's ideas," he declared, "were more remote from the plan than his were known to be, but is it possible to deliberate between anarchy and Convulsion on one side, and the chance of good to be expected from the plan on the other." Unfortunately, the obstinate ones did not yield. In his eagerness to see the document christened, Hamilton immediately went to the desk and wrote in the names of the states, ready to receive the signatures of their delegates. As Yates and Lansing had withdrawn in disapproval, he alone sponsored the Constitution for New York.

From that moment Hamilton put aside his own regrets for inadequacies of the reform and strove first to commend it for its promise and then to prove it useful in the performance. He began by proposing that friends join him in a series of newspaper essays which would explain the Constitution to the people of New York in preparation for the ratifying convention. Madison and Jay became his partners. William Duer wrote some pieces that were similar, but they did not appear over the common signature of "Publius." Gouverneur Morris and perhaps a few others were approached, but did not come into the collaboration. Soon known as *The Federalist*, these papers, written by peculiarly qualified authors, formed the foremost commentary on the Constitution. From an early date they lay to the hands of judges who must interpret the fundamental law.

Tradition has it that Hamilton wrote the first number, the introduction to the rest, in the cabin of the sloop bringing him from Albany to New York. For a time the authors read each others' manuscripts, but as the number of essays multiplied and pressures on the writers increased there was scarcely opportunity for each man to review his own sheets before they were wanted by the printer. A rough division of labor averted serious overlaps. Jay, from his diplomatic experience, treated foreign relations, Madison discussed the failures of ancient and modern confederacies, and Hamilton dealt with military and fiscal concerns. The essays appeared, usually a couple of times a week, in one or more New York newspapers, beginning in late October 1787 and continuing until early April 1788; then eight numbers were first published in book form and reprinted in the newspapers.

Of the eighty-five numbers, Jay wrote five; doubtless he would have contributed more but for an attack of rheumatism. The authorship of most of the others by Hamilton or by Madison or by the two jointly is certain, but much ingenuity has been used by scholars and partizans to attribute some twenty essays to one or another of the chief writers. Political philosophies have been compared, stylistic peculiarities have been searched, even supposedly habitual spellings have been identified in the inquiries. In lists that Hamilton and Madison happened to make they differed as to which wrote which piece, so similar were their views and so fallible their recollections. Roughly, it is agreed that Hamilton wrote two-thirds of the whole.

The essays were addressed "To the People of the State of New-York." They were a painstaking exposition and at the same time, a vigorous defense of the Constitution. At many points they commended the proposed national plan as similar to the Constitution of New York. Indeed, features of the Constitution which were objected to as conferring too much power were shown to give less than was exercised in the state. For further comparisons Hamilton had acquainted himself with provisions of the basic laws of other states, including Maryland, Delaware, Virginia, Massachusetts, and New Hampshire. Generally, the tone of the writing was calm and patient, but there were occasional sarcastic sallies against Governor George Clinton and Richard Henry Lee, whose pieces were also appearing in the newspapers.

The scheme of the papers, stated in the first number, was to demonstrate the necessity of union, the inadequacy of the Confederation, the need for a government at least as energetic as that proposed, and the conformity of the Constitution to republican principles. The series was the longest and by far the ablest of those that were offered. Numbers of the anti-Constitution pieces discredited themselves by their shrillness.

While Hamilton did not slight any part of the document, those who knew his favorite advocacies would recognize the emphasis he gave them; for example, the importance of a wide representation of the people and a vigorous single executive. As a lawyer arguing for his client he sometimes put a good face on problems which had troubled him. For instance, he had worried about the extensive geographic area to be embraced under a representative government. No reader could escape his perfect knowledge of the Constitution, his goodwill and wisdom. He not only met opposition arguments, but went further and posed alternative provisions to show that they were less desirable than the ones adopted by the convention.

The whole work was free of flattery; for persuasion, Hamilton relied on candor. An illustrative passage, which spoke his deep political conviction, occurs in No. 71 of *The Federalist* (March 1788) in which he is addressing the body of citizens: "It is a just observation, that the people commonly *intend* the PUBLIC GOOD. This often applies to their very errors. But their good sense would despise the adulator, who should pretend that they always *reason right* about the *means* of promoting it. They know from experience, that they sometimes err; and the wonder is, that they so seldom err as they do; beset as they continually are by the wiles of parasites and sycophants, by the snares of the ambitious, the avaricious, the desperate; by the artifices of men, who possess their confidence more than they deserve it. . . . When occasions present themselves in which the interests of the people are at variance with their inclinations, it is the duty of the persons whom they have appointed to be the guardians of these interests, to withstand the temporary delusion, in order to give them time and opportunity for more cool and sedate reflection. Instances might be cited, in which a conduct of this kind has saved the people from very fatal consequences of their own mistakes, and has procured lasting monuments of their gratitude to the men, who had courage and magnanimity enough to serve them at the peril of their displeasure."

One object of bringing out the essays in book form, two volumes, in addition to having them appear in New York newspapers, was to influence the vote in other states which had not ratified. The set was in two editions, a cheaper (of which Hamilton sent many copies to Governor Randolph, at Madison's wish, for distribution in Virginia) and a finer, such as Hamilton presented to Washington. Hamilton himself wrote the introduction to the first volume and edited the papers for both volumes. The authorship of the essays was known before a French edition of 1792 disclosed it (with the names of Madison and Jay misspelled). Five editions appeared in Hamilton's lifetime.

Chapter 9

STRUGGLE FOR
CONSTITUTION
IN NEW YORK

Before the opening of the New York convention which was to pass on the Constitution, Hamilton made intensive efforts to give it a favorable turn. Besides preparing his twice-a-week *Federalist* essays, he electioneered for delegates committed to ratifying, he inquired anxiously for the prospects in other states, and he arranged with John Sullivan and James Madison for expresses, at his expense, with news of success in New Hampshire and Virginia. The outlook in New Hampshire, following an adjournment favored by friends of the Constitution, was good. The Virginia convention had been in session ten days when Madison wrote (June 9, 1788) that he was hopeful, but apprehensive of a reverse. Eleazer Oswald, the formidable Philadelphia editor-opponent of the Constitution, was in Richmond closeted with the Antis. A week later Madison wrote that Oswald was communicating with foes of ratification in New York to bring about adjournment in both Virginia and New York, so that those states would be critical spectators of the new government when formed. Opponents in Virginia believed they could insist on amendments prior to approval. If the state rejected the Constitution the delegates from the Kentucky country would be the cause. Gouverneur Morris, in Richmond on business, was a close observer of the convention. He reported that "altho Mr. [Patrick] Henry is most warm and powerful in Declamation being perfectly Master of Action Utterance and the Power of Speech to stir Men's Blood yet the Weight of Argument is so strong on the Side of Truth as wholly to destroy even on weak Minds the Effects of his Eloquence." Hamilton was cheered when Massachusetts, after a contest, went for the Constitution, with satisfaction of the people of the state at the result.

Hamilton considered the outcome of election of delegates in New York uncertain, hinging on the choice in Albany County. A month later (May 19, 1788) he had to write Madison that he feared the vote was against them. Governor Clinton, "truly the leader of his party," talked down a national government. Opposition could not be overcome by reason, unless it had unexpected delayed effect. The hope was that if nine states consented, New York would conform, but even so, the state, swayed by Clinton's obstinacy, might hold out in any event. At the end of May he knew that "the elections have gone wrong." The Antifederalists won forty-six seats from nine counties (including all delegates from Albany), while the Federalists won only four counties and elected only nineteen delegates. All of the delegates from New York City were Federalists, overwhelmingly elected. Hamilton was fourth in number of votes; he received only twenty-two fewer than Jay, who topped the list.

Hamilton was profoundly disturbed by the power of the Antifederalist party. The more he penetrated their views, "the more I dread the consequences of the non adoption of the

Constitution by any of the other states, the more I fear an eventual disunion and civil war. God grant that Virginia may accede. Her example will have a vast influence on our politics."

When the convention met in the courthouse at Poughkeepsie, Hamilton figured that two-thirds of the sixty-five delegates were Antifederalist and that four-sevenths of the citizens in the state at large were of the same persuasion. Solidly Federalist were New York City and County, Richmond, Kings, and Westchester. Near-by southern counties—Queens, Suffolk, Dutchess—were divided, but more or less in favor of the Constitution. All above Dutchess was Antifederalist save the towns of Albany and Hudson. No matter what the news from the convention, New York City was in high heart for ratification, rang bells, fired cannon, and mounted a notable parade before the state entered the new union.

Governor Clinton was elected president of the convention. He was fair in his rulings, but his conspicuous position emphasized his leadership of the majority. The friends of the Constitution scored at the outset with agreement that no vote should be taken until the document had been gone through clause by clause. The resolution is in the handwritings of Hamilton and Robert R. Livingston. It ensured their hope that the delegates would be held together for at least two weeks—that they would not summarily reject the new government—and that arguments for the plan could have some chance of effect. This was a proper action on the part of the Antis, though in spite of their confidence it was their undoing. Said Robert Yates: "We yielded to a Proposal made by our Opponents to discuss the Constitution in a Committee of the whole, without putting a Question on any Part, providing that in the Course of the Discussion, we should suggest the Amendments . . . which we deemed necessary. . . . Fully relying on the Steadiness of our Friends we see no Danger in this Mode and we came into it to prevent the Opposition from charging us with Precipitation."

Both sides caucused on strategy—who should speak on what subjects and when. Usually Chancellor Livingston for the *pros* and John Lansing for the *cons* opened a topic and took first blows of the opposition. Hamilton was the chief champion of the Constitution and Melancton Smith was its chief opponent; they dominated the debates when tensions were greatest. While Melancton Smith was a cool analytical reasoner and an able foe, Hamilton had the better supporting team, especially Chancellor Livingston, John Jay, and James Duane, all resourceful men. Lansing and others loyal to Clinton, and Clinton himself in his several speeches, were organized to assist Smith, but few of them had the capacity or experience of Hamilton's corps.

It is difficult today to understand why so much endeavor was necessary to secure acceptance of the Constitution, not only by the large states of Massachusetts, Virginia, and New York, but by also North Carolina and New Hampshire, not to speak of the obstinacy of Rhode Island. Antagonism was compounded of distance and difference between communities with slow communication, the fear of authority such as had animated the Revolution, and the proprietary interest of local politicians. Objecting states had not the later experience of the utility of the Constitution; and remember, seventy-five years later states' rights were to precipitate civil war. All the more credit goes to those who urged the advantages of a firmer, more united government.

Hamilton's mind and emotions were passionately committed to approval of the Constitution by New York. The issue was really that of creating a nation or seeing the Confederation disintegrate. Though nine or more states might launch the new government, it could not prosper if New York held aloof, for the country would be cut in two, and it would lose its finest port and waterway to the interior. At one point in the debate Hamilton declared that "the establishment of a republican government, on a safe and solid basis . . . is an object of all others the nearest and most dear to my own heart."

Chancellor Livingston opened the debate. He was a tall, elegant man, of informed and polished speech. His official position of Chief Justice of the state added to his personal influence. Naturally, as introducer of the Constitution, his theme was the demerits of the Confederation. It was "defective in its principle, and impeachable in its execution, as it operated upon States in their political capacity, and not upon individuals; . . . it carried with it the seeds of . . . its own dissolution."

Next day, in a reproach to leading opponents, Hamilton set the serious tone in which the convention proceeded. He said that Lansing and Melancton Smith, in their replies to Chancellor Livingston's first address, had treated Livingston "as having wandered in the flowery fields of fancy; and attempts have been made, to take off from the minds of the committee, that sober impression, which might be expected from his arguments . . . I will not agree with gentlemen, who trifle with the weaknesses of our country . . . and suppose, that they are enumerated . . . to terrify with ideal dangers. No, I believe these weaknesses to be real, and pregnant with destruction." He was quick to say that a stable government must not be bought at the price of liberties. "If . . . on a full and candid discussion, the proposed system shall appear to have that tendency, for God's sake, let us reject it! But, let us not . . . accept doubtful surmises as the evidence of truth. Let us consider the Constitution calmly and dispassionately."

Hamilton early checked the gambit of assuming the worst conceivable consequences of the new plan. "The danger of corruption," he regretted, "has been . . . presented to our view in the most heightened and unnatural colouring. Events, merely possible have been magnified by distempered imagination into inevitable realities; and the most distant . . . conjectures have been formed into . . . infallible prediction." In the same spirit, villainous oppression had been discovered by supposing the lowest quorum, a bare majority of which would "decide in all cases on questions of infinite moment." He turned this back on challengers by reminding that such a danger belonged more to the small Congress of the Confederation than to the larger and differently operating legislature of the pending Constitution. With characteristic thoroughness, he traced out his rebuttal to the last detail.

It was necessary to destroy the contention that the existing scheme could be corrected here and there and would then serve admirably. "The fundamental principle of the Old Confederation [that the laws of the Union apply only to states in their corporate capacity] is defective. We must totally eradicate and discard this principle before we can expect an efficient government." Weakness in the head had invited resistance in the members. "We shall do well," Hamilton warned, "not to deceive ourselves with the favorable events of the late war. Common danger prevented the operation of the ruinous principle, in its full extent. But since the peace, we have experienced the evils, we have felt the poison of the system in its unmingled purity."

Hamilton constantly referred to the correspondence of the New York government to that prescribed in the Constitution—two houses of the legislature, the Senate to check the more spontaneous House; competent executive powers, and taxation of individuals. He was at pains to demonstrate that the states—the delegates were thinking in terms of New York, of course—would not be extinguished in the national plan. The central government and the state governments were coordinate, each with its sphere, the one general, the others particular to the concerns of their limited communities. No topic required more careful but candid emphasis than the need for vesting appropriate authority in the national organs. He appealed to history for his reasons. "In the commencement of a revolution, which received its birth from the usurpations of tyranny, nothing was more natural, than that the public mind should be influenced by an extreme spirit of jealousy. . . . The zeal for liberty became predominant and excessive. In forming our confederation . . . we appear to have had no other view than to secure ourselves from despotism." But this resistance to arbitrary power had antagonized necessary ability and resulted in imbecile government. Hamilton and his friends stigmatized two proposals of enemies of the Constitution that would cripple Congress. One was that no taxes should be collected unless the state had failed to furnish its quota of the requisition. Hamilton showed the madness of trying to coerce a refusing state. The defiant one would ally itself with others, and civil war would be the consequence. The other thrust at Congress was the reservation that the state legislatures be free to recall their members of the national Senate. There could be no doubt of the attachment of New York senators to the interests of their state, but at times, in obedience to their function under the Constitution, they must place national policy foremost. In this connection Hamilton repelled a rearguard action of opponents who pictured the United States Senate as composed of aristocrats. Hamilton declared that he did not know the meaning of aristocracy in America so long as any man was as much within the choice of the people for national office as he was for state office. If the voters selected for their senators individuals of talents, integrity, and wisdom were these to be suspected as aristocrats claiming inborn sway over their fellow-citizens?

After undercutting the attempts to rob Congress of sure revenue and to invade the independence of the Senate, Hamilton condemned the motive behind these restraints. It was easier, he said, "to calculate the evils, than the advantages of a measure; . . . to apprehend the danger, than to see the necessity of giving powers to our rulers." The Constitution offered a fortunate combination of freedom of the citizen and effectiveness of government. "Now what do gentlemen mean by . . . declaiming against this government? Why do they say we ought to limit its powers, to disable it, and to destroy its capacity of blessing the people? . . . Sir, when you have divided and nicely balanced the departments of government; when you have strongly connected the virtue of your rulers with their interest; when, in short, you have rendered your system as perfect as human forms can be;—you must place confidence; you must give power." Viewing the known and unguessed responsibilities of the national as compared with the more restricted state unit, "where," Hamilton asked, "ought the great resources to be lodged? . . . To what extent shall these resources be possessed? Reason says as far as possible exigencies can require; that is, without limitation."

Hamilton's friend Rufus King, then of Massachusetts, who was eager for approval of the Constitution everywhere, had arranged with John Langdon to send word as soon as New Hampshire, the ninth state to ratify, took the expected favorable action. Langdon dispatched his express rider from Concord on June 21, and General Knox at Springfield relayed the message to Hamilton at Poughkeepsie on June 24. King had foretold that "The accession of New Hampshire," bringing the new Union into being, "will present the Subject to your Convention in a new and indeed an extraordinary light." The next day Chancellor Livingston presumed to announce on the floor that since the old government was dissolved the decision of New York no longer hung on principle, but was shifted to the question of expediency. But King and Livingston were too sanguine. Melancton Smith still wanted to be shown that the Constitution was a proper instrument for New York, no matter if other states brought it into existence for themselves. One of his henchmen, John Williams, from far upstate, insisted on further amendment. No excise should be laid on a domestic product, and Congress should not impose direct taxes unless customs and excise proved insufficient and not then unless requisitions on the states had been refused. Smith and Williams feared that Congress would devour all of the revenue resources and annihilate the states.

For reply to this assault on the national treasury, Hamilton and Duane had an ace in the hole. They had the secretary read from Governor Clinton's complaints to the legislature in 1780–82 that New York bore an unfair share of public burdens because other states did not fill their requisitions and Congress was helpless to compel united contribution. The embarrassment of Clinton and Smith was deepened as Hamilton improved the occasion to show "that requisitions have been the cause of a principal part of our calamities; that the system is . . . rotten, and ought forever to be banished from our government."

Governor Clinton protested that he was "a friend of a strong and efficient government," but wanted to be sure that the Constitution promised a safe one. Hamilton pressed his advantage. Clinton talked falsely. Why during the war did he ostensibly approve an import duty for Congress and then block it by refusing to accept the prescribed mode of collection? Moreover, the preference now shown for import duties to the exclusion of direct taxes was against the interest of New York. As a commercial state New York must sacrifice revenue, while states more given to manufactures would escape similar contribution.

Debate between Hamilton and Lansing took a persistently personal turn, beginning with Lansing's reminder that Hamilton, now so generous in the role of the states, in the Philadelphia convention had given them short shrift. Chancellor Livingston expended sarcasm too telling to be tactful. Melancton Smith continued to demand amendments before the Constitution would be satisfactory to New York. If those who wanted to know how the convention felt, thought differently, and were free with offensive tactics, let them put the Constitution to a vote. This was a palpable touch, for a test at that time would have meant rejection.

James Madison, leading champion of the Constitution in the Virginia convention, had written Hamilton that the margin in favor might be as small as three or four delegates. Hamilton, with Schuyler's help, had sped to Madison news of New Hampshire's ratification. At the same time he begged for "further intelligence" from Richmond, "as our only chance of success depends on you." The gleam of hope in New York would brighten only if the Virginians approved the Constitution. Hamilton could not know that Madison, at that very time, was dispatching to him the yearned-for notice.

Shortly after noon on July 2 Governor Clinton, then discussing the power of Congress to contract loans, found his audience suddenly distracted. There was "such a buzz through the House, that little of his Excellency's Speech was heard." A rider had sprung from his panting horse at the door and handed in a letter for Hamilton. The news of Virginia's approval of the Constitution temporarily broke up the convention, for the Federalists celebrated by marching around the courthouse with fife and drum. If there was any immediate effect on debate it was to stir the Antis to submit new batches of amendments. In fact, the New York convention remained in session for three weeks after the ratification by Virginia was known at Poughkeepsie.

Debate on the Constitution, section by section, was completed July 7. Next day Hamilton wrote Madison of Federalist hopes; the Antis were showing disagreement among themselves. Their proposals were of three sorts: joining the Union only if amendments were first adopted, joining on condition that amendments be adopted later, and joining with recommendation of amendments.

On July 11 the Federalists decided to submit ratification to a vote. Hamilton drew up the motion, which was submitted by

John Jay. It was "that the Constitution under consideration ought to be ratified by this convention. Resolved further . . . that . . . whatever amendments may be deemed useful or expedient ought to be recommended." The day before, a committee of seven from each party had met to try to come to agreement on the question of amendments. On July 12 Jay complained to the convention that the Antis on the committee, instead of seeking mutual accommodation, had insulted the Federalists by insisting that all of the amendments be accepted as written. Hamilton followed to refute the idea of a conditional ratification. He begged the delegates not to hold him in ill will because of the vehemence of his support of the Constitution. His personal appeal had a conciliating effect. He argued that the convention was called to adopt or reject the new plan of government, not to take contingent action. No changes in the Constitution could be made except by a body equal in authority to that which framed it. Congress had no capacity to suspend any of its constitutional powers at the demand of a state which presumed to give law to its sister members of the Union. Even if Congress accepted New York with conditions attached, the other states would not stand for it. Hamilton "entreated the Convention in a pathetic strain to make a solemn pause, and weigh well what they were about to do, before they decided on a subject so infinitely important."

From this point on, the in-fighting brought Hamilton to his feet in the debate many times each day. Melancton Smith, unmoved by Hamilton's reasoning, offered a resolve which summarized the Antis' demands. The Constitution should be ratified only on several conditions. First another constitutional convention must be called to consider amendments. Until this was done the New York militia should not be continued in service out of the state for more than six weeks, nor should Congress regulate elections in New York. No excise should be collected in New York on domestic productions, except on liquor. No direct tax should be laid unless indirect revenue proved inadequate and the state had been requisitioned in vain. If these demands were violated, New York could withdraw from the Union.

Hamilton and Jay formulated amendments which Federalists would recommend; these made no great difference in the plan of government. But they were fearful that they could not budge their opponents from their obstinacy. New York would accept the Constitution with the reservation of a right to secede if her amendments were not adopted within several years, say, five or seven. Hamilton inquired of Madison whether New York could be received on this proposition. Hamilton must have felt sorely pressed to entertain the notion if he would do so after giving his own arguments against conditional approval. He now persuaded himself that if New York were accepted on her own terms, Congress would doubtless recommend certain amendments, and with the passage of time opposition to the Constitution would be dissipated.

Madison answered instantly and hurriedly from New York, where he was attending the Continental Congress. He gave a decided No to the Perhaps which Hamilton was willing to consider. "My opinion is that a . . . *conditional* ratification . . . does not make N. York a member of the New Union. . . . The Constitution requires an adoption *in toto,* and *for ever.* It has been so adopted by the other States . . . any *condition* whatever must viciate the ratification."

Meantime, James Duane entered a motion for unconditional ratification; it differed from Jay's by a harmless concession to opponents—New York delegates should procure from Congress a declaration that desired amendments would be considered in the constitutional way. Duane's motion was negatived, 41 to 20. Lansing, thus handsomely assured, proposed ratification on condition that a long bill of rights should not be violated and that a longer list should be submitted to a second constitutional convention. The vote of acceptance, 41 to 18, showed even more strength than before. If this recommen-

dation of the committee of the whole had been approved by
the convention, Hamilton's year-long, earnest efforts would
have been defeated. As it was, debate continued on Lansing's
amendments, which gave time for second thought among the
Antis. On July 23 Samuel Jones of Queens signalled the shift
by moving "that the words *upon condition* [in Lansing's resolu-
tion] should be obliterated, and the words *in full confidence*
should be substituted in their stead." Melancton Smith candidly endorsed this change of front. Until Virginia came in he
had hoped for previous amendments, but he was convinced
that this was now impossible. New York must be received into
the new Union, then he would work for amendments in the
prescribed fashion. The Federalists had persuaded him that a
second convention was undesirable. He was plainly moved by
the threat of secession of the southern counties from the state
if the convention refused unconditional approval of the Constitution.

Gilbert Livingston, brother-in-law of Governor Clinton, de-
fected. He had been "fully determined on previous amendments. . . . Nothing . . . but a conviction that I am serving
the . . . interests of my country, could ever induce me to take
another ground, and differ from so many of my friends on this
floor." Not so Governor Clinton, who would vote for what he
believed was the demand of his constituents of Ulster, conditional ratification.

The vote on Jones's motion for approval of the Constitution
"in full confidence" was passed, though narrowly, 31 to 29.
Next day more amendments were brought forward, but for
show, since—if the last vote in committee of the whole was
sustained—the Constitution was to be adopted anyhow. Lansing had one more arrow in his quiver. He would still make
approval contingent by reserving to the state the right to withdraw from the Union if in ———— years the amendments had
not been submitted to a convention in the prescribed manner.
Hamilton and Jay remonstrated against such a distrust of sister

states. Moreover, Hamilton read Madison's letter giving the opinion that "An adoption for a limited time would be as defective as an adoption of some of the articles only," Chancellor Livingston and Duane begged for a harmonious decision, and on this soothing note the question was put over to the next day, Friday, July 25.

That morning Melancton Smith repeated his recantation. Lansing's motion for conditional approval was voted down, 31 to 28. "The Constitution," a Federalist wrote in gratitude, "has . . . undergone an ordeal torture, and been preserved, as by fire." The devotion of Hamilton and his friends—Jay, Chancellor Livingston, Duane, Harison, and more—during six weeks of debate had changed a majority of two to one against to a bare majority of three for outright ratification. Certainly the adherence of New Hampshire, which made the new Union a fact, and, more important, the approval by Virginia had changed many minds as the impending isolation of New York bore in upon them. Then there was the fear at the end that the state might be torn apart by separation of the southern counties, which were insistently national. This is not to discount the arguments of the staunch minority of Federalists. Without their commitment and talents the convention would have promptly dismissed the Constitution. As it was, they held the delegates together until favoring events, reinforced by reasoning, could prevail.

The convention, on recommendation of the committee of the whole, formally ratified the Constitution, 30 to 25. The great object won, the Federalists gracefully proposed a circular letter to the other states urging a general convention to consider amendments. Lansing and Smith were properly placed on the drafting committee, and the hands of Jay and Hamilton appear in the manuscript. Hamilton, and also Madison, who later introduced the Bill of Rights in Congress, considered that the Constitution as drawn contained sufficient protections to individual and public liberty, but they went along with the strong desires of so many in the states. With all of their insight, they did not suspect the error of their omission. However, it is notable that Hamilton, at the very end, voted with Antifederalists against a motion of John Jay recommending that the President, the Vice President, and the members of Congress must be freeholders. (Even so, Jay's motion carried easily.)

After the convention accepted the Constitution, Governor Clinton, from the chair, pleased all, delegates and spectators, by promising to "endeavour to keep up peace and good order among" those who, until amendments were adopted, continued to oppose the new government. Hamilton reached New York City over the weekend and immediately presented the signed ratification to Congress.

The solidly Federalist business interests of the city, having anticipated that the New York convention would join the state in the new Union, had already mounted a grand parade in celebration. The many floats were led by the frigate *Hamilton*, but it was only one of several of the symbolic displays which proclaimed him a hero. Nicholas Cruger, "in a farmer's dress, supporting the farmers' arms," conducted six oxen drawing a plow. No one in the "pompous procession" could have been so proud as he, because sixteen years before he had sent from St. Croix an orphan lad who was now the champion of the Continent.

Chapter 10

PUBLIC CREDIT

Hamilton was a member of the expiring Continental Congress in 1788, but, like others, he attended irregularly; he was absent five solid weeks during the Poughkeepsie convention. He was diligent to have the incoming national government located in New York City as the initial capital. When the decision for this seemed doubtful, he offered to pay the expenses of Rhode Island delegates if they would come to Congress and swell the northern vote. Discreditably, he meant to hide his agency in this and have it appear that the money came from a Rhode Island source. He helped ready the city hall, with L'Enfant's improvements, to be the first United States capitol. He hoped that the permanent seat of government would be no farther south than Philadelphia.

Hamilton continued to encourage Nathaniel Chipman and his Vermonters to bring their government into the Union. Some thought he wanted a counterweight to the impending claims of Kentucky and Franklin for statehood. That is questionable because he led in having Congress declare the "clear and essential right" of the United States to the free navigation of the Mississippi, a principal object of the westerners.

In affection for Baron Steuben and appreciation of his services to the Revolutionary army, Hamilton furthered his friend's petition for a pension and compensation for losses in coming to America as a volunteer, though the application was not successful until later.

Blocks of Hamilton's time were given to national and state politics. His consuming care was to have the national government prosperously launched. He urged on Washington, who cherished his retirement, the duty of accepting the presidency. This would ensure in the eyes of all, at home and abroad, the most promising auspices. Hamilton with other Federalists provided against the accident that John Adams, agreed upon for Vice President, might receive more votes than Washington. He proposed to friends that Connecticut, New Jersey, and Pennsylvania throw away seven or eight votes for Vice President, "giving these to persons not otherwise thought of." Hamilton's attitude toward John Adams at the time was trusting; the cautionary withholding of electoral votes from him implied nothing of the later sharp enmity between them.

The case was reversed in Hamilton's treatment of George Clinton. The Governor had befriended Hamilton during the Revolution, and Hamilton had urged his military advancement. But subsequent experience, long before Clinton's hostility in the Poughkeepsie convention, had brought Hamilton to regard him as the inveterate foe of the national experiment. As chairman of the corresponding committee named at a Federalist meeting, Hamilton rallied support elsewhere in the state for the election of Robert Yates, Antifederalist, as governor, and Pierre Van Cortlandt, the incumbent Federalist, as lieutenant governor. The fortunes of New York in the Union, it was argued—the volume of its trade and repossession of the frontier posts—hung on the ouster of Clinton; the Governor, who had had twelve years' tenure, conceived that his own consequence would be diminished if he cooperated in the new Union. In some fifteen letters published at short intervals in the New York *Daily Advertiser*, all signed "H. G.," Hamilton blasted Clinton's career from his first public appearance to the eve of the election. The political attack was what was customary at that period, though more drawn out than usual. The personal attack was in bad taste, particularly in a writer who concealed his identity.

"H. G." was answered with spirit by Marinus Willett and other friends of Clinton. The Governor was re-elected by a small majority. The Federalists did better in running John Lawrence for Congress from New York City and County. The New York Senators, Philip Schuyler and Rufus King, were stout Federalists. The choice of King against several prominent Yorkers took some maneuvering, as he had only recently come to the state from Massachusetts. His election gave the New York Federalists and the nation a foremost leader for many years thereafter. This, however, was at the serious cost of alienating the Livingstons, hitherto Federalists, who wished to send to the Senate James Duane, their kinsman by marriage. However, due to Clinton's delay in calling the legislature and setting an election day, New York was not represented in either branch of the national Congress in its first session.

Soon aftter his inauguration, President Washington asked Hamilton's counsel on the etiquette of his office. Others had proposed semi-royal forms of address. It was important to preserve the dignity of the chief executive without offending democratic demand. Hamilton suggested the happy mien which Washington adopted—frequent formal receptions, invitations to a few guests at a time to home dinners, and direct access to the President for chief public characters.

Economic prosperity, banishing the dreary business slump, greeted the new national government. President Washington described the smiling scene to Lafayette: "In the last year, the plentiful crops and great prices of grain have vastly augmented our remittances. The rate of exchange is . . . much in our favor. Importations of European goods have been uncommonly extensive, and the duties payable into the public Treasury proportionably so." Eagerness to capture the revenue from import duties first occupied Congress with an emergency tariff act. This necessarily delayed for two months the organization of the executive departments.

It was not until well along in May 1789, that Elias Boudinot, who was to second Hamilton's policies at critical junctures, broached the subject of the departments. He gave priority to head of the Treasury. Among other duties this officer should "form and digest plans for . . . improvement" of the revenue. Provision for the other departments, of foreign affairs, (State) and War, would follow. It was agreed that the heads of executive offices should be appointed by the President with the consent of the Senate. After some debate the President was given the right to dismiss a minister; this because, among other reasons, the President might otherwise be impeached for his subordinate's malfeasance. As to the Treasury, should it be managed by a single secretary or by a board, as it often was under the Confederation? Gerry had served on a committee of the old Congress to supervise the finances, and he was for dividing responsibility among three or more officers. This return to bad practice (as compared to the efficient administration of Robert Morris as Financier) was roundly condemned. Likewise, single executives for the departments of State and War were voted. As subordinates in the Treasury, Baldwin proposed "a Comptroller, Auditors, Register, and Treasurer," which was accepted.

Several took alarm at words in the bill which made it the duty of the Secretary of the Treasury to "digest and report plans for the improvement and management of the revenue, and the support of the public credit." This was to supersede an important function of the House, whose members were capable of forming fiscal policy. Fisher Ames rebuked this ignorant presumption by reminding that the state of the finances "presents to the imagination a deep, dark, and dreary chaos; impossible to be reduced to order without the mind of the architect is clear and capacious, and his power commensurate to the occasion; he must not be the flitting creature of a day." Without such guidance, Madison warned, the House would prove guilty of bungling administration, which was as much to be shunned as faulty construction of the Constitution. In the act as passed, July 31, 1789, the salary for the secretaries of the Treasury and State was fixed at $3500.

It was natural that President Washington, in his habit of consulting with qualified persons on important appointments, should seek Robert Morris's suggestion for the Treasury. Morris was now in the Senate, and, anyhow, he would not have served again as Financier. As reported by Bishop William White, Morris's brother-in-law, Washington asked his old and trusted friend, "What are we to do with this heavy debt?" Morris replied, "There is but one man in the United States who can tell you; that is, Alexander Hamilton." Morris told of Hamilton's services to him. Hamilton's long-time friend Troup said that soon after the inauguration Washington informed Hamilton of his wish to have him in charge of the Treasury when the department was organized. When this should happen, Troup was to wind up Hamilton's law practice, which, though more remunerative than a minister's salary, Hamilton would relinquish if he could be of important service to the country. Along in July, John Adams thought it probable that Hamilton would be called to an executive post, in which event Adams's son Charles, entered as a law clerk under Hamilton, must seek another master.

Hamilton was nominated Secretary of the Treasury on September 11, 1789, and the Senate gave its advice and consent the same day. He was given competent associates, particularly Oliver Walcott, Jr., as Auditor, whom Hamilton had not known before; Wolcott moved steadily upward, showed himself to be dependable, and became Hamilton's immediate successor. For Assistant Secretary Hamilton chose William Duer, who had been secretary of the Board of Treasury. Though Hamilton had every means of judging of Duer's fitness, his selection was a grievous mistake, as was proved in his brief tenure.

A fortnight after Hamilton took office, the President informed him of his intention to name Thomas Jefferson secretary of State and Edmund Randolph Attorney General. Jefferson did not sail from Cowes until near the end of October 1789 and did not know of his appointment until he reached Monticello at Christmas. He accepted the post with reluctance. Domestic engagements at Monticello delayed his arrival at Philadelphia until March 1790. Jefferson's lethargy contrasted with Hamilton's eagerness to embrace the opportunity to help establish the national government. Jefferson had been for five years abroad and was not a witness to the worst failures of the Confederation nor the resolve for repair by construction of the Constitution. Nominally, Jefferson was the first of the President's ministers, actually, the problems with which Hamilton dealt (and not all of them were confined to the Treasury) were of superior importance to the nation's welfare.

Hamilton, more than others in the government, had to submit the principles of the Constitution to the test of day-to-day administrative practice. All enforcement had been slack before, so that obedience to the laws of Congress was not automatic; it had to be learned. His domain of finance was clothed with suspicion; the extraction of revenue must be with a combination of circumspection and firmness.

An early concern was regulation of the customs, the main reliance for federal income. There was the problem of transition from varied state controls to uniform national supervision and collection. On this account, Hamilton's many circulars to customs officers contained a degree of flexibility. Not so with attempts to cheat the revenue, of which he had personal knowledge from his boyhood experience of commerce in the

West Indies. He required exact attention and records from his subordinates at the ports of entry and a report of any delinquency of shipmasters and merchants to the District Attorney. He commissioned cutters which cruised the coast to prevent smuggling. Every feature of the construction, equipment, and manning of these little vessels (each of some forty tons, costing, complete, about $1000) was strictly watched. Captains and mates were individually approved by the President. Rum was a necessary part of the ration of the crews, but the nature of their assignment limited the daily allowance to half a gill per man. The service of the revenue cutters became the United States Coast Guard.

Some have assumed that Hamilton's plans for coping with the public debt were peculiarly original with him. They were so in the speed with which they were resolved upon, formulated, and pressed, but he had his models and advice from others. He was too good a workman not to consult precedent and the best credited writings on public finance. Thus John Marshall said of him that "To talents equally splendid and useful," he "united a patient industry, not always the companion of genius." He searched the comprehensive economic encyclopedias of Anderson and Postlethwayt and the works of Dr. Richard Price, and he closely minded the funding system of the younger Pitt and the history of the Bank of England. Nearer home was the wisdom of Pelatiah Webster's "Dissertation on . . . the Office of a Financier-General" (1781) which preceded the appointment of Webster's fellow-townsman Robert Morris and applied to Hamilton a decade later. Such a minister must "point out, arrange and put into action, *the ways and means by which the necessary supplies of the public treasury* may be derived." The proposals must be clearly presented for the comprehension of Congress. The design, however, *"must be the work of* ONE MIND."

Hamilton asked for suggestions from James Madison, William Bingham, and Stephen Higginson, the two latter being

businessmen of Philadelphia and Boston. He followed
Bingham's outline closely; it is entitled to be called an immediate source of Hamilton's system. Other friends offered ideas;
among them were John Witherspoon; Oliver Wolcott, Jr., in
the Treasury; and Philip Schuyler, who was adept in actuarial
calculations.

Public creditors in Pennsylvania, at the end of August 1789,
submitted to Congress a petition for action on the debt, and in
it they set forth desirable measures of reform. The House, after
delays on other concerns, now promptly resolved that "an adequate provision for the support of public credit [is] a matter of
high importance to the national honor and prosperity," and
the Secretary of the Treasury, when appointed, should report a
plan at the next session. The petitioners precisely anticipated
Hamilton's design. "Immediately to pay off the public debt,"
they observed, "if not impracticable . . . is certainly unnecessary." The example of reputable nations demonstrated "that a
permanent appropriation for the punctual payment of the interest will enable the public creditor to enjoy, by the facility of
transfer, all the advantages of the principal, without . . .
straining [the country's] resources." It sounded as though the
petition had been written by Hamilton; it urged that wise, dutiful action would permit America "to convert her calamity
into a blessing." Material from numerous sources on most
topics in the first report on the public credit were available to
Hamilton—especially in Mathew Carey's *American Museum*, to
which he subscribed—supposing he had time to read these
writings. However, numbers of expedients urged by others at
the time the report was in preparation had been entertained
by Hamilton long before, in the decade in which the economy
of the country had filled his thoughts.

Hamilton prepared his report for the support of public credit
in less than three months after it was ordered by the House.
With appendices, it ran to some 40,000 words. January 14,
1790, was set for its delivery. Gerry and others insisted that it

be submitted only in writing, but Boudinot, sensibly, urged that Hamilton be invited to appear in person "in order to answer . . . inquiries . . . , for . . . gentlemen would not be able clearly to comprehend so intricate a subject without oral illustration." Hamilton in a few spoken words on questioned features could probably have shortened debate on the report. A correspondent of Theodore Sedgwick found the report "difficult to understand . . . while we are in our infancy in the knowledge of Finance." Only after a third reading was he "gaining ground." The fear of Hamilton's influence, in the flesh, was misplaced, because in the end—though after prolonged and often rancorous discussion—the report was approved.

Some in the House complained that Hamilton had made his text complicated on purpose, evidently to cow his readers into acceptance. Actually his exposition was a model of clarity, and throughout he was deferential to the judgments of the legislators. He wanted to be understood. He wrote to Angelica Church, "Tomorrow I open the budget [i.e. submit the report] & you may imagine that today I am . . . not a little anxious."

Anticipating that the Secretary would propose that the central government assume the war debts of the states, purchasers of these deeply depreciated securities promised themselves a rich harvest. In remote parts to which news from the capital would reach slowly, state certificates could be had as low as two shillings on the pound. James Jackson of Georgia protested for the back country of the South. "Since this report has been read in the House," he cried, "a spirit of havoc, speculation, and ruin, has arisen. . . . Three vessels, sir, have sailed within a fortnight from this port, freighted for speculation; they are intended to purchase up the State and other securities in the hands of the uninformed, though honest citizens of North Carolina, South Carolina, and Georgia. My soul arises indignant at the avaracious . . . turpitude which so vile a conduct displays." His facts were correct; for example, Andrew

Craigie, king of these operators, wrote from New York, December 30, 1790, to Daniel Parker in London: "Haskel left here four days ago for Charleston[;] he carried with him 25000 or 30000 Drs in Specie" with which to buy state debt.

Hamilton's most celebrated state paper first declared the over-all importance of keeping the public financial engagements. This was the national moral responsibility, necessary for the sake of future borrowing and beneficial to all elements in the population. If the debt were "an object of established confidence," it would serve many of the purposes of money and be the foundation of credit. The entire economy would feel the infusion of ampler media of exchange.

As a matter of policy, it was agreed that the debt owed to foreigners must be discharged precisely according to contract. A contention already current concerning the manner of providing for the domestic debt was that a discrimination should be made between the holder by transfer and the original owner. The purchaser should be paid only the three or four shillings he had given, with interest, and the remainder should go to the first possessor, who, doubtless from necessity, had parted with his security for a fraction of its nominal value. This proposal Hamilton flatly rejected. The government had made the certificates transferable and must honor them by whomever they were presented. Otherwise they would not rise in value and serve the ends designed. Further, the Secretary intended that the war debts incurred by the states should be assumed by the national government. This would prevent lack of uniformity in treatment of state creditors, and it would put less strain on tax resources of the states, since they did not have customs revenue. Hamilton did not conceal the strengthening of the central government which would result if all creditors looked to it for satisfaction of their claims. These two positions of the Secretary—no discrimination between holders and assumption of the state debts—were to provoke most of the strenuous debate on his report.

The public debt in all its parts was in such confusion that exact statement of it was difficult; in fact, in some instances it was impossible. Hamilton placed the foreign debt at $11,710,378.62 (of which arrears of interest were $1,640,071.62); the liquidated (definitely ascertained) domestic debt was $40,414,085.94 (of which arrears of interest were $13,030,168.20); the unliquidated domestic debt, chiefly Continental bills of credit, paper money, was some $2,000,000. To this total of $54,124,464.56 must be added the debts of the states, estimated—high, as it turned out—at $25 million. On the grand total of $79,124,464.56 the annual interest, allowing 4 per cent on the arrears of interest, would be $4,587,444.81.

How now provide for this debt? The government could not meet its running expenses and also the interest on the debt at the contractual rate without imposing taxes injurious to the whole society. The Secretary hoped that creditors "will cheerfully concur in such modifications of their claims" as would be fair to them and convenient to the treasury. Acceptance of any change in original terms must be "voluntary in fact, as well as in name." Any domestic creditor who wanted to demand exact compliance with the government's promise would be satisfied, though he might have to wait longer than claimants who made the concessions now asked.

It was reasonable to accept a reduction in the stipulated interest, because the rate of interest was falling and the government could at any time borrow to advantage and discharge the principal. The Secretary believed that the rate of interest would fall from 6 to 5 per cent in five years and to 4 per cent in twenty years. He therefore proposed a new loan to the full amount of the national and state debts, to be subscribed wholly in evidences of the debt, on any one of several options which he offered. Each plan involved a reduction of interest, each contained features favorable to the creditor and others desired by the government. For example, for every $100 subscribed, the creditor could have two-thirds funded at 6 per cent, redeemable at the pleasure of the government, and receive the other third in western lands at 20 cents per acre. Or the subscriber could have the entire sum funded at 4 per cent, irredeemable by any amount exceeding $5 a year, and also receive western lands to the value of $15.80.

Besides this conversion loan, Hamilton proposed another for $10 million which was to be subscribed half in specie; the interest would be 5 per cent and the principal was not to be redeemed beyond $6 per year.

Lastly, Hamilton outlined the means of payment. Installments of principal of the foreign debt should be provided by new loans abroad. Interest on the whole debt plus $600,000 ordinary government expenses would be $2,839,163.09. This amount could be raised by existing customs duties, with additional duties on wines and spirits (including spirits distilled in the United States), teas, and coffee. All of the drinkables were luxuries, and some of the alcoholic ones were consumed to a harmful extent that should be discouraged. Hamilton took pains to favor the domestic (especially the small) producer, and to render excise inspection effective but not oppressive.

Reliance on the saying that "public debts are public benefits" would be liable to dangerous abuse unless "the creation of debt should always be accompanied with the means of extinguishment." Net proceeds of the post office to a maximum of a million dollars and a loan of $12 million on the credit of commissioners should constitute the sinking fund to discharge the principal of the debt. Since provision for the debt was now to be made, it would be proper for the sinking fund commissioners to purchase evidences of the debt at market value though below par.

Two features were in abeyance. The taxes proposed were to be applied to the national debt only, as assumption of the state debts had not been enacted. Also, Hamilton begged leave to submit a plan for a national bank later in the session.

Even a paper so highminded and earnest in the public interest could not escape reproaches, mainly for offering a harvest to predatory speculators, but also for assumption of state debts, the excise, and other features.

Chapter 11

FUNDING AND
IMPLIED POWERS

Congress, in its first session, besides providing emergency revenue and erecting executive departments, commanded the Secretary of the Treasury to submit plans for setting the new national government in operation. The second session, 1790, was mainly occupied with debate on the proposals for support of public credit. Now came birth pangs of a different sort from decision on the Constitution. Legislation to carry powers into effect, where property claims were concerned, drew criticism inspired by personal interest. This was the case with the conflict over funding the domestic debt. The question of assumption of the war obligations of the states, while pecuniary, was more political, for it roused the jealousies of those who did not want to see the importance of the national government magnified.

Full provision for the foreign debt was promptly agreed to. The usual plea of objectors—postponement—met the design

for funding. Delegates from North Carolina were not in attendance, and ought to be heard. How could means of repayment
be fixed when the exact amounts of debt in its various compo-
nents were not known? Time enough for discussion when all
was liquidated. The public back at home must be consulted.
This procrastination was voted down, but then opposition
took a less plausible turn. Funding, it was charged, would
saddle the country with debt indefinitely. Better submit to
severe, even direct, taxation and carry a heavier burden for a
shorter time. (Actually, those who urged this fiscal heroism
would have been the last to submit to it.) Then there was the
favorite vague optimism that sales of western lands would suffice to clear the debt.

Hamilton had the hearty support of William Loughton
Smith of South Carolina; Boudinot of New Jersey; Sedgwick,
Ames, and Gerry of Massachusetts; FitzSimons of Pennsylvania; Sherman of Connecticut; and other Federalists. Smith,
undoubtedly briefed by Hamilton, and an apt pupil, was his
floor manager in the debate. Boudinot, besides being in agreement with Hamilton's proposals, had an affectionate concern
for his protégé of years before. The Massachusetts protagonists
of the Secretary's plans were among the ablest in the chamber.
Of the opponents, Jackson of Georgia was the noisiest and
most sensational, a champion of the oppressed whose type
would not soon disappear. Madison, also an opponent, carried
far more weight than Jackson because of his character, though
his lack of understanding of the problem and its remedies is
surprising in a man of his high intelligence. The break between Hamilton and Madison over the issues of funding and
assumption was as unfortunate for the Federalists as it was
beneficial to the Antis, who were shortly to be known as Republicans. Whether Jefferson, who now entered the government as Secretary of State, alienated Madison from his earlier
nationalist views is disputed. In any event, Hamilton lost his
valuable colleague of the Constitutional Convention and the

Federalist papers, and thereafter he had to count Madison as a persevering foe.

The debate on Hamilton's fiscal policies, in Congress and the country, marked the birth of political parties in America. The hope entertained by most of the founding fathers that the new government could get under motion without the embarrassment of obtruding "factions" was naïve. Their knowledge of established political rivalries in other nations should have taught them otherwise. Besides, the unanimity for which they hoped would have proved harmful, for the checks and balances built into the Constitution are static as compared to the active confrontations of established parties. The Federalists, in the first dozen years of the nation's life, laid a foundation of sovereignty and solvency, but they were not superseded too soon for the development of democratic institutions.

Smith and FitzSimons listed the essential features of the report to be discussed. Boudinot made it clear that Congress was not in position to scale the debt. "Instead of being . . . arbitrators . . . we are parties to the contract. . . . We cannot judge in our own cause . . . we owe a debt contracted for a valuable consideration. The evidences of our debt are in the hands of our creditors, and we are called upon to discharge them." In proposing terms, he said, "Each party is as much to be consulted . . . as it was at the time of the first contract." Holders of securities who reloaned on any one of the several options offered must do so with their full consent.

Aedanus Burke of South Carolina broached the chief issue of contention by moving that "a discrimination be made between the original holders and their assignees, and that a scale of depreciation be prepared accordingly." Madison expanded on this proposition as a moral mandate. Of the four classes of creditors, original holders who never parted with their securities must be paid in full. Intermediate holders through whose hands securities had passed could never be traced, so they presented no problem. What of the relative claims of original holders who had sold, certainly at a fraction of the face value of their securities, and present holders by assignment? Madison thought justice required a compromise between them: "let it be a liberal one in favor of the present holders, let them have the highest price which has prevailed in the market; and let the residue belong to the original sufferers." This was administratively practicable, for present holders would produce their certificates, and original holders who had alienated could be discovered from the records. The world would approve this discrimination, for the country was discharging the whole amount of its debt.

A battery of Federalists answered this. Their points in reply were in Hamilton's report, but they put them with spirit. The evidences of the debt were, by their terms, transferable. Those who sold did so for their own reasons. The purchasers took the genuine risk that the securities might never be redeemed, as they would not have been without the "revolution in the Government" (under the Constitution). Congress was bound to the actual holders, however they came by their paper. Sympathy for unfortunates who had parted with their securities for a trifle—the impoverished veteran, his widow, and his orphans might as well have been weeping in the gallery—must not obscure the legal commitment to the purchaser though condemned by the name of speculator. How could the public borrow in future if it broke its promise given in the past? Wadsworth, a good witness, believed that seven-eighths of those who had sold had not done so from necessity.

Actually, in a high proportion of cases original holders who had alienated could not be discovered, for certificates had often been issued in the names of clerks or agents. Obviously, the discrimination could not be applied to the Continental currency, which in its declining value may have changed hands numerous times every day. If new securities to replace the old were not made transferable they would lack a desirable quality; if transferable they would invite fresh speculation.

The debate on a possible discrimination need not have worn on for the long fortnight which it did, for the Federalists always had the votes to enact Hamilton's plans. On February 22, 1790, Madison's motion for a discrimination was rejected, 36 to 13. Permanent funds should be appropriated to payment of interest and principal; arrears of interest (indents) should be treated in the funding operation as principal.

It was harder to carry through Congress Hamilton's proposal to assume the state debts than it had been to secure funding of the national debt. Opponents feared that the federal government would be obliged so far to preempt sources of revenue as to starve the states. The Treasury might require a land tax and other direct taxes, which was not to be tolerated. If state creditors looked to the central government for payment the latter would become, as the friends of assumption declared, "the centre of the wishes and affections of the country." On the other hand, the state objectors wondered whether their constituents were so politically tender. Would they not be glad to shoulder the burden of state debts onto the national treasury? When did a community rejoice in paying taxes?

The states most heavily in the red for the war—Massachusetts and South Carolina—did not clutch their debts as a precious bane. Sedgwick and Gerry of Massachusetts, strongly for the assumption, declared that their state's efforts to tax had brought on Shays's Rebellion. As the debate proceeded, South Carolina voices for assumption increased. States which had made progress in discharging their debts objected that they would be compelled to pay twice; they were not prepared for this discriminatory sacrifice. Should not the federal government reimburse the states for the debts they had paid? But where so much debt was active, why tax for what was dead?

One halfway measure proposed was that only debts above a state's proportion should be assumed, but this was discarded. Assumption meant rushing into financial danger, the national treasury might sink under the added load. The amount of the state debts was uncertain; better put the whole matter over until the accounts were definite. Here the answer was that the Secretary's estimate was enough to go on, the principle of assumption would be established, and later discovery and adjustments would bring all right. The state securities would gain value, serve as the basis of credit, and help to invigorate the economy. Otherwise the scene would be one of confusion and reproaches by many holders of state paper.

One way to put off the problem of state debts was to direct the Secretary to submit estimates of the cost of assuming them. Alexander White of Virginia (who, however, was to confer a favor later) insisted on giving Hamilton this trouble, though Federalists rightly objected that the Secretary was overtaxed with demands for reports and answers to petitions. Hamilton responded the very next day. He proposed no tax on houses, lands, livestock, or farm produce—the bugaboo that had figured in debate. Import duties should be increased 10 per cent, with additional duties laid on sugar, molasses, spices, salt, spirits, and manufactured tobacco. Carriages, licences to practice law, playing cards, sales at auction, and wine and spirits sold at retail were other proper objects. The only excise included was on snuff manufactured in America. The yield of these taxes the Secretary estimated at $1,040,000.

Hamilton's promptness in offering particulars and confining taxes largely to luxuries persuaded the enemies of assumption to shift from that topic back to funding of the domestic debt, including state debts. Southerners objected to the options extended to certificate holders. They were too many and too complicated. The promise of slow redemption held no attraction for impoverished creditors, but would tend to throw the debt into the hands of foreign speculators. A few alterations were made, including dropping supernumerary options. Then the Committee of the Whole adopted Hamilton's report, assumption included, though the vote was close. The cheering prospect, to the Federalists, that the House itself would follow suit was adventitiously destroyed. Debate on petitions of Quakers and others of Pennsylvania for stopping import of slaves riled Southerners against the drift of power to the central government. Delegates arriving from North Carolina revived attacks on assumption, and they got the whole report recommitted. Members from heavily indebted states replied angrily that the foes of assumption were inviting civil war.

The old question of location of the capital was then brought back on the boards. Most of the Southerners, insisting on the Potomac, were willing to the move from New York at the end of 1790 to Philadelphia for a temporary stay of ten years. Their alarm at proposals of Northern delegates for a site on the Susquehanna, or at Wilmington, or especially, Baltimore, drove the Potomac men to extra ardors. They forgot that they might have to offer assumption to their opponents as an equivalent. However, they succeeded in bringing the House to the Senate's bill—open the next session in Philadelphia and after ten years move to the vicinity of Georgetown on the Potomac.

After two defeats the friends of assumption got a third chance. The Senate approved assumption in an amendment to the funding bill. The foes were outraged that the Senate would transcend its powers by initiating taxes. Jackson of Georgia cried that state functions were being sucked into "the vortex of the all-devouring General Government." Nevertheless, the House accepted the Senate measure. Hamilton's proposals for the support of public credit had passed Congress. This was August 4, 1790.

How assumption of state debts came to be included in the funding is a story in itself. According to Thomas Jefferson's account, recorded three years after the event, one morning toward the end of June 1790 he and Hamilton met by chance before the President's house. Hamilton's "look was sombre, haggard, & dejected beyond description, even his dress uncouth & neglected, he asked to speak with me, we stood in the street near the door, he opened the assumption of the State debts, the necessity of it in the general fiscal arrangement & its indispensable necessity toward a preservation of the union." If Hamilton lacked influence to carry assumption, "he . . . was determined to resign." Hamilton continued that as colleagues in the Cabinet they should cooperate. Jefferson was glad to try to conciliate views; he "thought the first step . . . would be to bring Mr. Madison & Colo. Hamilton to a friendly discussion of the subject." He invited them both to dine with him the next day, when he explained that he did not understand the situation but "encouraged them to consider the thing together. They did so, it ended in Mr. Madison's acquiescence in a proposition that the question should be again brought before the house . . . , that . . . he should . . . leave it to it's fate." One or the other suggested "that as the pill [assumption] would be a bitter one to the Southern States, something should be done to soothe them, that the removal of the seat of Government to the Potowmac was a just measure."

In his narrative of the bargain, written a quarter-century later in his *Anas*, Jefferson revealed that he, for "preservation of the Union," urged that some members should change their votes to favor assumption, and that the South should have the capital on the Potomac as anodyne. Two Virginia members— Alexander White and Richard Bland Lee—obliged by reversing themselves, Hamilton, with the help of Robert Morris, similarly coaxed Northern votes to approve the Potomac, "and so the Assumption was passed."

However, as states' rights champion, Jefferson was profoundly embarrassed by his part in the deal, which threw "twenty millions of stock . . . to the stock-jobbing herd . . . added to the number of votaries of the Treasury, and made its chief the master of every vote in the legislature." He told President Washington, "I was duped into it by the Secretary of the Treasury and made a tool for forwarding his schemes, not then sufficiently understood by me. . . ." In his latest version of

the episode Jefferson added to his reproaches against Hamilton. The fact is that Jefferson's letters to members of Congress
urging them to fall in with the projected bargain showed that
he understood the assumption proposal and approved it in the
national interest. Only later did he lose his early enthusiasm
for political harmony, become Hamilton's bitter foe, and unworthily claim that he had been tricked. The kindest interpretation one can put on Jefferson's later excuses is that he suffered a lapse of memory.

In his first report on the public credit Hamilton promised to
submit a proposal for a national bank that would be an auxiliary to the Treasury. Famous as is his design of the bank, his
defense of the constitutional power of Congress to establish
the institution is yet more celebrated. Before treating either it
is proper to remark on the multiplicity of duties falling on the
Secretary, in spite of which he was able to concentrate his
faculties on major undertakings. In the interval of less than a
year since his first report was offered he had been anxiously
attentive to its disputed progress through the legislature. He
had constantly monitored the customs service. Providing for
the construction of revenue cutters and selection of their crews
were connected responsibilities. He let contracts for lighthouses and nominated their keepers. Of a different nature was
his opening of negotiations with Dutch bankers for all-important loans to the United States.

In this period Assistant Secretary of the Treasury William
Duer, whom Hamilton had appointed, resigned under unfavorable circumstances. While in a position to influence Treasury policies he was actively engaged in speculation in public
securities. Hamilton himself would have come under just criticism had he not accepted Duer's departure as necessary. Tench
Coxe, an economist and publicist devoid of the fortune which
permitted Duer's private operations, was chosen for the place
(April 1790). The move of the seat of government from New
York to Philadelphia occurred just at the time when the bank

report was in preparation. In addition, Hamilton was required to investigate all sorts of claims on the Treasury, and to respond to the assignments of Congress in distracting variety. Of course he could and did delegate some of these tasks to his fellow officers in the Treasury, but he was chargeable for every action taken and every paper signed. Few men would have been able to execute incidental detail, routine chores, and also summon energy for highly creative projects.

Hamilton's Report on a National Bank (formally, "On the Further Provision Necessary for Establishing Public Credit") was submitted to the House on December 14, 1790, in obedience to the order of the previous August. The report was only 15,000 words long; in the Columbia University publication of Hamilton's papers the editors' commentary on it requires two-thirds as many words. In planning the bank, Hamilton made painstaking use of the resources available to him, as he always did. Broadly, the Bank of England was his model, but he consulted the writings of Adam Smith, other European theorists, and the ablest American authors who had discussed the subject. He also relied on his knowledge of the Bank of North America (obtained especially through Robert and Gouverneur Morris), his Treasury dealings with the Philadelphia bank, and his intimate acquaintance with the founding and operation of the Bank of New York.

As this country had only three banks (that of Massachusetts, in Boston, was the third), and the members of the House were substantially ignorant of their function in society, Hamilton began his report with an explanation of the public services of banks. He tactfully addressed his instruction, he said, to the generality of citizens, but in fact it was meant for and needed by the members of the House. The operations of financial institutions were a mystery to the average person; they were therefore suspect, particularly if a connection with government existed.

The Secretary first referred to the historic acceptance and

uses of banks. "It is a fact well understood, that public Banks have found admission and patronage among the principal and most enlightened commercial nations. . . . Trade and industry, wherever they have been tried, have been indebted to them for important aid. And Government has been repeatedly under the greatest obligations to them, in dangerous and distressing emergencies." He pointed out the chief advantages of banks. First was the multiplication of the services of specie through note issue and loans in the form of book credit. Here he gave a clear account of what seemed to many then—and has to some since—a subtle process. Second was the facility of government in obtaining financial aids, especially in emergencies. Third was assistance in the payment of taxes, both by loans to individuals and by the greater plenty of money and quicker circulation in the community.

Hamilton also recited the alleged disadvantages of banks, disproving most of them but candidly admitting genuine drawbacks when they occurred. The gravest supposed objection was that banks, by substituting paper, drove the precious metals from a country. Hamilton showed that, on the contrary, by promoting industry, banks augmented products for export and thus attracted gold and silver from abroad. In demonstrating the utility of banks he was careful to distinguish between their notes and the paper money emitted by government. The bank currency was self-limiting because it returned upon the issuer for redemption, and the amount must bear a strict proportion to the capital and other cash resources available for this purpose.

He queried whether the Bank of North America could serve the nation's need, but found it lacking in essential respects. Its charter was now from a state (Pennsylvania), it ran for too short a term; the capital of $2 million maximum was too small for the extensive operations, in the Secretary's view; and there was no rotation of directors to reduce the chances of mismanagement. Hamilton appreciated the help of the Bank of

North America to the government during the war, and he did not brush it aside as totally incapable of serving the nation; indeed, his report concluded with the possibility that the Pennsylvania institution might be altered to obviate the necessity of organizing a new bank.

He gave his specifications for a Bank of the United States. It should have an exclusive corporate charter from Congress for twenty years. The capital should be $10 million; the $8 million subscribed by individuals or bodies should be one-fourth in gold and silver coin and three-fourths in 6 per cent public debt. The national government would subscribe $2 million in cash (which it was borrowing abroad), and the bank would immediately lend that same amount to government in its notes or as book credit. Without the government subscription, the specie resources of the bank would be insufficient.

The public debt subscribed by shareholders would appreciate in value, and could always be promptly converted into cash if need be. One-fourth of the twenty-five directors of the bank, exclusive of its president, should give place to newly elected ones every year. Stockholders should vote for directors in proportion to the number of shares held, but in a diminishing ratio, so that none would have more than thirty votes. All directors must be American citizens. The government would have no appointees among the directors, though the condition of the bank should be regularly reported to the Secretary of the Treasury. An "essential ingredient in its structure" was that the bank "shall be under a *private* not a *public* Direction, under the guidance of *individual interest*, not of *public policy. . . .*" Otherwise a feeble or too sanguine public administration would be liable to excesses. "The keen, steady, and, as it were, magnetic sense, of their own interest, as proprietors, in the Directors of a Bank, pointing invariably to its true pole, the prosperity of the institution, is the only security, that can always be relied upon, for a careful and prudent" management.

Though the idea of branches would appeal to areas remote from the center where the bank was located, Hamilton discouraged the Congress from establishing such, at least in the beginning, because supervising them would be difficult and their errors would endanger the parent institution. (His wisdom was proven when the successor bank suffered grievously from irresponsible conduct of its numerous branches.)

Within a few days of submitting his report, Hamilton offered the draft of a bill for incorporating the bank. The bill, only slightly altered, was promptly passed by the Senate. Debate in the House did not begin until six weeks after the Senate bill was received. The same members from the same sections of the country (mainly the South) as had opposed the funding and assumption also opposed the bank, and its support came from the same Northerners. Jackson of Georgia blasted the proposal with a variety of charges, but he and others of his persuasion, Madison especially, principally denied the constitutional power to create a corporation. Indeed, incorporation was more opposed than the bank itself. "Reviewing the Constitution," said Madison, "it was not possible to discover in it the power to incorporate a Bank . . . he well recollected that a power to grant charters of incorporation had been proposed in the General Convention and rejected." He rejected any broadening of the specific authorities given to Congress. The "general welfare" must be served through taxes only, and this bill laid no tax. Congress could pass laws "necessary and proper" to its assigned capacities, but these means must be "technical and direct. . . . The doctrine of implication is always a tender one," not to be abused or the Constitution itself would be destroyed. Stone of Maryland, who had the merit of animated speech, declared, "When implication first raised its head . . . he started from it as a serpent which was to sting and poison the Constitution." By implication, "Congress . . . may do any thing." Madison, forgetting his usual discretion, fell into the same error of assuming that if

Congress were allowed an inch it might take a mile; if it could incorporate a bank, "Congress might even establish religious teachers in every parish, and pay them out of the Treasury of the United States."

Gerry, Ames, Sedgwick, Boudinot, and others dispelled these exaggerated fears. Why the cry against implied powers? All that Congress had done in two years was by way of reasonable deduction. No amount of foresight of the framers could include in the fundamental law all of the measures to which the legislature must be competent. Sedgwick similarly brought the debate back to common sense. Where a power was clearly delegated, "all the known and usual means for the attainment of the object expressed are conceded also." The words "necessary and proper" "did not restrict . . . to enacting such laws only as are indispensable."

The debate became repetitious. Actually, any objections to the bank—not the question of its legality, which Hamilton had not raised—were answered in the Secretary's report. The House was eager for decision, which was overwhelmingly favorable, 39 to 20; nearly all of the votes against were from Maryland and southward, though five Southerners voted aye.

Since the constitutionality of incorporating a bank was so much in controversy, President Washington—a few days before the bill reached his desk—asked the opinions of the Attorney General and the Secretary of State. Both were opposed. In requiring Hamilton's view, in writing, of the "validity & propriety" of the measure, Washington enclosed the adverse pronouncements of Randolph and Jefferson. It was suitable to allow the Secretary of the Treasury these arguments for his rebuttal, since he was in the minority in the Cabinet and the disputed proposal was his.

This was on Wednesday, February 16. The President urged prompt receipt of Hamilton's defense of the bank; in eight more days the bill would become law without his signature. Hamilton worked double tides to justify his plan. After five days he wrote the President that he had been "sedulously engaged" in drawing up his paper, but would need one or two days more. When he submitted it, one week after he was bidden, he mentioned that it had occupied him the greater part of the night. Mrs. Hamilton helped with the copying. His defense was as full as his report to Congress had been. Though he wrote under pressure, he had the benefit of the debate in Congress. He made notes of Randolph's negative arguments, and he had no difficulty in countering those of Jefferson, which were partly irrelevant. His paper for the President largely took the form of a refutation of the objections of his Cabinet colleagues. His own Treasury experience told him how important the bank would be to the support of public credit, as a source of loans, an aid in collecting of taxes and in making payments throughout the Union.

Hamilton's defense of the bank is always cited for his reliance on powers implied in the Constitution. As has been seen, he did not originate this argument; it had been prominent, pro and con, in the discussion in the House. Rather, he gave it elaborate statement, and he gave his liberal interpretation of the Constitution an application far beyond the establishment of the bank alone. Thus, *"this general principle is inherent in the very definition of Government and essential to every step in the progress to be made by that of the United States; namely, that every power vested in a Government is in its nature sovereign, and includes by force of the term, a right to employ all the means requisite, and fairly applicable to the attainment of the ends of such power."* He was careful to refute the extravagant predictions of opponents, for he cautioned that such ancillary instruments must not offend against "restrictions . . . in the Constitution," or be immoral, or "contrary to the *essential ends* of political society."

Hamilton taxed Jefferson with confining government within impossibly narrow limits; to carry the enumerated powers into effect, said the Secretary of State, the Constitution restrained the government "to the *necessary* means; that is to say, to those means, without which the grant of the power would be nugatory." Hamilton rejoined that "It is essential to the being of the National government, that so erroneous a conception of the meaning of the word *necessary*, should be exploded." "Necessary" often meant no more than needful, useful, or conducive to. Hamilton had no difficulty in showing that the practice of government was against Jefferson's rule. Hamilton had been concerned with the construction and maintenance of lighthouses, beacons, and public piers. These protections and conveniences "must be referred to the power of regulating trade. . . . But it cannot be affirmed, that the exercise of that power, in this instance, was strictly necessary; or that the power itself would be *nugatory* without that of regulating establishments of this nature." The "general administration of the affairs of a country, its finances, trade, defence &c ought to be construed liberally, in advancement of the public good. . . . The means by which national exigencies are to be provided for, national inconveniencies obviated, national prosperity promoted, are of such infinite variety, extent and complexity, that there must, of necessity, be great latitude of discretion in the selection & application of those means." Such an observation surely appealed to the common sense of President Washington.

The Secretary went on to show how the bank would be a handmaiden of the Treasury in loans, collections, and payments, and would also stimulate the economy of the country.

The President was convinced by Hamilton's showing, signed the bill, and the capital was immediately oversubscribed, July 4, 1791. Jefferson told Monroe, "the bank filled & overflowed the moment it was opened." Hamilton himself did not suspect that "so rapid a subscription would take place," or he would have provided for wider distribution of the shares.

Hamilton's counsel of liberty with wisdom in meeting na-

tional needs was more courageous than the doctrinaire absten-
tion of Jefferson, Randolph, Madison, Giles, and the cohort of
"strict constructionists" of the Constitution. Those who fenced
themselves in were fearful of power, though used by themselves. If they took the first glass they might become drunk-
ards. They confessed to a lack of self-control. Actually, on their
program of denial, in order to stay within the Constitution
they would have been obliged to amend the fundamental law
until it became a confusion of statutes. This has been the case
with many state constitutions; from time to time they require
a cleanup of the clutter. Those who solemnly limited themselves in the name of prudence were unmindful of the saying
that "nothing is so conservative as progress." Hamilton, with
the faculty of foresight, had provided for an enormously expanded nation. While the present certainly figured in his
plans, the future was as vivid in his mind. This demanded
elbow room for the national government. The history of
America since his day proves his prescience in assigning the
major role to the central authority.

Chief Justice John Marshall's opinion in *McCulloch vs. Maryland* (1819), upholding the constitutionality of the Second Bank
of the United States, was mainly a repetition of Hamilton's
earlier appeal to implied powers. Some have said that by approving the authority of government to erect a corporation
Marshall was opening the economy of the country to capitalist
domination. This is questionable; it is perhaps an example of
the *post hoc* fallacy. But the same may not be said of Hamilton's motive a generation earlier. In his report on the bank he
gave all of his reasons for wishing it. He could not have been
more candid in declaring its service to the economy, including
enterprise in commerce and industry. A corporation was the
means of collecting together many small investments in a
country which had few individuals of great wealth who, if
more had existed, would not have been willing to risk all they

had in untried ventures. Transferable shares increased the safety of investors.

Hamilton's concern for the prosperity of the whole community is too obvious in his advocacy to require refutation of the charge that he had an invidious preference for the moneyed interest. He wanted to aid those capable of expanding production because they would benefit the entire society. The notion that Hamilton was the champion of capitalism in a selfish or class sense clashes with the historical fact that the national government which he helped so powerfully to project became in the fullness of time a welfare state. As these lines are written the President of the United States is about to announce plans for using the authority and resources of the federal government to curb inflation, spur production, and conserve energy. This is a far cry from a self-sufficient, not to say exploitive, private capitalism.

Chapter 12

BORROWING IN
AMSTERDAM

The report on establishment of the mint, in late January 1791, overlapped with the consideration by Congress of that on the bank. The mint report, though offered with diffidence because the subject was new to Hamilton, was accepted with only minor alteration. The recommendations were more important for the future than at the time, for United States coinage commenced on a minimum scale, while reliance continued to be on foreign currencies. Hamilton's memoranda, some of which were supplied to him by Tench Coxe and others, and his drafts of the report testify to his vexing search for satisfactory guidance. He resorted to European works written as far back as the early part of the century; in particular, he consulted the conclusions of Sir Isaac Newton on the relative values of gold and silver in the markets and at the mints of the trading countries of his day. He was influenced by resolutions of the Continental Congress for a mint and the reports of Jefferson, Robert and Gouverneur Morris, and others looking to an American coinage. Of these Jefferson's contributions were the chief, especially his choice of a decimal system.

Hamilton and Jefferson at this time were on the best of terms. Hamilton submitted his mint report to Jefferson in advance and they were in cordial correspondence over the problems involved. Jefferson, in his Report on Weights and Measures six months earlier, had included the dollar in his uniform system of weights. Hamilton had agreed to this in principle, but on closer examination rejected it. Jefferson's plan disregarded the exchange relationships at home and abroad which Hamilton was bound to regard. To fit into Jefferson's too-neat scheme, the American silver dollar must be heavier in pure metal, and therefore more valuable, than the Spanish milled dollar, then in universal use in this country. It would be too inconvenient not to have the two exchange on a par. Furthermore, Hamilton must conform the dollar as closely as possible to the value of the monetary unit in the countries with which America chiefly traded—England, Holland, and France. The contrast is that between closet philosopher and practical statesman.

Hamilton would have preferred to make gold the single standard, as least liable to variations in value, but his urge for the fullest currency possible persuaded him to utilize silver equally. He went to pains to hit on the ratio of pure metal in gold and silver dollars at the mint that corresponded as closely as might be to their relative values in the market. In recommending that the dollar should contain 24¾ grains of pure gold or 371¼ grains of pure silver (a mint ratio of 15 to 1), he slightly overvalued silver, so it was principally that metal which came to the mint. A generation after Hamilton's death gold became more plentiful, was overvalued at the mint even when the ratio was changed to 15.98 to 1, and silver was banished. The post-Civil War spectacular cheapening of silver, which led to decades of coinage controversy, is no part of

Hamilton's story, except that the gold standard, which he had first preferred, finally prevailed.

Hamilton recommended coinage of a half-cent to assist the poor in small purchases, which would also enable them to "labor for less." In the same behalf of a full circulation, foreign coins should continue in use for a year, the Spanish dollar for longer. He outlined modest quarters and a small staff for the mint.

The Amsterdam bankers who had served the Continental Congress during the Revolution opened a loan of 3 million florins, though not authorized by Congress and before Hamilton had presented his plan for funding the debt. Hamilton expressed his gratification at the zeal of the bankers, now combined under the formidable style of Wilhem and Jan Willink and Nicholas and Jacob Van Staphorst and Hubbard, but he cautioned against a repetition of such volunteer action. Still, it was an augury of the cordial cooperation which was to mark Hamilton's many dealings with the firm on behalf of the United States Treasury. He and President Washington had no difficulty in validating the unsolicited loan as part of the $14 million ordered by Congress in August 1790. Hamilton launched formal borrowing by forwarding to the bankers certified copies of the acts and of his own authority as Secretary of the Treasury.

Hamilton was relieved to learn that projects to purchase the American debt to France, one of Dutch bankers and the other of American speculators, had been dropped. He preferred to discharge the American debt to France directly, for that would best preserve the credit of the United States. William Short prevented the proposed mischief. Short, formerly Secretary of Embassy in Paris under Jefferson and now Chargé d'Affaires, was named by Congress as Hamilton's agent in borrowing in Europe. Informed and active, he was a fortunate choice, for the Secretary could not himself leave the busy scene at home. Hamilton's only amendment of the service of Short as proxy was to render him more amenable to the habits of Dutch lenders where their practices coincided with the interest of the United States in the long run. A feature of Hamilton's success in borrowing was his response to traditions of European loan markets which he was unable to visit personally. He purchased much by judicious concessions.

Promptly on taking office, Hamilton assured Jacques Necker, the French Director-General of Finances, that the United States debt to France would be faithfully discharged, but begged that installments of principal would be deferred for a few years if the interest was punctually paid. Lafayette assisted to this end.

Naturally, Short pressed the Willinks to obtain loans at the lowest possible interest and charges. The bankers at one point required 4½ per cent charges to cover premium to the lenders, brokerage, notary's fees, seals, paper for the bonds, and their own commission. Short insisted on 4 per cent, while the interest rate remained 5 per cent. With Short's consent, the bankers referred the dispute to Hamilton. He agreed to the charges, as they were paid only once and the lower interest achieved was a saving during the life of the loan. Hamilton also accepted the custom whereby a subscriber to a loan, if he paid an installment on the last day of the month, received interest for the whole month. While Hamilton's grand object was to be able to borrow at lowered rates of interest, he was mindful of the extraordinary demands for money in Amsterdam. This was because Europe was going to war and a Dutch tax of 1 per cent on all loans for foreign powers impended.

He was rightly gratified that the United States under these circumstances borrowed at less interest than other governments and that the American bonds, though only for small quantities, were frequently above par. The Willinks assured him that the credit of the United States was "sufficiently established and strong, to effect this without a Reaction from the political Circumstances of any Country whatever." The bankers reported that a loan at 5 per cent interest and 4½ per cent charges was embraced by the lenders "with all the Eclat you could wish, and has established a new Proof of the Degree which the Credit of the United States has attained here, to the great Satisfaction of their Friends."

This harmony with Amsterdam was temporarily broken when Gouverneur Morris, in Paris, told Short that a loan for a million dollars could be made "in a place not in Holland." This turned out to be Antwerp, Belgium. Hamilton agreed that it was desirable "to be able to resort to more markets than one." Short negotiated an Antwerp loan for 3,000,000 florins at 4½ per cent interest and 5 per cent charges. The Willinks were offended that Short had favored the Brabanders (*sic*) "at our very Noses" with bonds which they would have bought through Amsterdam. Short had behaved as though the Willinks were mere brokers, while the fact was that their influence and judgment were at the service of the United States, and they advanced interest. It was best to preserve a standing relationship with a banking house. "Whenever a Debtor borrows . . . here, there, and wherever He can find Lenders, It argues . . . that either the Wants are immensely great, or the means of satisfying them very confined," to his discredit.

This was Hamilton's conviction, in accordance with which he acted thereafter, relying on the one great market of Amsterdam, but he approved Short's application to Antwerp as a salutary inducement to the Willinks to persuade their lenders to accept 4 per cent interest as soon as possible. Hamilton suggested that the United States would soon be able to borrow at home at that rate. He would continue to borrow in Amsterdam rather than Belgium even if the Dutch laid the 1 per cent tax. Since the rate of exchange in the summer of 1791 was so much (upward of 20 per cent) in favor of Amsterdam over Paris, the Secretary instructed Short to pay off the whole of the debt to France as rapidly as he could secure loans in Holland, though this had not been his original intention. He refused to take advantage of the depreciation of assignats of 10 per cent, but still made a substantial saving by the exchange. This was an example of the advantages to be seized in unforseen circumstances, but for which the Antifederalists in Congress did not want to allow Hamilton freedom. His situation was sufficiently awkward due to slow communication, but then to have limits prescribed by legislators ignorant of his problem was troublesome. In fact, Hamilton allowed Short suitable discretion, confirmed his actions where desirable, and himself would meet the criticism when it arose. If hostile Congressmen could have heard the advice of the Amsterdam bankers for flexibility they might have been less rigid, though political animus might have ruled anyhow.

Hamilton used the resources of the Bank of the United States in conjunction with his operations in Holland. In the spring of 1793 he applied for conditional control of the bank's bills on London to the extent of $100,000 because he had to make a payment in Amsterdam which might not be covered by a loan there. If the bills were not needed, the bank would not suffer loss by the accommodation. This arrangement, too complicated to be referred to Congress, illustrated the Secretary's anticipation of contingent demands upon the Treasury.

Hamilton needed to take comfort in his success in funding the debt, in approval of the Bank of the United States, and his ready borrowing abroad, for untoward political developments in New York State were to bring him to grief. General Schuyler had been elected to the United States Senate in 1789, along with Rufus King, but had drawn the short term, which expired March 4, 1791. Hamilton's friend Robert Troup wrote him from Albany in disgust: "About an hour ago the election of Senator was brought on in the assembly. Burr suceeded by a decided majority. He has a decided Majority also in the Senate. The thing therefore may be considered as settled. The twistings, combinations, and maneuvers to accomplish this

object are incredible. . . . The Chancellor [Robert R. Living-
ston] is singularly happy. . . . We are going headlong into the
bitterest opposition to the Genl Government." A few hours
later William Duer supplied more detail. "Mr. Burr was this
day elected by both houses, to succeed General Schuyler, by a
large Majority in the Senate, and of five in the House of Representatives [Assembly]. This is the fruit of the Chancellor's Co-
alition with the Governor [George Clinton]. . . . Our Political
Situation, my Freind has a most Gloomy Aspect." "Strange
unions," another informed Hamilton, "have been brought
about by our artful perservering Chieftain [Gov. Clinton]. . . .
Many who were Federalists sucked into his Excellencys Vortex, & the Chancellor's family become one of the principal sat-
ellites of this Noxious planet. Hence it is that a blessed accession of strength will be added to the Senate of the U States in
the person of Col. A. Burr. . . . He is avowedly your Enemy,
& stands pledged to his party, for a reign of vindictive declamation against your measures. The Chancellor hates, & would
destroy you."

The Federalists, unfortunately, in distributing patronage,
had omitted the eligible and influential Livingston tribe. At
the least the Chancellor should have been rewarded with an
enviable appointment. But Jay had been made Chief Justice of
the United States, King had been preferred for the national
Senate, and Gouverneur Morris had been chosen for President
Washington's informal diplomatic agent in London. Burr saw
the opportunity to divorce the Livingstons from their Federalist faith. He persuaded Governor Clinton to name Livingston's
brother-in-law, Morgan Lewis, Attorney General of New York.
This brought the disgruntled Chancellor and his kin into the
Antifederalist camp, and the adventitious partnership of Clinton and Livingston ousted Schuyler and seated Aaron Burr in
the Senate.

This was the overt commencement of the enmity between
Hamilton and Burr. Something of Burr's tactics is revealed in

the hatred that he came to inspire in Jefferson also. Burr had more talents than principles. His selfish ambition damaged others—it was fatal to Hamilton—without benefiting himself. The good in him—courage as a soldier, skill as lawyer and politician, unalloyed affection for his accomplished daughter, Theodosia—was overborne by his flouting of integrity.

Hamilton, as Secretary of the Treasury, was rarely able to devote himself to one duty, however important, without other responsibilities obtruding upon him. This was the case when negotiations were in progress for loans in Holland. Hamilton was drawn into informal diplomatic conversations with Major George Beckwith who was in and out of this country as the confidential agent of Lord Dorchester, Governor of Canada, Dorchester, in turn, was acting for and reporting to the British Cabinet. Beckwith's history during the Revolution as handler of General Clinton's correspondence with spies, including Arnold's treason, did not commend him to American trust, except that his enemy status at the time excused his assignment. In his relations with Hamilton he seems to have been straightforward. Some critics, most impressed by Jefferson's career, have charged that Hamilton was too straightforward with the British agent. Beckwith was less concerned with the prospect of completing execution of the peace treaty than with discovering the policy of the United States should Britain go to war with Spain, and perhaps France also, following the Spanish seizure of Nootka Sound. The latest indictment of Hamilton * runs to length and requires close attention because wherein he erred is not readily apparent.

It is said that Hamilton intruded into the province of the Secretary of State, revealed Cabinet secrets to Beckwith, deceived President Washington about what passed between himself and Beckwith, and disparaged Jefferson and Gouver-

* Julian P. Boyd, *Number 7, Alexander Hamilton's Secret Attempts to Control American Foreign Policy* (Princeton, 1964).

neur Morris, the latter being Washington's informal emissary in England on an errand similar to Beckwith's here. The background of the episode, as of much else in those years, was preference of the Federalists for close commercial and cordial political relations with Britain, contrasted with Antifederalist (soon Republican) partisanship for France. Hamilton was involved in the first place because Jefferson was tardy in assuming his duties as Secretary of State and ere long left his desk for two months on a political junket through New England. Even so, Hamilton, repeatedly, for the record, declared to Beckwith that their talks were unofficial, and that if formal exchanges with Britain were to come about they would be in the hands of the Secretary of State. Meantime Hamilton reported his conversations with the Britisher to President Washington. A more substantive reason for frequent communications betweeh Hamilton and Beckwith was that each found the objects of the other congenial—up to a point, that is, on Hamilton's part. For whether, in the event of war between England and Spain, the United States would attack Spain in America in order to get possession of New Orleans was necessarily left in doubt, and the possibility that this country would become the ally of England was in more doubt.

Hamilton's desire, all along from the close of the Revolution, was to restore economic relations with the erstwhile enemy. He admired the British constitution and Britain's commercial and fiscal system, and he believed that the fortunes of the United States would be fastest advanced by trade ties with the mother country. Britain was stable; France, in contrast, was plunged into internal revolution with a violence that Hamilton rightly suspected would become more and more irresponsible. He was not impressed by America's moral obligations to France as ally in the Revolution, for he held that France had aided America, financially and militarily, not because she loved the rebel colonies more, but her historic foe less. France, economically exhausted, offered little to this country as a trading partner.

Of still more consequence, while Jefferson manifestly championed the independence of the United States, he was less committed than Hamilton to the process of improving the country's opportunities. He had been absent as minister to France (1785–89) when the Confederation had sunk to its lowest ebb and had been arduously replaced by the new Constitution. His abortive effort with John Adams to form a commercial treaty with England had persuaded him of the obstinacy of that court. Hamilton, on the other hand, had been constantly and deeply concerned in the domestic scene, devising ways and means for revival. In modern military terms, the Secretary of State may be likened to the airman on reconnaissance; the Secretary of the Treasury was the foot soldier, albeit an exceedingly lively one. In 1790 Jefferson was forty-seven years old and Hamilton was thirty-five, which, taken with the temperamental differences between the two, made a distinction in their emotional ardor. Hamilton did not restrain his patriotic eagerness, though it meant poaching on the preserves of colleagues. This was a fault of commission, but it did not impugn his motives.

Hamilton was frequently high-handed in his actions, but he could not be accused of underhanded maneuver. He was candid in his public life, often rashly so, as when he broke off his connection as aide de camp to General Washington, later recklessly attacked President John Adams, and finally spoke his utter distrust of Aaron Burr. Jefferson, by contrast, was subtler, not to say on occasion devious.

Actually the contretemps between the Secretary of the Treasury and the Secretary of State vis-à-vis Beckwith's inquiries had no ill effect in American foreign policy. The Nootka dispute between England and Spain was soon composed, and the United States did not resort to force to secure New Orleans, but got that port and the vast Louisiana Territory by Jefferson's purchase. Hamilton said nothing to Beckwith concerning Jefferson's leaning toward France which Beckwith did not know already; Hamilton's few words describing Gouverneur

Morris's tendency to intoxication with his own ideas was no more than the truth; besides, Hamilton loyally allayed Beckwith's suspicion that Morris was associating with his old friend Luzerne, the French Ambassador to London, for wrong motives.

Most of all, Hamilton's purpose of seeing the peace treaty with England fully complied with, and establishing trade relations with England, was secured in the Jay Treaty of 1795, of which he, Hamilton, was the chief promoter, architect, and defender. By the time Louis XVI and Marie Antoinette had been executed, England and France were at war, and the Reign of Terror was in full career.

> "We have vast quantities of land, cheap or to be had for the taking. We are an agricultural people. Why go in for manufactures? We export our tobacco, rice, grain and with them buy foreign fabricated wares. If manufacturing is to be stimulated at home that will involve raising duties on imported goods, which will increase the prices we must pay for them and also for what is made in this country. Moreover, if foreigners are hampered in selling us the products of their industries they will be less able to buy our staple agricultural exports. A man knows best how to apply his labor and capital. He should not be induced by government to enter an occupation that he does not choose of his own accord. That would be uneconomical. Where nature is so bountiful, why resort to artificial means of production? The bribes of government to encourage manufactures will go to a small class, at the expense of the majority of taxpayers and consumers. The democracy we cherish is best preserved in a rural society where individual citizens are independent. Manufactures will promote the growth of cities, where wage-earners live at the will of others."

The above were among the objections made to Hamilton's Report on Manufactures, submitted to Congress on December 5, 1791. The report had been ordered by the House nearly two years before, but other duties and the time-consuming collection of materials were responsible for delay. The deferred date of submission was desirable anyhow, because the public mind was more willing to accept government intervention in a novel field. Even so, this was the only one of Hamilton's chief proposals which was not acted upon at the time, but waited some years for full acceptance.

Hamilton is perhaps best remembered for his promotion of industry, though protective tariffs were not his sole means of encouragement. His establishment of the public credit is gratefully acknowledged, but the techniques to that end are not so easily recalled. His "home market" and "infant industry" arguments, readily grasped, were repeated for a century and a half after he put them forward.

In this report he gave his most explicit statement of his idea of what constituted national wealth. In much of the argument he ran counter to the teaching of Adam Smith, whose *Wealth of Nations* had been published fifteen years earlier and had become the handbook of many leaders of opinion in America. Smith eschewed mercantilism, a government-guided economy. He championed individual initiative in the optimistic belief that if every person followed his private interest all would be working for the public benefit. Hamilton, on the contrary, held that in a young country, with little capital and experience and devoted principally to agriculture, the helping hand of government would be necessary to stimulate enterprise and vary the forms of production. While Adam Smith defined national wealth in terms of aggregate of goods, Hamilton cherished rather the capacity for creating goods. The same policy was adopted long after his day in developing countries, which in their emergence from stagnation and poverty gave attention to roads, harbors, power plants, and the scientific approach to agriculture. The wisdom of his emphasis first on the means of production, not on increase of consumption goods, was illustrated in the ruin of the Confederate states by defeat in the Civil War. Having little industry, an outmoded labor system, and much ignorance, they were long in rising from prostration. On the other hand, Germany, beaten in two world wars, each time recovered rapidly because of knowledge and skills that permitted replacement of the advanced productive system.

In Hamilton's demonstration, a solely agricultural country was inferior in capacity to one combining commerce with tillage of the soil, and the addition of industry redoubled its prosperity. Different types of production were mutually fertilizing. Hamilton was at special pains to show that industry benefited the farmer, for a domestic demand for his raw materials was preferable to the fluctuations of foreign markets, plus the saving in carriage both of his crops and of the manufactures which he required. More broadly, a varied economy of agriculture, commerce, industry, and finance, with a diversity of opportunities inviting enterprise, was lively and inventive, whereas agriculture alone tended to become routine and lethargic.

In all of this reasoning Hamilton had to meet the axiom of Adam Smith that agriculture was the most productive pursuit. In this Hamilton was obliged to agree, but he held a brief for manufactures because they made an addition to national wealth otherwise absent. Also the fabrication of raw materials, as has been mentioned, interacted beneficially with the application of energies in other directions.

In his Report on Manufactures Hamilton made a further contribution which became influential, especially in the American economic thought of his followers. Adam Smith had equated the economy of a single community with that of the whole world. In his theory, the competition of producers in one street or town offered the example of free trade that should be embraced by the cosmos of merchants. Not so, said Hamilton. Between the local mini-economy and that of the universe of markets the nation interposed its needs. A country in the early stages of progress required the fostering care of government to encourage novel undertakings which without public subsidy would be too hazardous to attract effort. The demands of national defense required a degree of national self-sufficiency not to be left to private choice in the sorts of production. True, if all countries were more or less advanced and varied in their economies, free trade was desirable. But while most governments were placing their national interests foremost, and were restricting their imports to shelter their immature domestic industries, world free trade would spell injury for backward partners. The United States was emphatically in this category of rising countries whose policy must reject the dogma of nonintervention of government in the economy.

Hamilton never took refuge in a rule dictated by theory. A country experienced Protean departures from any expected pattern of behavior. Legislators and administrators, not to speak of individual enterprisers, must be prepared for constant adjustment to changing circumstances. A country's economy could not rely on the proposition of automatic operation. Hamilton's contemporary Antifederalists (Madison and Jefferson, for example) who rested their faith in laissez faire, the policy of let-alone, or the policy of, in fact, no policy, were wearing blinders. Hamilton plumped for the continuing exercise of judgment. This was the arduous, courageous system of conduct in a statesman.

If Hamilton and colleagues who shared his views had not given central government a prominent role in the first dozen years of American national life, the Republicans who took over from them, holding to more permissive doctrine, would not have been able to succeed as well as they did. Even so, Jefferson and his Republican successors in the presidency were obliged to adopt Hamiltonian policies which, before taking responsible office, they had decried. In particular, Jefferson, who had preferred a dispersed agricultural society, came to nourish manufactures as advocated by Hamilton.

The Report on Manufactures was inspired by Hamilton's desire for association, cooperation, and deliberate social planning; he disapproved of leaving national progress to chance. Hamilton, in fact, was a holdover from the mercantilist age, utilizing government as an indispensable engine of national improvement. He has been mistakenly regarded as the patron saint of American acquisitive capitalism. In his program for national development moneyed men had his solicitude. They were capable of effective economic action, formed a tolerably cohesive interest, served his public purposes as clients. He wished to utilize them, but he was not their partisan except for the role they could play in rounded development of the American economy. To make him their special pleader aside from the essential service they could render to the community at large is to belittle his intentions and achievement.

It is not surprising that a narrow, less worthy view of Hamilton's contribution has prevailed in the minds of many. Insistence on paying the nation's debts redounded, of course, to the benefit of creditors, numbers of whom had bought up their depreciated securities at a fraction of the face value. The Report on Manufactures sought public aid for the class of industrial enterprisers. His close friends with whom he worked in the Federalist party were in the main men of means. Too much of his career, in the Treasury and afterward, was taken up with political infighting. Except for his recollections of agriculture in his native West Indies he knew little at first hand of American life on the land. He was an urban dweller, and much of the wealth concentrated in large towns was in immaterial forms.

In spite of these temptations to cast Hamilton as strategist for property, the least attentive reading of his career reveals his concern for the welfare of all of the people. Toward the close of his busy life he regretted that as leader of the Federalists he had not exerted himself more to acquaint the mass of citizens with the purposes of his party. His preoccupation with establishing the political integrity and economic prosperity of the United States had not allowed sufficient time for educating the broad electorate. Hamilton's portrait on our ten-dollar bill conveys an impression of him that would be corrected, perhaps, if his image were on our dime or quarter.

The Secretary, in preparation for the Report on Manufactures, assigned the United States marshals and others to gather information for him on the character and extent of industries existing in the country. This survey was encouraging, especially as it exhibited "the vast scene of household manufacturing" which he emphasized.

Hamilton recommended the use of both tariffs and bounties to encourage American industry. The ideal way was to lay import duties and pay the proceeds in bounties. Bounties and premiums went directly to the producer to be helped and did not raise the price of the commodity. He indicated the type of assistance that the industries described in his survey should receive. Import duties should be raised, even be prohibitive, on finished goods where this country could supply its own needs. Import duties on raw materials which we could not soon furnish at home should be lowered.

Labor for factories would not subtract from the already inadequate number of workers on the land. Farmers' wives and children would find welcome employment in industry. More important, factory workers "would probably flock from Europe to the United States" if they could use their skills here. In any case, efficient power-driven machinery would lessen the need for labor. He praised the success of certain European mechanics, immigrants, who had constructed machines in America. However, government should commission cautious persons to procure machinery from Europe—cautious because the operation must be secret to escape laws forbidding such export. Foreigners were showing eagerness to invest their funds in industry in this country.

Hamilton at this time was practicing what he preached, for he was giving every assistance in equipping the factories of the Society for Useful Manufactures at Paterson, New Jersey.

(Also, while he was preparing his Report on Manufactures, he was having an affair with one Maria Reynolds. Chronologically, that episode should follow immediately, but it is reserved for treatment at the point five years later, when Hamilton's enemies chose to mistake his illicit romance for misconduct in the Treasury.)

Chapter 13

PANIC AND PATERSON

Of course speculation in securities, federal and state, commenced long before the national government was organized. With the prospect of action on the debt by Congress, buyers' hopes and purchases quickened. The small circle of these adventurers in New York were of the mind of Andrew Craigie: "The public Debt affords the best field in the world for speculation, but . . . I know of no way of making safe speculations but by being associated with people who from their Official situation know all the present & can aid future arrangements either for or against the funds." Use of privileged information for one's own financial advantage, or sharing inside advices with friends has by no means disappeared from public life, but two centuries ago the "conflict of interest" was not censured. Members of Congress such as Robert Morris, Thomas FitzSimons, and Jeremiah Wadsworth, patriots all, indulged their opportunities without pangs of conscience or blame from the community. They had excellent means of judging the course of events, but were not so perfectly placed as William Duer, Assistant Secretary of the Treasury.

To be sure, Duer could not be certain what Congress would do with Hamilton's proposals, but he was surely privy to them, which was the closest one could come to knowing the future. While in the Treasury, he was eagerly speculating in public securities for himself and in conjunction with intimates similarly engaged. Fortunately, he quit his official post after six months, but not soon enough to absolve Hamilton of criticism for tolerating his practices so long. The affection which Duer inspired in associates even after his recklessness had carried into dishonesty is puzzling. He had performed disinterested services during the Revolution, and until his debacle he bore the reputation of an ingenious financier. His social connections were enviable; George and Martha Washington attended his marriage to the daughter of Lord Stirling, which allied him with Lady Stirling's relatives, the Livingstons. He was a familiar of the Schuylers and of other families of like acclaim. Hamilton warned Duer more than once that he was over-sanguine, and when it was in fact too late for remonstrance he urged, "If you cannot reasonably hope for a favourable extrication do not plunge deeper. Have the courage to make a full stop. . . . God bless you and take care of you and your family. I have experienced all the bitterness of soul, on your account, which a warm attachment can inspire. . . . Assure yourself in good and bad fortune of my sincere friendship and affection." Some years later Hamilton secured the consent of Duer's creditors to his release for a time from debtors' prison to permit him to make a last, vain effort to retrieve his affairs.

The speculators in public securities were, typically, merchants in the coast towns, principally New York and Philadelphia, who were accustomed to taking risks in shipping and in purchase of enormous tracts of wild lands. Brisk demand in Europe for American wheat and opening of the China trade put them in funds. They generally accurately forecast that Hamilton would be named Secretary of the Treasury, and from his known principles they surmised that the policy of the administration would be to secure a provision for the debt. Thus William Constable, a large-scale operator in depreciated paper, wrote to one of his correspondents in June 1789, "your Friend Hamilton will I think be Secretary of the Treas in wh case we may count upon the most Efficacious Measures being adopted to put the Debt on a respectable footing, & to provide for the punctual payment of the interest."

Constable busied himself to worm out the details of what would be proposed. Two months before the Secretary's first report was made to Congress, Constable informed his confederate Craigie: "I dined with Hamilton on Saturday. He is Strong in the faith of maintaining public Credit. . . . I tried him on the subject of Indints [indents, certificates of interest due on the public debt]—'they must no doubt be funded tho it cannot be done immediately' was his remark, 'they must all be put upon a footing,' meaning these as well as the funded Debt. In short I am more & more of opinion that they are the best object at present." Perhaps Hamilton disclosed too much to a friend in the intimacy of his home.

On the other hand, six weeks later Constable was more vague about the source of his expectation that the indents "will be funded with the principal." And to FitzSimons he wrote (December 1, 1789), "Your presence here would be of infinite advantage as We might . . . find out the intention of the Chancellor of the Exchequer." Hamilton's old comrade in arms, Henry ("Light Horse Harry") Lee of Virginia, congratulated him on his recent appointment and continued, "From your situation you must be able to form with some certainty an opinion concerning the domestic debt. Will it speedily rise, . . . what will become of the indents already issued? These queries are asked for my personal information, perhaps they may be improper, I do not think them so." Hamilton copied his answer on the back of Lee's letter:

> I am sure you are sincere when you say you would not subject me to an impropriety. . . . But you remember the saying in

regard to Caesar's wife. I think the spirit of it applicable to
every man concerned in the administration of the finance of a
country. With respect to the conduct of such men, suspicion is
ever eagle-eyed. And the most innocent things may be misin-
terpreted. Be assured of the affection and friendship of your A.
Hamilton.

The darling object of speculators was debt of the Southern
states, as they expected that this would be consolidated with
that of the federal government. Constable prized "such as may
have been issued early in the war & have drawn no Interest,
prefering [sic] always such as have been issued to the line of
the Army." Foreseeing a market in Europe for £1,000,000 of
South Carolina debt at 4s, "I wish to God," he wrote Gouverneur Morris, "you and your friends would give me Orders to
Strike at a large sum of it." Earlier, South Carolina debt had
got down to two shillings in the pound, as no provision had
been made for the interest. Later, when it was certain that
North Carolina would come into the Union, its paper, with
four years' interest due, was at 1s. 10d., a most desirable purchase.

Constable was still pumping Hamilton, who, he concluded,
"does not intend to take up the State Debts immediately—a
thing devoutly to be wished as it will afford us some oppty
[opportunity] to get hold."

As soon as the Constitution went into effect, one speculator
voiced his fear that public securities would advance too fast
for his plans: "indeed my only apprehensions are that the arrangements will be taken so early as to raise the price in the
markett before ourselves & Friends can make such extensive
purchases as I could wish."

The method of the speculators to conserve their liquid capital was not to buy securities outright, but to borrow them if
possible. Prior to adoption of the funding plan, one partnership gave lenders 3s. 4d. in the pound in cash and security
for return of the securities at any time not less than a year af-

terward; the owners of the securities were to receive any interest the government paid on them. It was expected that the borrowed paper could be sold for 10s. If the funding were
adopted, the increase in the quantity of certificates offered
"must fall the mkt;" if funding were rejected the result would
be the same, "& of course We may replace at a more reasonable rate." Said the proposer of this scheme, "I know the hazard that attends such an operation but I think it may be
risqued." When calculating on the rise, the usual thing, the
speculators would sell their borrowed securities, pay the
owners the lower premium price when borrowed, and retrieve
their security. Americans acting as agents for European buyers
found themselves "always in advance" because they paid for
the stocks "every shilling on the Nail & we only draw on
transmitting the Certificates." Thus to earn the commission,
resources of the American agents were strained. The principals
in Europe were urged to buy shares in the Bank of New York
in the name of the American agents; "we shoud then be able
to make what Discount we might require." This dodge seemed
to justify the criticism that banks served stockjobbers and denied credit to merchants.

The promise that government would honor all public debts
was enough in itself to produce a scramble for securities. The
outlook for the invigorated American nation attracted the confidence of overseas investors, for the French Revolution and
preparations for war of the great powers clouded the European
scene. Hamilton regretted the excesses of speculation that led
to panic, chiefly in New York City, in the spring of 1792, but
he was not surprised. He approved of an active market for evidences of the debt as the means of overcoming depreciation
and rendering the obligations useful as the basis of credit and
currency. The short-lived madness was unfortunate for him
because it excited the charges of his Antifederalist political
foes. It caused fatal embarrassments of the Society for Useful
Manufacturers in which he had centered hopes. It strained the

resources of the Bank of New York, already beset by the threat of competition from the branch of the Bank of the United States and additional institutions being promoted in the city. Treasury borrowing in Holland was not shaken, but the bankers there required from Hamilton an explanation of American financial disorder in case their lenders should be alarmed. The bankruptcy of close friends was a sorrow to him. The panic coincided with an effort of New York Federalists, Schuyler and Hamilton prominent among them, to unseat Governor Clinton. (A personal anxiety of Hamilton at this time was the blackmail demands of Maria Reynolds's husband.)

Nevertheless, Hamilton met the crisis with steady nerve. After reaching a high point in January 1792, securities declined for five weeks. The panic was touched off by the failure of William Duer on March 9, 1792. Duer was struggling to retrieve his situation when he appealed to Hamilton from New York in dire distress (March 12). Would the Secretary defer suit against him, ordered by Oliver Wolcott, Jr., Comptroller of the Treasury, for his debt to the United States of $200,000? News had spread of what Duer referred to as "my having skipt Payment." But his public transactions, he declared, were not blended with his private dealings. He was hastening to Philadelphia, where "Every Farthing will be Immediately accounted for. If a Suit should be brought on the Part of the Public, under my present distrest Circumstances, My Ruin is complete."

Hamilton answered at once that it was too late to turn aside the blow, as Wolcott's instruction to the United States Attorney had been issued the day before. Hamilton could only urge his friend not to incur further liabilities; he should assign his assets first to "Institutions of public Utility" (this would doubtless include the Society for Useful Manufactures), and next to all fair creditors.

In December 1791, Duer and Alexander Macomb had made an agreement for joint speculation "in the Debt of the United

States and in the Stock of the Bank of the United States & Bank of New York." Macomb told Constable "Duer & I are upon an adventure which before the end of the Year may amount to a pretty large Sum." They relied on their "joint Credit at the Banks." They promptly acquired 400 shares in the Bank of New York. Low at the moment, these would rise in value, Duer assured Macomb, because Hamilton wanted to merge the branch of the national bank with the Bank of New York, and then the branch would disappear. Duer was guilty of duplicity toward his trusting partner. He really did not expect the discontinuance of bank competition in New York. He gave secret orders to Walter Livingston to sell short a hundred shares of the Bank of New York which Duer held privately. Apparently he meant that Macomb should remain bullish, helping to raise quotations on bank stock, while Duer four months hence would reap a profit when shares had fallen.

Robert Troup, on March 19, 1792, informed Hamilton of the "convulsion [in New York City] . . . immediately owing to . . . Our Friend Duer's failure. This poor man is in a state of almost complete insanity; and his situation is a source of inexpressible grief to all his friends. On Saturday night his friends met at his house & staid with him till near 12 o'Clock when we broke up in confusion without being able to agree upon a single measure." A follow-up meeting at Troup's house Sunday drew up "a notification . . . by which we said that from the magnitude & variety of Duer's operations he would not be able to make any specific propositions to his creditors till next saturday when we requested a meeting of the creditors." This had allayed threats of violence. "The truth is that the notes unpaid amount to about half a million of dollars & Duer has not a farthing of money or a particle of stock to pay them with." His land in Maine was heavily encumbered, but his friends were endeavoring to open a loan on that security to satisfy as far as possible "the voracious appetites of his note holders," among whom were "some low & turbulent spirits." Duer's "total bankruptcy" endangered his person and might bring odium upon the funding system.

It developed that Walter Livingston, Duer's principal creditor, had endorsed notes for him to the amount of $203,875.80 exclusive of $12,360.37 for shares in the manufacturing society. Duer assured Livingston that he had property to cover all of Livingston's engagements for him, but the next day, March 23, 1792, Duer was arrested for his debts at the instance of his commercial creditors. "I am now secure from my Enemies," he cried, "and feeling the Purity of my heart I defy the world." The melancholy scene from which Duer was physically removed was described by James Madison: "The gambling system . . . is beginning to exhibit its explosions. D[uer], . . . the Prince of the tribe of speculators, has just become a victim of his enterprizes . . . and . . . every description of persons, from the Church to the Stews, are among the dupes of his dexterity and the partners of his distress."

Hamilton stepped in to support the market for public stocks by buying for the sinking fund. His agent was William Seton, cashier of the Bank of New York, who was supplied largely with loans from that bank, on security of the certificates purchased. The first $50,000 was made available on March 25, 1792. Seton was to buy 6 per cents at par even if they had fallen below, and if possible at auction as more public than in private sales. However, Seton, this time, must not declare that he bought for the sinking fund since on Sunday Hamilton could not get the expected formal authorization. Seton should announce the reassuring news that Amsterdam bankers were lending the government three million florins at 4 per cent; if foreigners were so confident of our credit why should citizens sacrifice their holdings of public securities? Hamilton counseled that banks should allow time for paying up, and individuals could reduce pressure on the banks by giving credit to each other. "If there are a few *harpies* who will not concur . . .

let them be paid and execrated." New Yorkers should refuse to be panicked.

As these measures were having effect, Seton was supplied with another $50,000 and was directed to use $100,000 more if "a pretty extensive explosion" demanded. On April 9 Seton reported that the "many failures daily happening" would be overshadowed if "Mr. Macomb cannot or will not comply with his engagements," amounting to some $500,000. The next Monday would bring the test whether securities had improved or Macomb would have to accept large quantities and pay the difference between the prices promised and the lower prices prevailing. Seton pled that government assistance, known in advance, might "save the City from utter ruin." It was too late. Next day Seton informed the Secretary that Macomb had failed. Hamilton, by express, rushed him authority to expend $150,000 for the sinking fund. Eighty eager sellers awaited him, and all he could do was to distribute his funds among them. Seton thought he had alleviated distress on what would prove to be the worst day.

Nicholas Low, a director of the manufacturing company, gave Hamilton the bad news that the failure of John Dewhurst, another director, probably meant the total loss of money ($50,000) entrusted to him for expenditures abroad. Another New York businessman was no more cheerful: "The failures already taken place here, and many more . . . yet to come, will ere long . . . injure . . . Philadelphia, and in this City . . . many who were . . . worth handsome fortunes . . . 3 or 4 months ago, are now . . . probably not worth a groat, in case they were to pay all their debts." Seton's returns of purchases for the sinking fund in eleven days in early April 1792 showed that he bought from 95 individuals and firms, usually to the extent of $1000 each, but in some cases much more. The commissioner of loans' sixteen clerks could not record transfers fast enough to keep current. The scene in New York was reflected in Philadelphia, but not so severely. Treasury purchases for the sinking fund were completed May 10, 1792, when Hamilton thanked Seton for his faithful service. Seton's judgment was the more important because the Secretary of the Treasury was two days removed from the crisis in New York City.

This was perhaps the earliest instance of the federal government coming to the aid of a particular locality, an action not then so generally approved as later. The help which the Secretary rendered illustrated the wisdom of his insistence that the Treasury required a surplus to take care of emergencies and that it should not be limited to the penny of prescribed disbursements.

The Society for Establishing Useful Manufactures, chartered by New Jersey in November 1791, was a mistake in all respects. Like Hamilton's Report on Manufactures, of which the society was intended to be the companion piece, years were to pass before its object could be achieved. Hamilton said that his reputation was "deeply concerned" in the fortunes of the Society. He was not formally a promoter of it, and never a director, though he may have drawn the charter of incorporation, but he gave it more attention than did any of its investors. Really his project, he failed in it, with help from the neglect of others, the money panic that greeted its commencement, and bad judgment and inexperience on the part of all. On paper it was the first sizable industrial undertaking in the United States, meant to demonstrate the feasibility of manufactures in the predominantly agricultural country. Fifty years later William Gregg, in South Carolina, a section similarly exclusively devoted to the planting economy, succeeded with his cotton factory, but then he could pattern after matured enterprises in New England and the Middle states.

Early in August 1791 six organizers of the manufacturing society meeting at New Brunswick requested Hamilton to

engage "artists" (artisans) who could direct labor in the spin-
ning and weaving of cotton and printing of cloth. Four months
later he reported to the first—and only fully attended—meeting of the thirteen directors of the society, who had been
elected by the stockholders. He had made contracts with
Thomas Marshall to superintend the cotton mill, William Hall
for the printing department, Joseph Mort as an assistant where
he could best be used, and George Parkinson as a foreman.
William Pearce was on the point of being hired; he had devised a double (hand) loom, which "as far as without seeing it
worked, it can be judged of, promises to answer . . . Expectations." Mort was willing to go to Europe to recruit workmen.
Hamilton left the society free to dismiss any of these candidates who proved unfit. The directors confirmed Hamilton's
choices.

The selection of mechanics to equip and operate the plants
was crucial. In spite of having gathered materials on manufacturing ventures, Hamilton had only a layman's knowledge of
machinery and technical skills. He seems to have closed with
key figures in haste, without sufficient inquiry into their particular abilities. Marshall was a recent immigrant to this country, but Hamilton accepted him promptly, and he took the
others with no better knowledge of them. Marshall was the
only one who remained in employ for as long as five years,
and he departed in debt to the society.

Hamilton was present to advise at two meetings of directors,
several days each, in the spring and summer of 1792. He was
deputed to write William Duer, governor of the society, and
now in debtors' prison, hoping that funds of the society had
not been lost in Duer's bankruptcy, of which there was much
fear. Following widespread prospecting for location of the society's development, Hamilton agreed on the vicinity of the
great falls of the Passaic river. Ten days later the committee to
buy lands, accompanied by General Schuyler who had knowledge of waterpower, met at the falls. It was concluded that

water could be taken from above the falls, be carried on a short aqueduct across a ravine, and be led thence into a canal descending the hillside, thus providing mill seats. Farms were purchased for £3293. The property afforded ample space for the town—tactfully named for Governor William Paterson of New Jersey—which would contain homes of workers in the mills.

This involved revoking contracts for lands at Vreeland's Point, at the head of navigation on the Passaic river (now the city of Passaic), which Samuel Ogden had bought at the direction of Duer. It was judged to be preferable, from an engineering standpoint, to be adjacent to the falls, though it meant contending with seven miles of land carriage for all materials and products.

Hamilton met with the directors at the falls at the tavern of Abraham Godwin in July 1792. In accordance with a map prepared by one Willis, $20,000 were appropriated for the canal. A carding mill, a plant for spinning and (hand) weaving, and a printworks were to be erected. A sawmill would provide lumber for fifty modest homes for workers, and loans would be made to the supervising mechanics if they wanted to build better homes for themselves. United States funded debt would be security for a bank loan of $70,000 to cover construction costs. An adjourned meeting at Newark learned no more of funds entrusted to Duer, but he remained as governor, though his situation in prison did not recommend a corporation whose capital had not been completely subscribed. Creditors were pressing, and the term "Manufacturing Script" was mentioned as means of payment.

Hamilton had saddled the society with Duer, the financial visionary, as governor; he now added the engineering visionary, Pierre Charles L'Enfant. L'Enfant had overrun the appropriation for remodeling the city hall in New York as temporary national capitol, and only six months before had been dismissed as designer of the federal city on the Potomac. (He was afterward reengaged for the plan of Washington, D.C., the execution of which gave him enduring fame.) He was better suited for layouts of grand public enterprises than for serving a private industrial corporation. He proposed to scrap the scheme of surface canals winding down the hill, saying that the ground was too porous and the water would escape into caverns. He revived Duer's project of a canal seven miles long to Freeland's, but now, in L'Enfant's fancy, to be carried in a stone aqueduct built on arches, ancient Roman fashion. If leaks occurred in the bed of the aqueduct they could be detected and plugged. Meantime the directors were content to order machinery constructed for the cotton mill, and they hired a wagoner to haul back and forth between the falls and Vreeland's Point.

L'Enfant, as engineer and town planner for the society, assured Hamilton that "your favorit Child will be carefully nursed and bread up to your satisfaction without Involving the parents in to Extravagant . . . Expence." Ere long the ebullient designer was reporting to Hamilton that he was felling trees and clearing immense roots in the path of the canal. "I am in hope in a few weak to be enabled to make a beginning of the foundation of the grand acqueduct."

It was believed necessary to import skilled workers from England, though none would prove as extraordinarily competent as Samuel Slater, who served the Browns in Rhode Island. Hamilton was to advise on the delicate project of importing forty or fifty workers and some machinery, in defiance of the British laws which prohibited their export from the kingdom. For the purpose $50,000 was appropriated. The agents of the society would meet an eager response from those solicited, for, said a letter from Dublin, "The people are every where panting to go to America . . . Emissaries from America are at this hour dispersed through England, Scotland and Ireland, to enveigle our husbandmen and mechanics." George Hammond, the British minister, warned his government that the society's agents were "employed in the chief manufacg towns in England for express purpose of enticing skilful workmen, and procuring correct models of machines." Thomas Digges, who had sent over William Pearce, the inventor of the double loom, was distributing a thousand copies of Hamilton's Report on Manufactures as a stimulus in his recruiting of workers in Ireland and northern England.

This was the last hopeful action of the society. Two days were needed to get a quorum for the meeting of the directors in April 1792. By then the financial panic in New York had felled Duer, Dewhurst, and Macomb. The acting treasurer explained that "in this critical moment when every hour brings its misfortunes and the property of every man [is] at hazard none of them can . . . leave town." Deputy governor Nicholas Low and a committee drafted an appeal to Hamilton for advice, which they sent by messenger. With the society's business at a standstill, "It is natural for us . . . to look up to you as the founder of the institution." Would he "be kind enough to furnish us with your ideas . . . and assist us in our operations as far as in your power." Governor Duer, immured, was too distracted to be of help.

Hamilton's response was read to a sparsely attended meeting held ten days later at Powles Hook. If loss of funds by several means was not too great, the prospect would be bettered by securing a superintendent, an accountant, and a cashier, all of unquestioned competence and integrity, who would be responsible under the directors. Hamilton would help to get a loan if that was necessary. He advised them to try to attract only *"a few essential workmen"* from Europe for a cotton factory, leaving the print works for later, and to postpone the suggestion of a lottery until conditions were propitious.

The directors named a committee to query Duer on the disposition of monies entrusted to him. He assured them that the funds were safe and would be faithfully applied. Macomb, as ordered, had furnished Dewhurst with bills drawn on Macomb's correspondent in London to the sum of £10,975.12.2 sterling, which was to be spent abroad for workmen and materials. Dewhurst had properly receipted for these bills, and Walker, the accountant pro tem, reported that the bills had been remitted and the skilled workmen and machines were expected soon.

The society was to enjoy no further comfort. The directors feared that, after Dewhurst's failure, the bills in the hands of his partner would be seized by Dewhurst's creditors in England. The British packet that sailed from New York April 9 would carry the news of Dewhurst's bankruptcy, but it had to call at Halifax first. A swift pilot boat was dispatched at the cost of $850 in hopes it would reach England in time to salvage the funds. The directors begged Hamilton to confer with Dewhurst in Philadelphia; he could get only a promise to try to indemnify the society for loss on his account, and meantime the society should be represented by an able attorney in London.

The report to stockholders at a meeting in October 1792 stated that the bills Dewhurst remitted to England "are in a State of Jeopardy little short of desperate." Immediately on their receipt, his agent in London had "pledged the said Bills to divers Persons, for the private Debts of the said John Dewhurst." Dewhurst soon went to England, where it was expected that he would take advantage of the bankruptcy law.

Duer was superseded by Nicholas Low as governor, and a year later Low was empowered to accept an offer of Macomb to pay $12,195 in full satisfaction of the society's claim against Dewhurst, provided all rights to the bills were assigned to Macomb. It seems this offer was rejected, for the directors requested the London house of Phyn, Ellice & Inglis, on which Macomb had drawn, to make a settlement. That firm accomplished nothing in a year, and William Constable, then in London, was given the assignment.

Hamilton's advice was followed: the society reduced the number of experienced workmen solicited abroad to the minimum that could instruct the unskilled hands—many of them children—to be had locally. It also declined proposals for manufacturing flax, hemp, chip hats, and for calico printing, and extended time for the third payment on stock.

The society made ineffectual efforts to procure a general superintendent for its day-to-day conduct. Nehemiah Hubbard declined the post in spite of Hamilton's plea that judicious management would retrieve losses. L'Enfant was supervisor of construction, and anything but a businessman. Finally, Peter Colt was placed in charge. He had been Treasurer of the State of Connecticut, and gave the enterprise at Paterson his constant care. He was what Hamilton called "a *totus homo* to the Institution." However, in the beginning he applied to Hamilton for information and direction. Hamilton made himself responsible for payments to Scottish firms for shipping stocking frames and skilled workmen to Paterson. In July 1793 he was creditor to the society for $1811.10, mostly for advances to mechanics.

The *New York Diary* attacked the society as got up by stock-jobbers who "meant nothing more than to possess themselves of a great number of shares, raise them to an exorbitant price, sell out, and after realizing a handsome fortune, care very little if the whole . . . went to the devil." Actually, shares on which the original deposit was $25 rose to $50 at one point, but at the time of the *Diary's* blast they had fallen to 8 or 10 shillings. Nevertheless the charge that some directors were more concerned with speculation than with manufacturing was accurate. In contrast to Hamilton's voluntary sacrifices for an undertaking "of . . . real public importance," Macomb had agreed with six others "to purchase up three thousand shares of the . . . manufacturing Society, in order to have the management of the Direction, and by that means to promote its interest & *our own.*" Duer, governor of the society, had proposed the scheme.

In spite of the attention of Colt and Hamilton the works

were endangered by dissatisfaction and desertion of the technical specialists. Pearce had gone to Philadelphia to see about his patents and seemed on the point of being wooed away permanently to a manufacturing project there. Hall was off on his own concerns, while Marshall was in New York demanding that his salary be doubled. Joseph Mort, still in the society's pay, had long been absent in Virginia. Would Hamilton remonstrate with L'Enfant for his "extraordinary long Absence?" He had left Colt no knowledge of his plans for waterpower and homes for workmen. L'Enfant returned to Paterson full of complaints; he suspended all construction until the directors met to hear his grievances. Hamilton was unable to meet with the directors, but counseled which of the temperamental mechanics should be let go, which satisfied in their demands. Colt was obliged to go to Hartford because his family had smallpox, of which one child died and another was long in hospital. Two payments on shares were in United States funded debt and for half the original subscription. Hamilton himself had yellow fever.

When Hamilton recovered, he went to Albany for convalescence, and on the way he stopped at Paterson (October 1793). He learned that the auditing committee two weeks before had reported, on the basis of ill-kept records, that the affairs of the society were in a "deranged situation." Little actual manufacturing was going on. The directors had been as negligent as all the others; they should meet regularly "& enter into thorough and minute examination of all . . . transactions of the society."

The next month (November 1793) brought even more discouraging developments. Two foremen had wrongfully taken machinery of the society to Wilmington, Delaware, and its recovery was problematical. A lottery promoted to raise $100,000 had not prospered and was contracted to $39,000. With the new year, 1794, L'Enfant left, taking with him wanted papers and Willis's map. The society could not pay a treasurer, and the director elected to that office declined to give bond, so the governer was to serve as treasurer also. The intention to build a hotel was abandoned. However, fancies persisted. The superintendent was to plant white mulberry trees "for the culture of silk worms." (Actually, more than a century later Paterson became the chief center of silk manufacture in America.) To give the factory children a modicum of schooling, a teacher was engaged at 10 shillings a week to instruct them on Sundays.

From this time on the enterprise drooped to its finish. The calico printers were dismissed. Town lots were offered at lowered prices to any who would build homes. Drawings in the lottery were postponed. A special meeting for important decisions held at the beginning of 1795 fetched only three directors. And in August of 1795 the governor was to sell deferred stock at a minimum of 14 shillings to discharge debts. The next month Hamilton, now out of the Treasury, was elected a director, but he is not recorded as attending in this capacity. In 1796 the superintendent was to stop further manufacturing and sell goods on hand at auction. The cotton mill was to be leased. In July of 1795 more stock was to be sold on lenient terms to satisfy creditors. The faithful Peter Colt was released with regret. The stockholders were to consider dissolving the corporation. After a lapse of four years the directors met and ordered the remaining United States stock to be sold at a price.

Hamilton had done more to inaugurate and bolster the experiment than had anyone else, but he had overreached. His approval of Duer and L'Enfant was disastrous. He could give to the society only what time he could snatch from his heavy responsibilities in the Treasury and his political activities. Even with the best will, he had not the needed knowledge or energies to permit him to focus on a complicated pioneer enterprise involving engineering, manufacturing, town-building, and recruitment of machinery and skilled labor from abroad. The directors were merchants and speculators, not industrialists. The project was premature and on too large a scale. For years thereafter investors were attracted to expanding commerce and the opening of western lands.

A generation later Hamilton's hopes began to be realized. The war of 1812–14 convinced people that the country should be more self-sufficient. Manufactures, small and well managed, took their rise, the Second Bank of the United States was chartered, the tariff of 1816, the first that could be called protective, was passed. The "American System" associated with the name of Henry Clay embraced the manufacturing and the means of transport that Hamilton had advocated.

The Society for Establishing Useful Manufactures shared in the resurgence ten years after Hamilton's death, as real estate proprietor. Under the stimulus of war the town of Paterson was "flourishing beyond the most sanguine expectations." A schoolhouse and church were to be erected to serve the expanding population. The State of New Jersey exchanged its hundred shares for land. Roswell L. Colt, son of the old superintendent, bought the remaining shares above par. The corporation prospered from real estate holdings and power leases until it was taken over by the city of Paterson in 1945, after a life of more than a century and a half.

Chapter 14

STORM IN THE CABINET

It is hard to know how Hamilton found enough hours in the day and night to discharge his official duties and engage himself in private activities as well. He was looked to by Federalists everywhere as their leader, particularly in the State of New York. There, in the election of 1792, the effort was renewed to unseat Governor George Clinton. Hamilton and his friends had supported Robert Yates as the likeliest candidate in 1789, without success. He was persuaded to try again, but withdrew from the race. He pleaded financial reasons, but Hamilton suspected that Aaron Burr, willing to desert the United States Senate if he could obtain the New York governorship, was the cause of Yates' retreat.

A group of friends of both Hamilton and Burr visited Hamilton and Schuyler to induce them to turn to Burr, whom they quoted as being devoted to the Union and attached to Hamilton and his policies. They had no chance of success. Burr had defeated Schuyler for the national Senate, and Hamilton was steadily distrustful of Burr, whose "integrity as an Individual," he said, "is not unimpeached. As a public man he is one of the worst sort—a friend to nothing but as it suits his interest and ambition . . . he cares nothing about the means of effecting his purpose. . . . In a word, if we have an embryo-Caesar in the United States 'tis Burr."

To oppose Burr as much as Clinton, the Federalists prevailed on Chief Justice John Jay to be their champion in place of Yates. Twice before he had refused to stand for elective office, and he consented now with the condition that he would not "make any efforts to obtain suffrages," relying solely on his known character. In the acrimonious campaign that followed, the shafts of Clinton and the Livingstons were aimed at Hamilton as though he were the Federalist candidate.

Jay would have been the winner if the votes of Otsego, Tioga, and Clinton counties had been allowed. But they were not. The canvassers threw them out on the ground of technical irregularities of a kind which had been ignored in previous elections. They declared that the count stood, for Clinton 8440 votes, for Jay 8332—a victory for Clinton by 108 ballots. The decision, made along party lines, so stirred opposition that the canvassers appealed to New York's Senators, King and Burr, for their legal opinions. After two days' conference Burr confirmed the canvassers' verdict, while King gave precedent to reinstate the rejected votes. The canvassers then burned the disputed ballots, but the contest was continued in protest meetings of Jay's supporters at which threats were made to snatch Clinton violently from the usurped governor's chair or at least to have the legislature order a new election.

Hamilton cautioned Rufus King against "a ferment . . . raised which may not be allayed when you wish it." The opposers of Clinton were the "friends to order & good Government, and . . . it will ill become them to give an example of the contrary." He deprecated talk "of Conventions and the Bayonet." Hamilton, who was "out of . . . reach of the contagion," was cooler, momentarily, than was the staid John Jay himself.

Burr was ubiquitous in his pretensions. If not the New York governorship, then the vice presidency of the United States claimed his notice. "If the enemies of the Government are secret and united we shall lose Mr. Adams," Rufus King warned Hamilton. Burr's partisans were active in Connecticut and Pennsylvania; Jefferson and his friends might so reduce the votes for Adams that he would decline the office. Hamilton thought Burr's bid was nothing more than "a diversion in favour of Mr. Clinton," Hamilton would exert himself against Burr. Clinton's elevation to the national government would be "very unfortunate," though he was "a man of property, and, in private life . . . of probity." Burr, on the contrary, was unprincipled as a public and a private man. "I am mistaken, if it be not his object to play the game of confusion, and I feel it a religious duty to oppose his career."

The country could have been spared the virulent political dispute between Hamilton and Jefferson which filled the newspapers in 1792–93. More accurately, the quarrel was between Hamilton and the proxies of Jefferson, for Jefferson swore before heaven that he penned not a line of what Hamilton attributed to him in the controversy. Jefferson did not discourage the thrusts of his partisans at Hamilton, but Hamilton on his part pursued the fight with unmistakable zest and persistence. The tilts involved the close supporters of the opposing champions, to the point that the mutual accusations pitted against each other the Federalist and Republican parties. This fierce battle of principles and personalities has fixed in the minds of many a mortal antithesis between Hamilton and Jefferson. This has obscured the republican attachments of Hamilton and the desire of Jefferson to see the national government strong and prosperous. Near the end of Hamilton's life he had much to do with making Jefferson President of the United States, and in that office Jefferson adopted important policies of Hamilton's. Though in the main at odds with each other, they were complementary figures in the historical development of the nation, for the fact was that Jefferson's liberty called for Hamilton's stability, and the central government which Hamilton fostered would have become dictatorial and been short-lived without the political vitality of individuals and localities.In telling the story of Hamilton or of Jefferson it is easy to spice pages with their antagonisms, but, beyond a point, that subtracts from the positive contributions of each. So far as relations between the states and the federal authority are concerned, it is plain that Hamilton's espousal of the latter has been warranted in the course of events. Similarly Hamilton's expectation of an industrial economy in America, rather than persistence in an agricultural society which was Jefferson's hope, was what matured.

For some months in the first flush of the new national government Jefferson and Hamilton cooperated as friends. Hamilton's trust in James Madison was older, and it seemed to him enduringly firm. In a long letter to Edward Carrington of Virginia in May 1792 Hamilton described the destruction of these cordialities. It is the best window to the hostilities because Hamilton was unbosoming himself to a friend, not dealing in the asperities of newspaper polemics. He assigned what he conceived to be causes of the differences.

In France Jefferson "saw government only on the side of its abuses. He drank deeply of the French Philosophy, in Religion, in Science, in politics. He came from France in the moment of a fermentation which he had had a share in exciting, & in the passions . . . of which he shared both from temperament and situation." He came to America "electrified *plus* with attachment to France and with the project of knitting together the two Countries in the closest political bands." Hamilton inferred from Jefferson's encouragement of the demolition of the regime of Louis XVI that the Virginian was suspicious of all government not the most democratic and local. Hamilton said, with much reserve, that Jefferson and

Madison "have been found among those who were disposed
to narrow the Federal authority."

Aside from French influence uniting with his native bent,
Jefferson was a rural man, an individualist. Other than Washington's Mount Vernon, Jefferson's home on its hilltop in
Virginia was the most cherished in America. There Jefferson
was lord of all he surveyed, and he felt self-sufficient. Of
course here was a cruel paradox, for at Monticello, so far from
celebrating the rights of man, he ruled over chattel slaves.

Great as was Hamilton's distaste for Jefferson's leanings,
was his regret and resentment at the defection, as he saw it, of
James Madison. One may doubt Hamilton's statement that he
would not have assumed the burdens of his Treasury post
unless he was sure of being able to rely on the support of
Madison. After Jefferson appeared on the scene Madison suffered a sea change. Hamilton all but imputed Madison's surrender of his nationalist views to the dominating influence of
Jefferson. Together they were at the head of a faction *"subversive of the principles of good government and dangerous to the
union peace and happiness of the Country."*

Hamilton, for his part, was cast in the British mold, like the
British was attached to constitutional government, and much
preferred steady progress over sweeping, violent innovation.
He reminded his touch-and-go opponents of the old saying
"That it is much easier to raise the Devil than to lay him."
Hamilton was an urban man, living cheek by jowl with his
neighbors, and consequently highly conscious of rules of community conduct. (Only near the end of his life did he acquire a
small country estate.)

Though Jefferson made gestures in the direction of economic
competence, actually he had no such equipment. He admired
the laissez-faire evangelism of the French Physiocrats, which
practically forswore deliberate economic controls, and he embraced a lighthearted economic naturalism which shrugged off
social resposnsibility. Jefferson had faith in individual compe-

tition. Hamilton, on the other hand, was impressed by the merits of association for a chosen desirable result. In America, a young country with vast lands and a sparse population, co-operation was essential to progress. For Hamilton, govern-ment, agreed authority, was the engine of social improvement. Government could prompt, subsidize, and correct economic action. One day competition and the regnant profit motive might safely take over, but that was in the future, Meantime, for the good of the society, nurture was superior to nature. Jef-ferson in his thought was doctrinaire, Hamilton was selective.

Besides these environmental and temperamental distinc-tions between Jefferson and Hamilton, which contributed to their enmity, was the circumstance that Hamilton had been constant through the trials of the Confederation and had worked unceasingly for reform, while Jefferson had been abroad for the five years during which American government and economy had sunk to the depths. For a decade Hamilton had helped to forge the tools of national betterment, and, fol-lowing adoption of the Constitution, he eagerly seized them. Jefferson had been reluctant to accept President Washington's invitation to his Cabinet and had excused his tardy appear-ance at the capital.

The accusations on both sides ran the gamut of supposed misdeeds of the antagonist. The ready organ for Hamilton's barbs was John Fenno's *Gazette of the United States,* while the assaults of Jefferson's friends were sure to appear in Philip Freneau's *National Gazette.* Other papers picked up the offen-sive charges. Both sides used *noms de guerre.* Hamilton signed himself "American," "Fact," "Amicus," "Catullus," "Me-tellus," "T.L.," and maybe other names, and he sometimes employed several at once. As the controversy waxed and al-legations and answers became more detailed, even readers avid for political squabbles must have found the fracas hard to follow. In spite of that, sometimes the little sheets, except for stale news clipped from foreign publications and reports of

debates in Congress, would contain little besides the screeds
known to issue from the camps of Hamilton and Jefferson.

In late July 1792 Hamilton, as "T.L." addressed Fenno's *Gazette of the United States* (Federalist):

> The Editor of the "National Gazette" [Freneau] receives a salary
> from government. Quere—Whether this salary is paid him for
> *translations;* or for *publications,* the design of which is to vilify
> those to whom the voice of the people has committed the ad-
> ministration of our public affairs—to oppose the measures of
> government, and, by false insinuations, to disturb the public
> peace? In common life it is thought ungrateful for a man to bite
> tha hand that puts bread in his mouth; but if the man is hired
> to do it, the case is altered.

Hamilton had established that Madison had promoted Jefferson's invitation to Freneau to be translator from the French in
the Department of State and then had urged him to set up a
Republican newspaper in Philadelphia. Madison protested, to
Edmund Randolph, that he made no link between the clerkship under Jefferson and the object of a party press. He concluded that he would not make a public reply to Hamilton's
malicious insinuation. Freneau replied formally to Hamilton's
continued attacks on Jefferson as *"institutor* and *patron"* of
Freneau's paper and as a man who used public money to support his political mouthpiece. In an affidavit sworn before
Mayor Matthew Clarkson, Freneau declared that the Secretary
of State had nothing to do with his paper; "the Editor has consulted his own judgment alone in the conducting of it—free—
unfettered—and uninfluenced." Hamilton refused to withdraw his accusation; Jefferson was no less culpable because
Madison had been the go-between.

Hamilton, over one or another name, showed that Jefferson
had been equivocal about the Constitution and leaned toward
the calling of a second convention. He had been willing to see
America's debt to France shifted to the shoulders of private in-

vestors in Holland, which was discreditable, as he thought the nation might default. Since Jefferson was the enemy of order and union, the proper thing was for him to resign his post in the government and assume frankly the role of leader of the opposition.

The Jeffersonians damned Hamilton as leader of the "monarchical party," "monied aristocracy," "Monocrats," "corrupt squadron." The funding system was regularly pilloried. "An irredeemable debt . . . is hereditary monarchy in another shape. It creates an influence in the executive part of the government, which will soon render it an overmatch for the legislative. It is the worst species of king's evil." Hamilton's supposed dictum—neglecting his cautions—that a national debt was a national blessing was the subject of repeated mockery.

President Washington deplored the rupture between his ministers, now paraded in the public prints. In August 1792 he wrote to both of them, in similar terms, remonstrating against the mischief they were causing and begging them to desist. To Hamilton he expressed his mortification that "men of abilities, zealous patriots, having the same *general* objects in view . . . will not exercise more charity in deciding on the opinions . . . of one another." He hoped for "liberal allowances . . . instead of wounding suspicions, and irritating charges, with which some of our gazettes are so strongly impregnated, and cannot fail, if persevered in, . . . to . . . tear the machine asunder." The President assured Hamilton of his "sincere and affectionate regard" and invited him to drop in at Mount Vernon if his projected southern journey brought him that way. He lamented to Jefferson, "How unfortunate . . . that, while we are encompassed on all sides with avowed enemies and insidious friends, internal dissensions should be harrowing and tearing our vitals." Just at this time the President had issued a proclamation against the violence of westerners protesting against the whiskey excise.

The wrangling ministers gave Washington only qualified assent to his remonstrance. Hamilton agreed that harmony was essential to energy in the government, but he must for a while longer defend· the Treasury against dangerous thrusts of the party of his opponent. He regretted that he could not visit Mount Vernon—evidently expecting that Jefferson would be a guest there on his return from Monticello. Jefferson avowed his innocence of any public attacks on Hamilton, but, to the President, he condemned his policies. Jefferson was unworthily insinuating about Hamilton's origin. He wanted to quit his office of Secretary of State, and would then answer his profaner.

A few weeks later Jefferson, at Mount Vernon, gave the President an earful of abuse of Hamilton such as he said he had refrained from uttering in print. Washington's offer to be mediator in calming the dispute went unheeded. The talk happened, unfortunately, before breakfast. Jefferson had just come from hearing colicky George Mason affirm that Hamilton had "done us more injury than Gr. Britain & all her fleets & armies." Jefferson was in the same heightened temper in blasting the "monarchical" party of which Schuyler and Hamilton were leaders. Washington brought him to earth with the statement that no such party existed in this country. Jefferson then shifted his anathemas to the funding system, and received a reply that would have been music in Hamilton's ears. The President agreed there were two views about it, but "for himself he had seen our affairs desperate & our credit lost, and . . . this was in a sudden & extraordinary degree raised to the highest pitch."

The newspaper war was wearing itself out by the close of 1792, but the fray found a new forum in Congress. Jefferson and Madison devised inquisitorial resolutions which were introduced in the House by Giles of Virginia early in February 1793. The investigation of Hamilton's conduct in the Treasury thus begun was intended to drive him from office. His foes believed that he could not answer the charges until a later session, and meantime would stand discredited. He replied with such speed and fullness of exhibits that the forced enquiry justified him. John Jay, who had had Hamilton's ardent support in his campaign for governor of New York, loyally wrote, "The thorns [your enemies] strew in yr way will hereafter Blossom, and furnish Garlands to decorate yr administration. Resolve not to be driven from yr station."

It is probable that Hamilton's letters of April 5 and 8, 1793, gave President Washington his earliest news that France had declared war on England, Russia, and Holland two months before. Hamilton assured Washington of the "universal and ardent" desire for a peaceful posture on the part of this country. He at once considered the rights, duties, and options of the United States as a neutral. Jefferson and Randolph identified the queries the President laid before the Cabinet meeting as Hamilton's work. It was agreed by all that a proclamation should issue "preventing interferences of the citizens of the United States in the war between France and Great Britain."

Anticipating contingencies—as the Secretary of State gave no evidence of doing—Hamilton had urged Chief Justice John Jay to draw a proclamation. Jay, on the point of leaving New York, hastily complied, but, pending further consideration of our obligations under the treaties with France, avoided use of the word "neutrality." Rufus King and others regretted the omission, since that was the whole sense of the proclamation.

In spite of Hamilton's urging of the proclamation, Jefferson declared that the New Yorker endangered the fact of neutrality by his pro-British behavior. "H. is panic-struck if we refuse our breach to every kick which Gr/ Brit. may chuse to give it . . . every inch of ground must be fought in our councils to desperation . . . to hold up the face of even a sneaking neutrality. . . . Some propositions have come from him which would astonish Mr. Pitt himself with their boldness."

Washington's Cabinet decided that the minister of republican France should be received. He was Edmond Charles Genêt, sent to displace Ternant, who had represented the executed Louis XVI. Young Genêt's flushed complexion was a sign of his fevered rashness. He landed at Charleston and, amid the applause of citizens of French extraction, immediately issued letters of marque to sail against allied shipping. The French consul then condemned and sold the first prize brought in. Hamilton called this "a dangerous commitment of our peace, without even the ceremony of previously feeling the pulse of our government." Genêt, who received the cheers of Democrats as he journeyed up the coast, did not present himself at the capital until he had been in this country a month. His mission from the Directory in France was to draw the United States into the war on the side of France, and he tried to start military operations by projecting attacks by Americans on East and West Florida and New Orleans. The President directed Jefferson to receive Genêt with courtesy, not cordiality. Jefferson thought the reserve was Hamilton's doing, but ere long he himself was calling the revolutionary envoy "Hot headed, all imagination, no judgment, passionate, disrespectful & even indecent towards the P[resident]." Alexander Dallas, secretary of the Commonwealth of Pennsylvania, expressed his Republican chagrin to Gallatin: "Every step that Genêt has taken seems a greater display of vanity than talents, and leaves us who love his cause to deplore that he was ever deputed to support it."

Hamilton was among those who described Genêt's direct collision with the federal government. The British brig *Little Sarah*, captured by *L'Ambuscade*, was brought to Philadelphia and renamed *Petit Démocrate*. The warden of the port informed Pennsylvania's Governor Mifflin that the prize was being fitted out for privateering with a crew of 120 and that her four guns had multiplied to fourteen and six swivels. This was against President Washington's orders to detain all privateers.

Mifflin sent Dallas, to request Genêt to suspend departure of the privateer. But Genêt would give no satisfactory assurance; he complained bitterly of his treatment by the authorities and crowned his career of errors by declaring that "he would appeal from the President to the people."

At this Mifflin forbade any pilot to take the vessel out, and drafted 120 militia, including artillerists, to prevent her departure if attempted. Next morning, Sunday, Jefferson tried his persuasion on Genêt with such satisfaction to himself that he induced Mifflin to countermand his forcible preparations. Genêt told Jefferson that *Démocrate* would not be ready for sea before the President returned from Mount Vernon. Jefferson reported this to Monday's Cabinet meeting. Hamilton and Knox were so little impressed that they urged the Governor— Jefferson dissenting—to set up a formidable battery on Mud Island.

Hamilton wrote out his reasons for mistrust. He said that Genêt had previously violated our neutrality and gone back on his own promises. His threat to go over the head of the President was an intolerable insult. We had pledged to the British minister that no more French privateers would be fitted out in American ports; to permit it would be to invite British retaliation. The French government was ill served by Genêt, and would not protest if this illegal marauder were sunk in attempting to escape. Jefferson gave contrary arguments. He believed that Genêt would hold the vessel for the forty-eight hours till the President's return. If not, she was ready to resist restraint; if we fired on her war would result. Better let her go and complain to France against the violation. He was suspicious of Britain and correspondingly admiring of France and her "most sacred cause that ever man was engaged in."

Before the battery on Mud Island was ready the *Petit Démocrate* dropped down the river to Chester, soon put to sea, and afterward took four prizes.

The clamors against American neutrality betokened the for-

mation of a French party which had a skeleton of organization
in the democratic societies fostered by Genêt. To counter these
cries Hamilton published his "Pacificus" papers in June and
July 1793. He often began by listing the arguments of his opponents, which he answered in his text. The President, in
whom the Constitution reposed relations with foreign powers,
had the right to issue the proclamation holding this country
aloof from the European war. We did not thereby abandon our
treaty obligations to France, except that we were released from
protecting the French West Indies because our alliance was
defensive and France was waging offensive war. Hamilton indulged some reflections on the "very favorite topic of gratitude
to France [for help in our Revolution] since it is at this shrine
that we are continually invited to sacrifice the true interests of
the country; as if 'all for love, and the world well lost,' were a
fundamental maxim in politics." The fact was that France did
not send military and naval assistance until the patriot army
had promised eventual victory by defeating the enemy at Saratoga. The French had their reward in seeing Britain deprived
of her best colonies. If we owed gratitude, it was to Louis XVI,
slain by those who now claimed our loyalty. Further, if we
embarked with France we could give her no aid proportional
to the injury we would do ourselves; anyhow, France could
not win against all the rest of Europe.

The sympathizers with France were embarrassed because
Genêt made an ass of himself. Jefferson could do without the
pointed thrusts of Hamilton. He sent the first numbers of "Pacificus" to Madison with his appeal: "Nobody answers him, &
his doctrines will therefore be taken for confessed. For God's
sake, my dear Sir, take up your pen, select the most striking
heresies and cut him to pieces in the face of the public. There
is nobody else who can & will enter the lists with him." Madison, thus assigned an arduous role which Jefferson himself
avoided, protested that he needed information to escape "vulnerable assertions" which would invite Hamilton to "trium-

phant replies." Jefferson several times obliged. Still Madison was plaintive: "I have forced myself into the task. . . . I find it the most grating one I have ever experienced." His "distaste to the subject" combined with "excessive lassitude from the excessive . . . heat." He submitted his first number of "Helvidius" for Jefferson's revision, and Jefferson must contrive to get it into Fenno's paper without the agency of either of them being discovered. Poor Madison, laboring under duress, could offer no better than a lackluster performance, so different from his convincing contributions to the *Federalist* when he was Hamilton's colleague, not his critic. The fact was that Madison wanted peace as much as Hamilton did, and Genêt's antics made pro-French argument untimely.

Vexed questions concerning the rights and duties of the United States under international law and our treaty obligations could not be got speedily to the courts, and for that reason Jefferson wanted the Justices of the Supreme Court to advise in advance on situations that might arise. President Washington was prevailed upon to make the reference. Hamilton thought such decisions belonged, when cases arose, to the executive, with the help of the Attorney General. Nevertheless, Hamilton propounded a score of queries, and Jefferson half as many, on which the Justices were requested to pass. They met and explained that they could not pronounce on hypothetical propositions. This was their correct position, but the variety and intricacy of the cases put to them must have compelled them to refuse the assignment. The many possible situations which Hamilton cited showed how intimately he was involved in preserving United States neutrality. His "No Jacobin" pieces in Philadelphia and New York papers in August 1793 were in the same behalf, though they were in the main too technical to attract readers.

Chief Justice John Jay and his brethren would not commit themselves unless and until an actual case came before them in their proper judicial capacity, but in the meantime working rules were required for guidance of collectors at the ports. The President, prompted by Hamilton, requested Cabinet members and the Attorney General to draw up the instructions. They were sent not only to the customs officers, but also to the state governors and the ministers of the belligerent powers. Hamilton's colleagues thought he leaned over backward to conform to our treaty with France, and so omitted one of his directions. Even so, good friends and, reportedly, the British minister, blamed the Secretary of the Treasury for Gallic leanings in the regulations.

Hamilton's "No Jacobin" pieces were discontinued because he was stricken with yellow fever. What with convalescence and a relapse, he was incapacitated for two months, September and October 1793. His two essays signed "Americanus," written in the further effort to keep this country at peace, appeared in January–February 1794. In them he deflated emotional pro-French appeals by coming down to cases. He showed in sober detail that the United States could be of no military aid to France, explaining that essential money from Holland would be sacrificed instantly we became the ally of her enemy. He also recited our lacks in all the other means of waging an unpopular war at a great distance.

Among the propaganda shrillings of the "Democratical Societies" fostered by Genêt in Philadelphia and numerous other towns was the warning that if France were subdued America would be the next to fall to the foes of liberty. Hamilton effectually removed this bugaboo; the allies would be too drained by worsting France to attack us, even if they had a motive for it. He exploded the excited claim that France was the champion of freedom in the world. He found the opposite in "the horrid and disgusting scenes which have been, and continue to be, acted." He perceived only "atrocious depravity in the most influential leaders of the revolution . . . among these, a Marat and a Robespierre, assassins still reeking with the blood of their fellow-citizens, monsters who . . . are predominant in influence as well as iniquity." If France should ultimately be victorious, "after wading through seas of blood," she might "find herself . . . the slave of some victorious Sylla, or Marius, or Caesar," an apt forecast of the event of a decade later when Napoleon placed the crown of emperor on his own head.

Hamilton scouted the parallel which his opponents drew between the French and American revolutions. Hamilton, as spokesman for the Federalists, viewed the French revolutionists much as most Americans a century and a quarter later looked on the Bolshevists in Russia who dissolved all social and moral ties and mocked religion. However, Hamilton hoped that France would one day come back to sanity, order, and progress.

Jefferson said of the split between Americans over the European war that "parties seem to have taken a very well defined form in this quarter. the old tories, joined by our merchants who trade on British capital, paper dealers, and the idle rich of the great commercial towns, are with the kings. all other descriptions with the French. the war has kindled & brought forward the two parties with an ardour which our own interests merely, could never excite."

In this contest the Federalist came off best. Hamilton's policies, domestic and foreign, were approved by President Washington. Jefferson left the Cabinet on the last day of December 1793. After Genêt's caprices Jefferson called his ambassadorial appointment "calamitous" and said he would "sink the republican interest" if the party did not abandon him. Jefferson's letter rehearsing the mischiefs of Genêt and requiring his recall had the benefit of contributions by Hamilton and Randolph. It was thoroughly discussed in Cabinet meetings, for it would be closely examined by friends of France in this country and her enemies abroad. (As it happened, the complaint against Genêt was to be transmitted to the Directory by the American minister to France, Gouverneur Morris, who was no more popular there than was his counterpart here). When it

came to the final draft, Hamilton objected to Jefferson calling
the cause of France that of liberty, and got the allusion
stricken. He was for publishing the letter to the people
forthwith. The President chimed in on this when Knox called
attention to a lampoon which placed King Washington on a
guillotine. Washington was, in Jefferson's words, "much inflamed; got into one of those passions when he cannot command himself; ran on much on the personal abuse which had
been bestowed on him; . . . that *by God* he had rather be in
his grave than in his present situation; that he would rather be
on his farm than to be made *Emperor of the world;* and yet . . .
they were charging him with wanting to be a King. That that
rascal Freneau sent him three of his papers every day, . . . an
impudent design to 'nsult him; he ended in this high tone."

The wish of Knox and some others to ship Genêt off
forthwith was rejected. Soon his party in France, the Giron-
dists, fell, and Fauchet, the minister sent to America by the
succeeding Jacobins, demanded Genêt's arrest and return,
which would have meant the guillotine. The administration
would not consent to this cruelty. Genêt married the daughter
of Governor Clinton, became an American citizen, and subsided into forty years of farming.

Chapter 15

ATTACKS ON CONDUCT
OF THE TREASURY

Hamilton's Republican foes, unsuccessful in their opposition to his political and fiscal policies, questioned his competence and integrity in the Treasury. William Branch Giles of Virginia, who made a specialty of fault-finding (later, within his own party), in the spring of 1792 moved for an investigation into the causes of St. Clair's defeat the year before by the Indians on the Wabash. The main culprit was William Duer, the army contractor, who was delinquent in furnishing supplies. St. Clair himself was unskillful, but he was also the victim of others' errors. The inquiry was only a glancing blow at Hamilton, who readily showed that the Treasury had been prompt in responding to calls when made. Hamilton's regret was that when the western settlers were complaining of the excise on their whiskey the government did not protect them against Indian attacks.

Frontal assaults on Hamilton erupted in Senate and House in the winter of 1792–93. The principal charge was that he had ignored the laws authorizing two foreign loans in August 1790, the first for $10 million for payment of the foreign debt, the second for $2 million for reduction of the domestic debt. Other accusations, with increased insinuations of dishonesty, proliferated. The Senate was quickly satisfied on the score of loans, surplus revenue, and bank deposits, but not so the House. There Giles moved five resolutions requiring a display of Treasury operations from the commencement virtually to the date of the demand. The first two resolves requested the President to report the authority for application of the funds borrowed and particulars of payments on foreign debts. The third directed the Secretary to exhibit all dealings of the Treasury with the Bank of the United States. The fourth would lay bare operations of the sinking fund. The fifth concerned unapplied revenues.

Giles supported his resolutions with a speech to which the House agreed, doubtless without understanding the accounting details. Giles was pained because the more he studied Hamilton's financial statements, the more he was confused. He suspected irregularities in the Secretary's conduct. If he was proved mistaken, he would acknowledge his error—a promise which he did not keep.

The most damaging charge was that, according to Giles, $1,554,853 "which ought to be in the Treasury" was unaccounted for. Also the government had paid as much as 17 per cent on borrowings from the Bank of the United States. Bank loans were taken out when sums larger than the loans were on deposit in the bank. How was it that large sums were drawn from loans abroad for purchase of the domestic debt when the sinking fund was always overflowing from domestic sources?

Giles had been dangerously specific with his injurious allegations. If his animus had not so prodded him he might have realized that Hamilton would be able to offer simple and convincing explanations of what Giles paraded as gross mismanagement, if not massive thefts. Having been so impugned, Hamilton felt at liberty to resent the implied accusations which he was disproving. As far as possible without halting the regular work of his department, the Secretary and members of his staff devoted their time to collecting the many and various materials required. He submitted his exhibits in a series, beginning ten days after the demand was addressed to him, and he completed the whole a fortnight later; all reached the House between February 4 and 19, 1793. This was an arduous labor, corresponding to the studied detail which Giles had stipulated. The only omissions in Hamilton's reports were those of which his inquisitor had not taken account, namely the transactions of the Treasury which needed time for completion, including the long credits, up to two years, for payments by importers on their customs bonds. For these Hamilton made the best estimates he could; otherwise he reported down to the last penny.

Besides misunderstanding Hamilton's figures, his critics failed to comprehend economies in administration of the Treasury which the Secretary could and did use. Most of these were of his own devising, others were made highly desirable, indeed all but necessary, on the advice of the bankers in Europe through whom he negotiated loans. Members of the Congress, including some Federalists, cherished the illusion that as legislators, if they chose, they could completely plan fiscal operations without assistance from the head of the Treasury. They conceived that it was demeaning to rely on the Secretary to originate proposals. He should be confined to obeying orders, to being no more than a superior clerk and record keeper. In this the legislators disregarded their own law which had created the office of Secretary of the Treasury, for that statute charged him with offering advice, propounding solutions to problems.

The notion that a considerable body of men, even a large committee, of unspecialized abilities could hatch wise schemes of public finance—taxes, for example—in any detail was fatuous. The legislators forgot their own former failures, which had dictated reposing responsibility in the hands of one capable Financier, Robert Morris.

As to the loans authorized in August 1790, the bankers in Holland had urged that they be floated without distinction of purpose on the part of the American government. The lenders were not accustomed to judging the object of a loan, but rather relied on the credit of the borrower. The lenders were men of habit who did not like novelty. Also, if the loans were made on both acts indiscriminately, they could be applied as circumstances rendered advisable. So long as monies were disbursed as stipulated by law, the source in this instance did not matter.

Giles's suggestion that Hamilton had mislaid $1,554,853 was "one tissue of error." Had Giles been attentive to the Treasury reports he would not have supposed any such thing. Or, though Hamilton did not say this, if Giles had really been seeking clarity rather than wanting to throw out a reproach, he could have spoken to Hamilton personally and been immediately satisfied. Anyhow, Hamilton pointed out that of the proceeds of foreign bills, $632,132.02 remained to be received. Second, the Bank of the United States and two of its branches had, from sales of Amsterdam bills, $605,883.08 yet to be carried to the Treasurer's cash account. Third, a large sum in import duties, as allowed by law, was outstanding in bonds, had never come into the Treasury. Thus the imagined vanished income had not been received, though how it arose and where it was, on its way to the Treasury, was evident in the exhibits if rightly noted.

The bother of the House about suspected misapplication of the loans of August 1790 was as readily dispelled. The law to incorporate the Bank of the United States authorized the government to subscribe $2 million to its stock, this payment to come from either of the August loans. At the same time the bank was to loan an identical amount to the government.

Hamilton observed that "nothing could have been more useless . . . than actually to draw from Europe out of the monies borrowed there, the sum necessary for the payment of the subscription to the Bank, and again to remit out of the loan, which was to be obtained of the Bank, a sufficient sum to replace such monies . . . destined for the foreign object." Such a criss-cross of monies over the Atlantic would have involved risk, loss of interest, and loss of time in applying the funds to useful purpose. Consequently, Hamilton proposed and the Bank agreed to "a merely formal [bookkeeping] arrangement," by which "in fact, no monies were either withdrawn from, or returned to [the foreign] fund." The law was complied with, Treasury procedure was followed, and the whole transaction was of record.

By intensive industry Hamilton had answered all of the queries of the House within a few weeks. This defeated the expectation of his prosecutors that he would be unable to respond before adjournment, and thus would rest for months under the imputation of wrongdoing. However, Hamilton's explicit answers to Giles's charges could not satisfy Jefferson, who thought that more could be made of Hamilton's alleged mismanagement. He drafted another set of resolutions raking Hamilton fore and aft, most of which Giles introduced in the House on the very eve of adjournment. However, Giles had the grace to reduce Jefferson's harshest censures. He did not call on the President to remove Hamilton from office; he was content with having his new set of accusations referred to the President. Giles did declare that Hamilton had been guilty of an indecorum toward the House in judging of its motives in demanding information.

Later Jefferson recorded that the effort to discredit Hamilton could not succeed because two-thirds of the members of the House were bank directors and stockjobbers. Jefferson, who complained that Hamilton poached on his preserves in the State Department, had endeavored, through Giles, to see his

Cabinet colleague dismissed in disgrace. Fauchet, the French minister, who was sympathetic with the Republicans, admitted that the "useless inquiry of [Hamilton's] enemies . . . proved . . . abortive." Hammond, the British minister, of contrary temper, was glad of Hamilton's "complete triumph."

At the very moment that Hamilton was being belabored in Congress, his conduct of the Treasury was winning praise in Holland. On June 1, 1793, the United States had to pay one million florins on principal and 470,000 interest on its loan in Amsterdam. The bankers saw no prospect of securing these sums by a fresh loan even at higher interest, since France had declared war on England and Holland. They passed their alarms to Short, who relayed them to Hamilton. As the fatal date approached when the credit of the United States would be damaged unless funds were in hand, the loyal bankers devised emergency measures: the existing loan could be extended, and the bankers would advance the interest from their own resources. This was April 27. Two days later the bankers were completely relieved by a letter from Hamilton, written March 15. He freed funds (495,000 guilders) in their hands by borrowing the amount from the Bank of the United States. By the packet sailing March 3 he had remitted 970,000 guilders in bills on London and Amsterdam. In addition was Robert Morris's bill on a London house at sixty days' sight for £12,096.15 sterling.

The Treasury's bankers in Amsterdam knew how to appreciate the "Exertions on your part, not only active and praiseworthy in the extreme, but likewise beyond what we could have . . . supposed probable . . . Intelligence of your Remittances coming forward at such a crisis . . . tended to raise an high Idea here, of the Credit and Resources of your Country, and of the Judicious management of them." After three years of Treasury operation from a discouraging start, and only two years of life of the Bank of the United States, Hamilton was able to command large sums in America to satisfy distant creditors. It would not have been amiss if the encomium of the Amsterdam bankers had been broadcast to the Secretary's Republican critics at home. The only excuse for his critics' partisan malice is that they did not know whom they were assailing.

The renewal of the attack on the Secretary of the Treasury provoked a sharp debate. William L. Smith, of South Carolina, who had been Hamilton's mouthpiece in Congress when funding was on the carpet, led with a speech Hamilton had prepared for him. He insisted that the first two resolutions and the last should be eliminated, not referred to the Committee of the Whole for discussion. The opening pair were too general; they admitted of exceptions. The last, sending the censures to the President, was intended "to remove the Secretary from office" unheard. William Vans Murray condemned the "unhandsome proceeding" by which the Secretary was meant to be condemned at the tag end of the session (only three days before adjournment) when he could not possibly answer. The objections to three of Giles's thrusts were upheld.

Robert Barnwell, South Carolina Federalist, observed that Giles was in retreat; his indictment had changed in hue "from the foul stain of peculation to the milder coloring of an illegal exercise of discretion, and a want of politeness in the Secretary." Barnwell approved Hamilton's use of discretion. We owed interest abroad, to be paid from domestic revenues. We had borrowed abroad to pay principal of the French debt. Unexpectedly the chance arose to discharge part of this debt by sending provisions to the French colonists in Santo Domingo, who were in distress because of the rebellion under Toussaint. Therefore Hamilton expeditiously paid principal with interest money here and interest with principal money there.

William Findley of western Pennsylvania, who had opposed Hamilton's measures all along, was now more than ever abrasive because he shared the frontiersmen's grievances against the whiskey excise. Findley hit at Hamilton's "self-important

plans" that were not born in any direction of Congress; in fact
the Secretary's presumption partook "of the nature of treason." Findley was embarrassed when he had to admit that he
had not examined the Treasury exhibits with which Hamilton
replied to Giles's former resolutions. Findley's speech stood as
a tirade. Giles spoke next; his address was considerably toned
down from his original charges. He hoped the justice of the
committee toward Hamilton would be tempered with mercy.
Mercer of Maryland, like Findley, had attended little to Hamilton's replies, but was sure he was corrupt. He went further; he
blamed the President for not keeping a tighter rein on the Secretary of the Treasury.

A battery of Hamilton's friends came next—Livermore of
New Hampshire, Hillhouse of Connecticut, Sedgwick of Massachusetts, and the ever faithful Boudinot of New Jersey. Madison, a fomenter of the attack on Hamilton, could not let
smaller fry be the only backers of the indictment. Though he
was shaky on Hamilton's accounts, he was positive that the
Secretary had diverted funds contrary to the will of Congress.
But Madison did not score; he was too intelligent to believe
that Hamilton's fault was more than nominal. Fisher Ames
took it that Hamilton was vindicated, and so begged for restoration of harmony. This did not suit the fiery Findley, who
repeated the by now familiar charge that Hamilton had robbed
our friends the French in order to enrich the Bourbon Bank of
the United States. Boudinot, evidently munitioned by Hamilton, wound up the debate with a stock of facts and figures. He
urged that his protégé deserved "the thankful approbation of
his country for his . . . strict attention to the true interests and
credit of the United States."

The Committee of the Whole disapproved all the resolutions
accusing Hamilton. In a night meeting held on March 1—
Congress was to adjourn next day—the House itself dismissed
one resolve after another, three to one, two to one, four to one,
five to one. On the last vote of censure even Findley deserted

his fellow Republicans. Only five in the House, including Giles and Madison, voted for all six of the impeachments.

Hamilton's vindication did not silence his critics. John Taylor of Caroline, a scribe of the Virginia Republican junto, promptly published a pamphlet repeating the arraignments of the Secretary of the Treasury as though they had not been elaborately answered. Hamilton and the Bank of the United States, he complained, were in collusion, each serving the other. The bank, "capable . . . of polluting every operation of the government," should be disestablished. The Treasury should be reformed in all its parts. Hamilton had been cleared in the recent probe only because his corrupt corps of supporters prevailed in making a hasty decision on the evidence; many who had not had time to penetrate the obscure exhibits chose to give the accused Secretary the benefit of the doubt. Others besides Taylor kept up the clamor.

Hamilton was unwilling to leave the verdict of his innocence anywise in doubt. In December 1793 he requested of the House "a new inquiry . . . without delay," and the more thorough the better. Giles would oblige. He moved for investigation of the Treasury generally, under headings from bookkeeping to sinking fund. Federalists were for rejecting Giles's motion out of hand, since the whole matter had been gone into and concluded. Page of Virginia gave the sufficient answer to that: the Secretary himself demanded the additional probe. A committee of fifteen was named, with Abraham Baldwin of Georgia, a notable Republican, as chairman and, of course, Giles a member. Hamilton said of the composition of the committee that a majority were "either my decided political enemies or inclined against me," while no member friendly to him had the knowledge of public affairs to counteract his opponents.

The committee required comprehensive records of Treasury operations from the beginning of the government, and its report in late May was composed chiefly of these. The old, scarcely concealed charges of peculation against Hamilton were flatly contradicted: "The Secretary of the Treasury, or any other officer of the Department, besides the Treasurer, never has the possession or custody of any part of the public moneys. . . . All warrants for the payment of money . . . are first signed by him [but] subject . . . to the check of the Comptroller . . . and to the further check . . . by the Auditor."

Hamilton inquired of the investigating committee whether they expected him to produce authority from the President to draw into this country proceeds of the Dutch loans of August 1790. The only question, he thought, was not of authority, but whether he had acted legally. The committee rejected this view. Hamilton answered that all public money could be taken into the Treasury and be issued for legal purposes without special authority. Still, since it was the President who had been empowered to make the loans, the Secretary had regularly sought his approval for drawings, which was usually given orally, though sometimes it came by letter when the Chief Executive was absent from the capital. The inquisitors insisted that Hamilton produce the President's sanction for each draft on the borrowed funds. Washington replied in much the same words Hamilton had used: "I cannot charge my memory," he said, "with all the particulars which have passed between us, relative to the disposition of the money borrowed." Aside from the letters, which spoke for themselves, the President did not doubt that his oral approval of measures were what Hamilton reported, always "upon the condition, that what was to be done by you, should be agreeable to the laws."

Hamilton should have been satisfied with this, but he was smarting under what he considered persecution, and he begged the President for more incontestable support. Could Hamilton, in "a full conference," recall to the President's mind all of the circumstances? Washington made no reply, but Hamilton need not have been troubled, for the committee was not interested in the supposed mandate of Congress that the two loans be handled in all respects separately. The committee gave the Secretary a clean bill of health. They were "satisfied that no moneys of the United States, whether before or after they have passed to the credit of the Treasurer, have ever been, directly or indirectly, used for, or applied to any purposes, but those of the Government, *except*, so far as all moneys deposited in a bank are concerned in the general operations thereof." Hamilton understood that this exculpation was unanimous.

With many persons preferring claims to the Treasury it was inevitable that some who were disappointed would allege that the Secretary was putting in his own pocket the money due them. These disgruntled, suspicious ones were apt to take their supposed grievances to Hamilton's known opponents. This was the case with Andrew G. Fraunces, a clerk discharged from the Treasury.

He took pains to make sure that John Beckley, Clerk of the House and a Virginia marplot, was informed of evidence that Hamilton and Duer had been partners in speculation. Fraunces, said even by Beckley to be a man of bad habits, put his charges against Hamilton in a pamphlet, appealing to the President and to the House. A committee of the House approved Hamilton's rejection of Fraunces' claim and said that the Secretary "acted a meritorious part toward the public." Another claimant was John F. Mercer of Maryland, who wanted compensation of a few hundred dollars for horses shot under him in the war. In one way and another Mercer aired allegations that Hamilton had favoured Duer and other paper men. Hamilton replied with heat. For a time it looked as though a duel would be the result, but the tiresome exchanges petered out.

Hamilton was in the midst of refuting charges against his conduct of the Treasury when, in early September 1793, he was stricken with yellow fever, then raging in Philadelphia.

Some said the contagion, beginning at the waterfront, was from coffee rotting on the wharves. Governor Mifflin, a politician, not a physician, propagated the certainty that the plague was brought to Philadelphia by refugees from San Domingo or other immigrants. Between mid-August and late November, 4000 persons died, most of them from yellow fever. Dispute over the source of the scourge was less important than differences over the proper method of treatment. Dr. Benjamin Rush, the most prominent medical man in the city, acted on the conviction that since the seat of the infection was in the "abdominal viscera, . . . their seculent corruptible contents [must be] discharged" by heroic purges (30 grains of calomel, 45 of jalap in three doses) even when the pulse could hardly be felt. After four or five evacuations, draw 8 or 10 ounces of blood from the arm. When fever subsided, resume the purges and ply the lancet.

Hamilton had the benefit of the contrary ministrations of Dr. Edward Stevens, his old friend from boyhood in St. Croix. On invitation of Dr. John Redman, president of the College of Physicians, Dr. Stevens published a long letter explaining his method. As the disease was debilitating, remedies should be "cordial, stimulating, and tonic." Thus it is known how Hamilton and his wife, who promptly also came down with the sickness, were cured. In its onset the disease was combated by rest, a full diet with old Madeira wine, cold baths, followed by brandy burnt with cinnamon; at night a gentle opiate combined with a few grains of volatile salts and a "grateful aromatic." Each day the patient was given a few doses of bark (quinine); vomiting was relieved by an infusion of camomile flowers, and small doses of a cordial mixture of oil of peppermint and spirits of lavender. The patient's mind must be kept serene; weakening evacuations were avoided.

When the Hamiltons recovered—by means, they believed, of Dr. Stevens's restorative treatment—they set out for the Schuylers' home at Albany. Their five children, the youngest only a year old, had escaped the disease; they had been whisked off to their grandparents earlier. The mayor and common council of Albany made no protest against these healthy youngsters entering the town, but took alarm at the approach of the ex-patients. General Schuyler was summoned to two meetings with officials to hear the precautions demanded. He agreed that the convalescents should stop at Greenbush on the east side of the Hudson and there be visited by the several physicians of Albany. If they were found free of the "putrid fever" their clothes should be burned, and they should don fresh garments from the Schuylers' home; then they could come on in an open carriage without servants or baggage. They would be quarantined in the Schuyler house, with guards posted at Schuyler's expense. General Schuyler was outraged at a rumor set afloat that when he embraced his daughter he clapped a vinegar-soaked sponge to his mouth and directly afterward left the room to wash his face and rinse his mouth.

At the Treasury in Philadelphia, Oliver Wolcott, Jr., the Comptroller, had taken over those of Hamilton's duties which had to be performed, but soon he too fled to a safe distance up the Schuylkill, leaving only two or three clerks in charge of the office, which was in a low place, "surrounded with infectious air, sickness and Death." As soon as he was well again Hamilton lost no time in returning to duty. He picked up four clerks in New York, considered resuming business in emergency quarters in Trenton, but accepted Robert Morris's invitation to be his guest at "The Hills" in the country outside Philadelphia. Hamilton was still ailing, but he answered the President's calls for advice on several counts. Among other services, he drew up parts of the President's speech at the opening of Congress. Hamilton thought it safe for the legislature to convene in Philadelphia, but, knowing the lingering terror of the place so recently in grip of the plague, suggested that Germantown would be a convenient way station to the capital.

Chapter 16

"WHISKEY BOYS"

Alexander Hamilton rarely had so many demands made upon him as he did in the autumn of 1794, when the "Whiskey Insurrection," which had broken out in the western counties of Pennsylvania, had to be suppressed. Most inappropriately, Henry Knox, the Secretary of War, was absent in Maine on his private affairs, so Hamilton administered that department when at its busiest. The Treasury, beside its usual work, had to provide funds in numerous quarters for the punitive expedition. Just at this time the government was perplexed to defend its neutral position in the war in Europe, for privateers of both main belligerents were illegally bringing their prizes into United States ports and vessels were surreptitiously fitting out for warlike cruising. These violations required directions to customs officials, and to make matters worse, the Attorney General, William Bradford, was out of reach on the frontier, where he was on the President's commission to argue the insurgents into obedience.

Governor Mifflin of Pennsylvania, at first obstructionist in the plans to discipline the lawbreakers of the transmontaine district of his state, had come round to recruiting the hither militia, but his lingering doubts were yet to be dispelled. This necessitated a tactful but firm correspondence in which Hamilton, who was alone possessed of the facts, wrote for Randolph, the Secretary of State. Mifflin for years back had been, off and on, critical of Washington. Relations of the national government with his offending province were not improved when his habitual drunkenness—now in forenoons, too—passed his authority to Alexander J. Dallas, his decidedly Republican secretary of state, who became the Governor's eager spokesman. This friction was barely below the surface.

As western resistance to the excise waned in the Carolinas, Virginia, and Maryland, it persisted and climaxed in the four frontier counties of Pennsylvania. Those who afterward loudly charged that Hamilton welcomed the opportunity to flex national muscles against a dissident locality did him a patent injustice. He had tried by every means to avoid physical coercion. He had recommended successive revisions of the excise laws in order to accommodate their administration, as far as possible, to the convenience of the objecting distillers. He had promoted the President's early proclamation against the disorders, and he had encouraged the dispatch of national and state agents to the troubled area to persuade the rebels to compliance. His final resolve to crush the uprising by an overwhelming march of 15,000 militia from four states was as thorough as the need for it was regrettable. The action had to produce not only outward quiet and cessation of overt acts against revenue officers, but also conditions permitting unquestioned efficient collection of the excise taxes in a district long accustomed to flouting the laws. This involved the corralling of suspected offenders for trial in eastern courts. Hamilton personally supervised these arrests in the centers of violence, which cast him more than ever in the role of punisher. His critics passed lightly over the fact that as Secretary of the Treasury he was responsible for collection of the national revenue under laws to which the great majority of distillers had dutifully conformed; they had already paid a million dollars in excise taxes. Hamilton had to be certain that correction was complete, that offices of inspection could be opened and maintained peaceably, and that names signed to submission papers would be followed by orderly payments into the Treasury.

Those who took out their chagrin at the success of the military expedition in clamors against the political motive of the Secretary were not deterred by the visible sanction of President Washington, who led the militia army to the foot of the western mountains. If anything, the President's subsequent condemnation, in his address to Congress, of the "democratical societies" which he blamed for the turmoil, made the outcries shrill against him personally.

Hamilton had to direct the forwarding to points of rendezvous the arms, ammunition, clothing food, forage, straw, tents, and all other camp equipment that would be needed by the various militia units. Some of the arms came from as far away as New London, Connecticut. This required correspondence with the governors, their military subordinates, and federal quartermasters and commissaries. He was mounting the concentration of more men than had marched at any one time during the Revolution, unless it was for the siege of Yorktown. With the designation of intermediate stations, the Virginia and Maryland contingents were to rendezvous at Cumberland, Maryland; the Pennsylvania and New Jersey militia would meet at Carlisle, Pennsylvania. Hamilton readily secured authority to increase the force to the total of 15,000 by the addition of 1500 men not at first contemplated. He stressed to the governors of Virginia and Maryland the President's design that the enlarged force should contain particularly formidable troops. Thus, to Governor Henry Lee he recommended that "as many . . . as possible may be drawn from places near the scene of action and may be riflemen. It is represented that the insurgents are impressed with more respect for a force of that kind and from that quarter, than for any other, which they expect to come against them. General [Daniel] Morgan whom it is understood to be your intention to employ can . . . be very useful in carrying this particular object into effect." This would be curing the bite with the hair of the dog.

Trustworthy participants afterward judged that a smaller army penetrating the disturbed region would have hazarded defeat—the worst possible consequence, against which Hamilton guarded all along. With the burden on the Treasury acutely in mind, he also guarded against needless expense. "Too much depends upon the event," he declared, "not to give . . . a vigorous support to the undertaking. Yet a just economy is always precious in public operations. The one in train will involve no trifling bill of Cost with the utmost possible care." As the number of men to be fed was so large, the contractors should provide rations at lowered price, otherwise they should buy on commission.

The western distillers justified their defiance of the excise with several complaints. Most serious was that, since they were distant from the eastern population, whiskey was their only product sufficiently valuable in small compass to bear the cost of transport by packhorse over the mountains. When they shipped their grain, hides, and other bulky commodities by flatboat down the Ohio and Mississippi to be loaded on coasting vessels for eastern ports they met with difficulties at the hands of the Spaniards at New Orleans. The westerners believed that these obstacles interposed in Spanish territory were tolerated by the national government in return for fishing rights granted to New Englanders and other easterners. Besides, the exit for gross articles by water was long-drawn, costly, and toilsome. Grain could be turned into whiskey; worth fifty cents a gallon west of the mountains, it could be carried east, two kegs to a packhorse, and sold in Lancaster or Reading for a dollar a gallon. The tax reduced this profit and limited by that much the iron, tar, and other manufactures which must be obtained in the east.

There was little currency in circulation in the over-mountain district with which to pay the excise. In new and primitive settlements exchanges were commonly made by means of barter. The western pioneers were conquering a wilderness by their own efforts, and they felt that the national government did nothing to serve them. The expeditions of General Harmar and St. Clair (1790 and 1792) against the Indians had met with failure; the tribes, munitioned by the British who still held the western posts, continued to terrorize the lonely clearings. Thus isolated and self-dependent, the westerners, suspicious of the national authority anyhow, became positively hostile under the coaxing of Citizen Genêt, who found them responsive to the pro-French democratic societies he fostered.

The most fallacious grievance, but one regularly put forward against an excise, was that government inspectors invaded private premises. Anticipating this charge, which was susceptible of all sorts of elaboration, Hamilton had stipulated that all buildings or parts of houses devoted to distilling should be plainly marked as such and be accessible to the revenue officers without entering living quarters. However, rumors of illegal entry were rife in sparsely settled communities, and means of correcting their falsity were lacking.

While Hamilton sternly condemned resistance to the law, especially the menaces against officers of the revenue, he genuinely pitied the ignorance and poverty of the body of insurgents. Many were illiterates, men who were unable to keep and render accounts even had they wished to do so. He was patient for several years of slim collections while he adjusted the excise to local convenience, hoping that opposition would diminish. But he found that his concessions were taken as evidence of weakness and retreat on the part of government. Distillers who complied with the law were looked on as traitors to demands of the defiant majority. "Tom the Tinker" (supposed to be one John Holcroft), in messages posted on trees and in letters to the Pittsburgh newspaper, threatened to destroy the stills of law-abiding neighbors. "Tom" published widely the names of those who failed to rally to attacks on officers and others held to be public enemies. While some distillers, in spite of well founded fears, continued to obey the law, there was no organized local counterpoise to the insurgents.

Hamilton scorned the few men of education and position in the district who encouraged or actually led the riotous mobs. One who later had the frankness to admit his error was Albert Gallatin. He had served as secretary of a protest meeting at Pittsburgh in August 1792 and, Hamilton believed, had written the defiant resolves adopted there. From that day forth Hamilton regarded Gallatin with bitter distaste. Hamilton pointed out, especially in newspaper pieces in 1794 signed "Tully," that it was perfectly right to urge the repeal or modification of a law held objectionable, but obstruction of the law while it was in existence was criminal. This was the offense which Gallatin and many others had committed.

As ground for meeting force with force, Hamilton prepared for the President a narrative of resistance to the excise in the four western counties of Pennsylvania. No sooner had the laws been passed than talk against them was rife, and compliance was discouraged by exciting public opinion against them. Other measures of government, such as funding, bank, and the salaries allowed to members of Congress, were similarly condemned in a spirit that showed opposition to the national authority, however manifested. These denunciations soon took on organized form in associations which refused to list stills for the taxes and in meetings which published resolves to hold all officers of the revenue in contempt and, of course, to lend them no aid of any sort. The next step was violence. "A party of men armed and disguised way-laid [Robert Johnson, a collector of the revenue] at a place on Pidgeon Creek in Washington county—seized tarred and feathered him cut off his hair and deprived him of his horse, obliging him to travel on foot a considerable distance in that mortifying and painful situation." The deputy marshal who was sent to serve processes against three accused in this attack "was seized whipped tarred & feathered, and after having his money & horse taken from him was blind folded and tied in the woods, in which condition he remained for five hours." A poor fellow named Wilson, "manifestly disordered in his intellects," who represented himself as a revenue officer, was worse treated. A party in disguise took him from his bed, carried him some miles to a blacksmith shop, stripped him of his clothes, burned him with a hot iron, tarred and feathered him, and at daylight dismissed him in this suffering state.

Not only officers, but private citizens who obeyed the law or spoke in its behalf were objects of assault. Modifications of the excise in supplemental legislation did not mollify the opposition. The property of complying distillers was destroyed and the victims were compelled to publish their losses and promise not to pay the taxes again. Serving processes against those accused in these attacks, the United States marshal, accompanied by General John Neville, the inspector of the district, was fired upon as the sequel to other menaces. Next day the house of the inspector near Pittsburgh was assailed by a hundred men, most of them with firearms, others with clubs. Though alone, the inspector, well provided with weapons and ammunition, beat them off. His prompt request for protection brought the reply from judges and militia officers that the law was too unpopular to be executed; the *posse comitatus,* if called out, would consist mostly of violators. The inspector, thus abandoned, did secure eleven soldiers from the fort at Pittsburgh. And none too soon, for the mob that quickly hove in sight had grown to five hundred. The inspector was obliged to escape by the back way. After brisk firing against the house and from within, the soldiers surrendered when outbuildings were set on fire, then the house itself was consumed.

The marshal and General Neville's son were made prisoners on their way to the scene of the fight. The marshal was repeatedly threatened with death, and was obliged to promise to serve no more processes to the west of the mountains. He and the inspector made their way to Philadelphia by a circuitous route to avoid the insurgents.

Hamilton's catalogue of violence against the excise was made too soon to include the muster of some thousands of militiamen from the western counties (August 1, 1794) on the field where Braddock had been defeated. David Bradford, of Washington County, though a deputy attorney general of the state, called himself the "general" of this impromptu force. He flourished about on horseback, urging the tipsy men to follow him in an attack on the near-by log town of Pittsburgh. The eastbound mail from that place had recently been robbed, disclosing letters of prominent citizens appealing to the national government to suppress the riots. The threat to burn Pittsburgh fetched Hugh H. Brackenridge and others to the bellicose camp. They professed sympathy with the insurgents, but discouraged the invasion. They succeeded in reducing the march next day to fewer members who contented themselves with burning a barn; before their mood became more dangerous they consented to be rowed across the Monongahela, and thence they stumbled home.

Hamilton accompanied the punitive expedition because, as the proposer, he ought to share the dangers into which his fellow citizens were brought. The President was entirely agreeable. Hamilton, pointing out that General Knox would have returned to the War Department, and that the Treasury was left in the competent hands of Oliver Wolcott, Jr., bought a horse ("easy gates of some blood"), transacted business until the last moment, and set out with the President in mid-morning of September 30, 1794, for Carlisle. There Washington took command of the 3000 early arrivals of Pennsylvania and New Jersey militia. The President was accompanied by his private secretary, Bartholomew Dandridge, who, however, had little to do since Alexander Hamilton, the super aide, was at hand. As always, when occasion offered Hamilton anticipated the President's wishes, supplied him with the information he needed, and wrote letters and orders at his direction. In this instance Hamilton had an original and intimate concern in the success of the march, and he contributed to it in every way to be expected of the head of the Treasury, besides acting in a semi-military capacity under the Commander in Chief.

Hamilton had an early opportunity to give counsel when the President was visited at Carlisle by commissioners from the western counties, William Findley and David Redick. They bore resolutions of a recent meeting at Parkinson's Ferry, representing to the President and to Governor Mifflin that their neighbors were prepared to submit to the laws and hence the expedition was no longer required. With Washington were Governor Richard Howell of New Jersey, Hamilton, and Dandridge. Governor Mifflin was invited, but he declined from press of business. The President described the meeting at length in his diary. He promised to listen with patience and candor to what they were deputed to report. "Mr. Findley began . . . viz That the People in the parts where he was best acquainted, had seen their folly, and he believed were disposed to submit to the Laws; that he thought, but could not undertake to be responsible, for the reestablishment of the public Offices for the collection of the Taxes of distilled spirits and Stills—intimating however, that it might be best for *the present*, and until the peoples minds were a little more tranquilized, to hold the Office of Inspection at Pittsburgh under the protection . . . of the Garrison . . . That the Civilian authority was beginning to recover its tone." Redick spoke to similar effect, except that he exaggerated by claiming that only one person—perhaps one of consequence, he meant—had refused to take advantage of the offered amnesty by signing a submission paper.

To these partial assurances or pleas Washington replied that only after the western people had been deaf to the government's earnest wish by mild means to bring them to a sense of their duty had coercion been reluctantly resorted to. In the absence of "unequivocal *proofs* of absolute submission" the march would proceed. The mission of the army was not to be executioner under military law, but to support the civil magistrates in trying offenders. It is known that Hamilton, particularly, brought the ambassadors from the west down to cases. Could offices of inspection in the four counties be opened with impunity? Could they be conducted without obstruction? And could the taxes be certainly collected? The Secretary of the Treasury would be satisfied by nothing less than the certain prospect of payments into the revenue as commanded by the laws. Hamilton's influence on the President to this end may be taken for granted. He wrote Washington's "public letter" to Attorney General Randolph covering the interview with the emissaries of the partially chastened insurgents. Washington wrote privately to Randolph, "I believe they [the rebels] are scared."

Findley thought he spoke for most observers when he said that Hamilton "gave the supreme direction to the measures that were pursued" in suppressing the insurrection. His "paramount influence" in military arrangements for the march was less blamed than was his zeal for accusing and arresting suspects. "While the President was with the different wings of the army, the secretary accompanied him, and appeared to act as his official secretary."

Amongst what Hamilton wrote for the President at Carlisle, and as he led the march to Cumberland, were important admonitions to Mifflin and orders to Governor Henry Lee of Virginia. Mifflin was told of Washington's deep regret that two soldiers had met violent deaths, and he was exhorted to exert himself to prevent the like in future, since the army marched to enforce the laws, not to break them. The orders to

Lee were to take command when Washington left to meet
Congress. They outlined what Lee should do if he met physical opposition in the troubled counties and stressed support of
the magistrates who would hear evidence against notorious offenders. To expedite the latter, District Judge Richard Peters
and District Attorney William Rawle accompanied the expedition. Washington was put out when he learned that Judge Peters, in his zeal, had arrested two of the accused before the
army reached the center of the disturbances. It would now be
harder to bag the leaders since they were now warned to flee
the country. Hamilton did not flinch from the distasteful task
of rounding up chief opponents of the law in what had become submissive communities. He urged that those who had
made off to escape punishment should be outlawed and their
property should escheat to government.

The temper of the punitive army, always dutiful toward its
object of vindicating national authority, was helped by the
swift conversion of Mifflin and his alter ego, Alexander J. Dallas. Mifflin, commanding the Pennsylvania militia, had earlier
been reluctant to discipline his western citizens, but when he
was told that militia near the mountains would not respond to
the call he toured the eastern and middle counties with such
effect that he was complimented by Washington and by Congress. Dallas, previously obstructionist, went on the expedition as paymaster of the Pennsylvania troops. With every
westward step he increased his blame of Gallatin, Findley, and
Smilie, his former allies. He believed they would escape the
law, but that they were "inconceivably obnoxious as the original perpetrators of the doctrines which have . . . produced
these violences." As to the dupes of the culpable leaders,
"Nothing but fear and coercion . . . will ensure their submission." That Mifflin and Dallas became firm endorsers of the
expedition was sufficient answer to critics who complained
that Hamilton had promoted the march to aggrandize the
power of the national government.

After the President and Hamilton rode from Bedford, Pennsylvania, to Williamsport and Cumberland, Maryland, to survey the southern wing, they returned to the northern wing at Bedford. From there Washington posted back in his carriage to Philadelphia for the assembling of Congress. Hamilton continued to keep the President informed of progress across the mountains, and he received encouragement to net miscreants who were fit objects of punishment. Hamilton by direction opened all public letters for the President, and he turned over those which dealt with the military to Governor Lee, now in command. The march over the mountains, made slower by heavy rains for days on end, took four weeks. Hamilton early determined that a competent force must be stationed at Pittsburgh after the army quit the scene of insurrection. He urged that Congress should authorize for this purpose 500 infantry and 100 horse. "Without this, the expense incurred will be essentially fruitless. . . . This business must not be skinned over. The political putrefaction of Pennsylvania is greater than I had any idea of. Without rigor everywhere, our tranquillity is likely to be of very short duration, and the next storm will be infinitely worse than the present one." The arms deposited at Pittsburg should include little artillery "in so disaffected a Country."

Hamilton and Washington had all along been apprehensive that major inciters to the violence would avoid seizure. So it happened, to their regret. David Bradford, the self-styled general at Braddock's Field, knowing what was in store for him, fled to Louisiana, which was as far as he could get from the scene. Others whom Hamilton held guilty escaped arrest for different reasons. Albert Gallatin had urged that the excise be brought into contempt, but he was judged by the Attorney General not to have committed an indictable offense. Brackenridge, described by Hamilton as "the worst of all scoundrels" for his two-faced conduct, had purchased immunity by aiding the commissioners. John Hamilton, colonel of a regiment of militia in the Mingo Creek settlement and sheriff of Washington County, claimed that he had been the friend of government all along, in spite of belligerent appearances. He tried to dissuade David Bradford from the rendezvous at Braddock's. When his effort failed he led his contingent to the field intent on preventing outrage; In the end he surrendered. The small fry who could be rounded up provoked sympathy for their poverty and ignorance; harsh treatment of them was opposed because the rebellion had been put down without bloodshed.

No sooner had General Daniel Morgan led his light troops into Washington County, which held "the most disaffected scenes," than the military seized twenty suspects who were turned over to the judiciary. Two days later, when Hamilton was at Pittsburgh, the prisoners had increased to 150. A few among them were "most conspicuous . . . for character or crime." Time did not allow "for preliminary investigations to apprehend the guilty upon process." Pleading the emergency, Hamilton agreed in the trespass on civil rights. Brackenridge, the lawyer, knew how to protect himself when examined by Hamilton, but he was sure that humble men were put at a grave disadvantage. In his short-circuit of legal procedure, Hamilton was encouraged by Washington, who wrote from Wright's Ferry, on the Susquehanna, his hope that the Secretary "by *Hook* or by *Crook*" could send three suspects whom he named "to Philadelphia for their winter Quarters." Hamilton was a notable defender of civil rights, but in the hurried roundup of supposed insurgents in western Pennsylvania he lapsed dangerously from his principles.

However, he forbore to press the excise law beyond fair limits. An office of inspection would be opened in every county; this had not been done previously, which excused some distillers for non-compliance. Infractions of the laws went back further, but it would be best to collect taxes only for the year ended the last July. In view of the lack of cash, whiskey would be bought for the army at 3s. 4d; Pennsylvania currency, per gallon, and the receipts of the army purchasing agent would be accepted at the Treasury for the taxes.

Hamilton mapped out with General Lee homeward routes of the army so that provisions and pay could be provided in advance. On November 19 he notified President Washington from Pittsburgh that the army was on its return march and that he in five minutes would mount his horse to follow. Actually, because he was considered to be in personal danger in the so recently rebellious region, he was escorted by a guard of six horsemen the hundred miles to Bedford and for a distance beyond. Addressed to him on the road homeward was a letter from General Knox, written at the President's request, bearing distressing news. It revealed the special reason for his repeated messages to his wife assuring her that he was safe and would quickly rejoin her. Knox explained that Mrs. Hamilton was "much alarmed" because "she has had, or has been in danger of a miscarriage," though the report from her doctors was satisfactory. It was a miscarriage, for she did not deliver another child until three years later.

On his return to Philadelphia December 1, 1794, Hamilton notified the President that he would resign as Secretary of the Treasury the last day of January. He called this to the attention of Speaker Muhlenberg in order to give the House, if it chose, an opportunity for further investigation of his department, which was to say of Hamilton's conduct of the Treasury.

A sequel of quelling the Whiskey Insurrection was President Washington's excoriation of the "self-created societies" which threatened to "destroy the government of this Country." These were the offshoots of the parent Democratic Society which Genêt had established in Philadelphia, "for the express purpose of dissension," Washington charged. The Senate, heavily Federalist, chimed in cordially with the President's censures, but the House, more evenly divided, had an animated debate before agreeing to compromise wording of its response to the speech. Critics were alarmed that the military was used to put down freedom of speech and assemblage. Those opposed to Jay's mission to England wondered how they were to attack his treaty if candid discussion was to be forbidden. A technical point involved Hamilton's account of the origin and progress of the rising, on which Washington had relied for his facts. Hamilton said that seeds of insurrection were planted by the excise law, which was passed before the societies were created. How, then, could he blame the latter? It was finally explained by Hamilton when he returned that early obstruction was fanned into outright rebellion by the Antifederalist meetings. Hamilton drafted the President's proclamation for a day of thanksgiving "for the seasonable . . . supression of the late Insurrection."

A delayed reaction to the discipline of the "Whiskey Boys", which reflected no credit on anybody, was the precipitate resignation of Edmund Randolph as Secretary of State in August 1795. It called in question the diplomatic spying of the day. The British intercepted a letter of Fauchet, the French minister to the United States, which the British placed under Washington's eye. Fauchet wrote that Randolph, in effect, had solicited a bribe to show that the British, not the French, had fomented insurrection on the western frontier. Offended by Washington's suspicion of him, thus aroused, Randolph hastily resigned. His published *Vindication* cleared him of wrongdoing, but his injudicious countercharges sent the President into a fury and left Hamilton unconvinced of Randolph's innocence.

Chapter 17

TREATY AND LEGACY

John Jay's treaty with Great Britain, made in 1795, was largely Hamilton's doing. It brought the peace treaty of 1783 into full operation, and purchased years of exchange between the two countries which were beneficial to development of the American economy. Jay's Treaty illustrated Hamilton's willingness—eagerness, in this instance—to take half a loaf rather than no bread. Devotion to his twin objects of peace and customs revenue required him to defend an instrument which had its own shortcomings and also a ready-made party of opposition. Hamilton's support of the Constitution, when first offered to the people, was more promising than his plea for approval of Jay's Treaty. Those who were against the Constitution were not yet a cohesive political force, and they were handicapped by loyalty to the Articles of Confederation, which had been discredited in actual experience. Agreement with Britain in 1795, on the other hand, meant disagreement with France as a belligerent in the European war, and accentuated the contest between partisans in America which reflected the struggle of great powers overseas. This division of sentiment colored the decade of life which remained to Hamilton, and, of course, it continued for years beyond his death.

Except for approval in the first flush of the French Revolution, Hamilton disagreed with all that went forward in that country in its internal and external affairs. He had neither idealistic sympathy nor emotional attachment for America's erstwhile ally. On the contrary, he admired the constitution and political temper of our recent enemy, Britain. Though he had helped to stir our violent break with the mother country and had served six years in the Revolutionary army, then he had been claiming for America the rights of Englishmen, he had not been crying up a novel egalitarian philosophy. In all of his plans for the United States, stability was the underlying essential. The scene in France was the reverse of harmony and orderly progress.

Jefferson's report on America's foreign commerce, ordered two years earlier, was submitted to the House on December 19, 1793. It invoked countervailing discriminations against the trade and shipping of countries with which we had no commercial treaties, mainly Great Britain. The report was correspondingly favorable to those nations with which we were in treaty, principally France. The whole was colored by the contest in America between partisans of the chief powers, Britain and France, then at war in Europe. Attachment of Republicans to the fortunes of France, and of Federalists to the efforts of Britain, intensified the party struggle within this country as long as the Napoleonic Wars lasted. The Republicans harped on our debt to France for assistance in our bid for independence, cried up revolutionary France as world apostle of liberty, and made light of the Reign of Terror and the stridency of Napoleon's invasions. The Federalists, Hamilton particularly, discredited supposed sympathetic motives of France and defined her object as damage to England, her ancient foe.

Jefferson's report, which nourished our trade with France and antagonized that with Great Britain, was the proximate

beginning of the Federalists' movement for commercial agreement with our former enemy and completion of obligations of
the two nations under the peace treaty of 1783. The result was
the Jay treaty of 1795, which caused sharp party controversy.
The Federalists contended that the Republicans, by stressing
Britain's depredations on American commerce, proposed to
draw us into war with that country as the ally of France.
Whether, in the absence of Jay's Treaty, that would have happened is problematical. As it was, the treaty vouchsafed to
America peace with Britain for the decade and a half in which
our national institutions became established. (The disquieting
interlude of quasi-war in 1798–1800 was with France).

Madison, then in the House, promptly embodied Jefferson's
recommendations in seven resolutions paying in their own
coin nations hostile to our commerce. Britain was the target of
attack, France was our friend. Import duties on a variety of
commodities should be increased. Tonnage rates on ships of
non-treaty countries (read Britain) should be raised, while
those on ships of treaty nations (France the chief beneficiary)
should be lowered. American citizens should be reimbursed
by our government for British seizures of vessels and cargoes.
To ward off the sure objection from Federalists, these steps
were to be taken gradually. Madison comforted his listeners
with the reminder that America had her own food in plenty;
with less reason he promised that our revenue would not suffer and that we would find substitutes at home for the ex-
cluded British manufactures.

The Federalists got the debate on Madison's propositions
deferred while they marshaled their forces to reply. In mid-
January 1794 William Loughton Smith of South Carolina fired
the opening gun in a detailed counterattack, every word of the
fifteen thousand in it prepared by Hamilton. Smith's merit
was that he spoke Hamilton's lines with conviction. Though
Jefferson's report on which Madison's resolves were based had
the benefit of material and advice from Tench Coxe, an econo-

mist of repute, on the whole its data could not bear close scru-
tiny, and its summaries were strongly flavored with partisan
sentiment. Hamilton's rejoinder was of a different order. He
had a good acquaintance with the facts and eager incentive.

Hamilton was determined to preserve the superior advantages of our trade with Britain, for the profit of American ex-
porters and the customs revenue flowing to the Treasury. To
his mind it was imperative that America should avoid a rift
with Britain that would incline this country toward France in
the European war. He showed that Britain was twice as good a
customer to us as France. Jefferson had conceded that three-
fourths of our imports were from Britain and her dominions
and that the credit she extended was to our young country "an
essential nutriment." Hamilton on his part had to agree that in
shipping France served us better than Britain. We were ex-
cluded from the British West Indies except for taking salt from
Turk's Island, while France admitted to her islands any of our
vessels which were of sixty tons and upward. After correcting
Jefferson's figures, Hamilton put our tonnage with French dominions at 82,510, that with the British at 66,582.

Jefferson and Madison, by their retaliatory penalties on Britain, would convulse three-fourths of our import trade, two-
fifths of our export trade, and two-thirds of our public revenues. Hamilton insisted that we could not hazard war with
our best customer and provider. The proud and resourceful
British nation would not be easily prodded into compliance
with our demands. America, for the nonce, was the weak trading partner, and she must bide her time to reach full economic
competence. Pending that development, we should seek favorable treaties, not indulge in politically inspired reprisals.

Madison came back with reinforcement of his resolves. Britain was dependent on us for raw materials and for sale of her
manufactures. America could do without superfluities, could
fabricate essentials in households, and could find elsewhere—
country not specified—the forfeited revenue from Britain. He

stretched credulity by naming revolutionary France a "settled order." Fisher Ames, floor leader for the Federalists, tried in vain to keep the discussion to economic terms and avoid fierce political tempers. Richard Bland Lee of Virginia called the British lovers of liberty. This provoked Smilie of western Pennsylvania, soon to be an actor in insurrection there, to ask whether British attachment to freedom was shown "by breaking our treaty, by withholding our posts, seizing our ships, attempting to starve France, by infringing the Law of Nations, in preventing our vessels from carrying there provisions, exciting the Indians to murder us, letting loose the Algerines upon us?" Giles chimed in with recent proofs of British perfidy. For the Federalists, Tracy of Connecticut wisely commented that Madison's resolves went too far for commercial reciprocity, not far enough to accomplish political objects.

Debate wore on, with intervals of interruption. Many members felt that war with Britain was imminent. Why proceed with adjustments in commerce when commerce was to be annihilated? The discussion should shift to military and naval defenses. To stem "the torrent of British injustice" Vans Murray would stop all intercourse with that nation until she satisfied us for past injuries. Both branches of Congress promptly approved an embargo for thirty days on all vessels intending for foreign ports. A bipartisan committee of fifteen was to find replacement for revenue thus lost. Knowledgable members declared that the Secretary of the Treasury was "the only person qualified to direct their judgment in a question concerning finance," but Page of Virginia proclaimed the competence of the committee "in a single day" to devise ways and means. The favorite appeal was to funds from sales of public lands. War loomed closer. Coast artillerists, 80,000 militia alerted, and a continental army in the event of hostilities were proposed. Dayton was for sequestration of all debts due from American to British citizens. Smith of Maryland, though he approved generally, would exempt property of British subjects in our public funds. Smith of South Carolina, Hamilton's spokesman, argued against sequestration of public or private claims. If we fought Britain, Holland was her ally: should we withhold debts from friendly Dutchmen? Before using any menace, said Boudinot, we should send a special envoy to London to secure peace. Giles retorted that war was probable, it was time for America to assert her rights. This belligerence was of the sort that stirred the Federalists to speed Jay's embassy.

It has been charged that Hamilton was too confidential with George Hammond, the British minister to the United States, and that the Secretary interfered in the functions of Jefferson. Hammond found Jefferson "so blinded by his attachment to France and his hatred of Great Britain, that he would without hesitation commit the immediate interests of his country in any measure which might . . . gratify . . . his resentments." After Jefferson resigned, Hammond viewed Randolph similarly. Hamilton himself insisted on strict neutrality, because "any event which might endanger the *external* tranquillity of the United States, would be as fatal to the systems he has formed for the benefit of his country as to his . . . personal reputation." It was the British who preyed on American commerce to the injury of France, the British to whom private debts were due, the British who had carried off 3000 slaves. The threat of war was with our recent enemy, cheered on by partisans of our late ally. Hamilton strove to redress this imbalance in American public sentiment. Naturally, he worked with the British minister to secure durable peace. Though there were obstacles, two circumstances favored the efforts of Hamilton and the other Federalists: most wanted the western posts evacuated and demanded compensation for depredations on our shipping.

What happened in foreign relations was more important to the Treasury than Treasury operations were to the State Department. Demarcations in the small Cabinet were indistinct. Hamilton's eagerness to forestall war was not checked by the certainty of causing internal conflict. Minister Hammond, on his part, countering the machinations of Genêt, valued his exchanges with Hamilton, whom he called "the most influential member of the administration." Not that Hamilton was always receptive to the British minister's proposals. Hamilton would brook no British interference in this country's relations with the Indians, and indemnity for American vessels illegally seized and sold was a must.

The spring of 1794 saw leading Federalists huddle on plans to negotiate a settlement of all points in dispute with Great Britain. The British order of November 6, 1793, had caused the capture of over two hundred American vessels in the West Indies, more than half of which were condemned. On March 10 Ellsworth, Cabot, and Strong met with Rufus King "to confer on the course most advisable to pursue." Ellsworth should urge on the President that these aggressions threatened war "unless some system calculated to calm the public mind . . . was speedily adopted." Besides devising defensive measures and additional taxes, "an Envoy extraordinary should be . . . sent to England to require satisfaction for the loss of our Property, and to adjust those points which menaced a War between the two Countries." The appointee should be a man who has "talents of the first order, enjoying the Confidence of the friends of Peace, of the Government, and whose character was unexceptionable in England." In the eyes of these friends, Colonel Hamilton's qualifications "afforded a very commanding preference."

The President, in his response to Ellsworth, said that he himself was sure of Hamilton, but doubted whether he had "the general confidence of the Country." In the next months Congress enacted an embargo for thirty days; the scene brightened when the British orders of the previous November were revoked. Hammond informed Lord Grenville, Britain's Foreign Secretary, that Jay, Hamilton, or King would be sent as negotiator.

Hamilton was vigorously opposed by the Republicans, especially Jefferson and Monroe. The latter argued to Washington that if Hamilton were the envoy and failed to bring Britain to terms, we could not expect France to be our ally in the resulting war. The Federalists called in Robert Morris to support their backing of Hamilton. Morris recommended accordingly to the President; in so doing he discountenanced the choice of John Adams or Jefferson. Actually, all things considered, the President secured Jay's consent to serve. Hamilton had a more intimate knowledge of political tempers and of commerce, but his position as party leader was against him. Jay, as Chief Justice, was above partisan contentions and commended himself for patriotism at home and wisdom abroad. Hamilton, reviewing the confronting situation for the President, removed himself from consideration and endorsed the selection of Jay. Aside from Jay's superior merits for the mission, Hamilton wished to be at hand to watch developments here, and he felt obliged to see the western rising against the excise quelled without delay.

Republicans opposed the appointment of Jay, but he was readily confirmed by the Senate. Hamilton, Ellsworth, Cabot, and King discussed with Jay the terms he should put forward in London. The inexecution of the treaty of 1783 should be adjusted and spoliations on our commerce should be compensated; then we would pay the private debts, which amounted to some half a million sterling. Hamilton was anxious for commercial privileges in the West Indies, and he would be conciliatory on Indian trade, navigation of the Great Lakes, and the period of evacuation of the military posts. He furthered the advice of the Federalist caucus in various ways, most specifically in writing parts of Jay's official instructions. The object was "to repel war, for which we are not disposed," but "to assert, with dignity and firmness, our rights, and our title to reparation for past injuries." Debts due British subjects were to be decided in our courts. The clauses covering our trade with the British West and East Indies were Hamilton's. Both Britain and the United States could trade with Indians across the frontier, no troops should be kept on the Great Lakes, and our products should be admitted to the British European dominions on an equal footing with those of other nations. However, Hamilton did not agree with the contention that provisions were contraband only if bound for a blockaded port; he would permit seizure if they were paid for. In his mind free ships did not make free goods. He would not have Jay sound out the ministers of Denmark, Sweden, and Russia with a view to the United States joining the Armed Neutrality. Those countries could be of no aid to us; they might engage us in difficulties. Hamilton kept in anxious touch with the progress of negotiations in London.

No sooner was the treaty delivered in this country than Hamilton made time for an elaborate analysis of it which had been requested by Washington. The President wanted "the favorable, and unfavorable side of *each* article stated," with a recommendation "on which side the balance is to be found." Afterward, he apologized for putting Hamilton to such pains, but he need not have felt guilty, for Hamilton knew how much hung on the President's decision. Also, later, Hamilton modeled his exhaustive public defense of the treaty—the *Camillus* essays—on his report for the Chief Executive.

Hamilton was ardently for ratification of Jay's Treaty, though he approved the Senate's rejection of Article Twelve of the commercial treaty, pending negotiation. This forbade us to re-export certain commodities which were products of the British West Indies but which were also produced elsewhere— including, in the case of cotton, the United States. Hamilton did not share the outcry against Article Eighteen, which permitted seizure of provisions as contraband provided they were

paid for. The British might abuse this right and the French
and French sympathizers would complain of it, but it was a
compromise we should accept.

Surrender of the western posts would end the Indian wars
and tend "powerfully to establish the . . . authority of the
general government over the Western country." Then and later
Hamilton warmly endorsed the privilege of both countries to
trade (mostly in furs) across the Canadian border. The contention of opponents of Jay's Treaty was that the British had first
violated the peace treaty by abducting slaves. Hamilton concluded that the first fault was ours in that some of the states
had obstructed payment of debts owed to British merchants.
As to the slaves, whom the British refused to return or com-
pensate for, their money value was inconsiderable compared
to other magnitudes involved. Many of the slaves were enemy
property by capture, and anyhow it was inhumane to return
persons to bondage.

Hamilton found the treaty honorable in refusing to sequester British property in our funds. He declared that the established rule of international law was that enemy goods
might be taken from neutral vessels. This was correctly stipulated in Jay's Treaty. The position of the Armed Neutrality and
those who wanted to supply non-contraband goods to France
was that neutral ships made neutral cargoes. Hamilton argued
that this license could not be upheld. The treaty did not violate
our prior commitments to France. We could no longer permit
France to sell her prizes in our ports, but that had been an informal, and unneutral, concession which should be ended.

In sum, Hamilton advised the President to approve the
treaty. It promised the United States immunity from the war
in Europe, peace in which our nation could develop. We
agreed to pay the private debts, but the treaty granted us more
benefits than we gave.

But briefing the President was not enough if New York was
to join the other port cities, from Boston to Charleston, in con-

demning the English treaty. A mass meeting in Wall Street, called by opponents, was no place for calm discussion, in spite of efforts of Hamilton, King, and their friends to have it so. The proceedings were disorderly beyond the power of the chairman, who stood on the balcony of the city hall, to prevent. Hamilton, attempting to speak, was hissed and hooted down, but not stoned, as was long afterward reported. As reason could not figure, the crowd divided physically, some drifting toward Trinity church, others sheering off to the Battery to burn the treaty. Another meeting was set for two days later.

This meeting was bigger than the first, though the report that 5000 to 7000 damned the treaty in all its parts seems excessive. The Federalists answered with action of the Chamber of Commerce supporting the treaty. The net result was to register a popular veto by New York, this in spite of Jay's election as governor of the state before the terms of his treaty were known. Could dispassionate examination and weighing of all aspects prevail with the President against excited clamor by opponents?

Hamilton immediately resolved on a thoughtful appeal in a series of newspaper essays signed Camillus. He had a right to count on the public tiring of hasty denunciations and the indecencies of effigies of the former Chief Justice seated in a dung cart or swinging from a tree limb. Hamilton's reliance was upon "the good sense of the people" who "will maintain their character . . . for deliberation and reflection." In thirty-eight numbers, reaching into the next year, he placed every feature of the treaty in a just light as it bore upon the interests of this country. His fully informed argument was that of the patriot, not the partisan. He had help from Rufus King, but the conception and main execution were his own. Jay's Treaty would probably not have been approved without the education of the public in Camillus' persuasive expositions. The pieces had not been long appearing when Jefferson took alarm

at their effect. He exclaimed to Madison: "Hamilton is really a
colossus to the anti-republican party. Without numbers, he is
an host within himself . . . We have had only middling performances to oppose to him. . . . For God's sake take up your
pen, and give a fundamental reply." But Madison, like Jefferson, preferred not to expose himself.

Hamilton had the satisfaction of writing Washington's
speech at the opening of Congress in December 1795. The
President announced that the Senate had advised approval of
the treaty with Britain; he had agreed and waited only for similar endorsement by King George. Concord at home and
abroad promised a "precious . . . foundation . . . for establishing . . . and maturing the prosperity of our country!"
In March 1796 the President laid the treaty before the House as
an accomplished fact. Here fury against the instrument exploded anew. The House called upon the President to furnish
it with Jay's instructions and other pertinent papers. Hamilton
advised the President to refuse. These documents were no
business of the House—the treaty-making power was vested
in President and Senate. Washington so acted. Thus rebuffed,
Madison led those who insisted that the House could refuse to
make the appropriation of some $100,000 to execute the treaty.
At this late date Madison and others rehearsed the treaty's
vices and proclaimed the power of the House to defeat it after
all. Here was a poser. Fisher Ames, in a famous oration, defended the treaty. He compressed the arguments in *Camillus*
and added his own emotional warmth. The Committee of the
Whole adjourned under the spell of his appeal, then, two days
later, the appropriation was narrowly carried by a vote of 51 to
48.

Hamilton resigned as Secretary of the Treasury the last of
January 1795. He had been, as was later pronounced, "the vital
principle of the first administration under the constitution."
His task, assigned to him by Congress but no less self-as-
sumed, was to liquidate the lapses of the Confederation and

achieve the solvency that was the condition of sovereignty. In this he had the steady support of President Washington. While the Secretary of State was nominally the first officer of the Cabinet, the role of Jefferson was in fact minor, and he retired more than a year before Hamilton did. Jefferson, with the rest, approved neutrality of the United States in the war between England and France. Thereafter, for a time, events in Europe were reflected in squabbles in American internal politics rather than in our foreign policy. Edmund Randolph, Jefferson's successor, was no more assertive than Jefferson had been. Hamilton was rightly accused of encroaching upon the functions of the Secretary of State, but his actual administration, at a critical juncture, of the War Department was at General Knox's wish.

Frequently President Washington put a question to several of his Cabinet advisers. A query to Jefferson and Hamilton in the autumn of 1790 had distinctly to do with foreign policy. If the dispute between Britain and Spain came to war, the former would doubtless send troops from Detroit through United States territory against New Orleans and other Spanish possessions on the Mississippi. What should be the answer of the President if permission for the march were asked, what the answer if it were undertaken without leave? Jefferson replied briefly and vaguely; we should give no answer to a request, then be guided by the event. Hamilton, by contrast, furnished the President with a comprehensive discussion: he considered the contingencies, cited applicable international law, and reached definite conclusions. If permission were asked, do not refuse. If not asked, and our post on the Wabash were forced, then demand satisfaction for the insult, and if that were not forthcoming, make war on the trespasser.

After leaving the Treasury, Hamilton, though no longer attending the daily conferences of Cabinet officers with the President, was hardly less at the service of the administration through assistance requested or volunteered. In fact, through his familiars in President John Adams's Cabinet, Hamilton powerfully influenced national affairs until the scales fell from Adams's eyes.

At the last of May 1794, Hamilton deferred his offer to resign at the close of the session of Congress, though, if the President had chosen his successor, he would of course quit at once. He wished to forestall efforts he felt were being made which would plunge this country into war with Britain. Also, western parts of Pennsylvania, then violently obstructing collection of the excise on whiskey, were to be brought into compliance. By the first of December he could do no more for the time being to further Jay's Treaty, and the western rebellion had been put down. He notified the President that he would retire two months hence, which gave Washington an ample interval to fill his post. The same intention, timely passed to the Speaker of the House, produced no further investigation of the Treasury.

During Hamilton's tenure in the Treasury, expenditures of the federal government doubled, from $3,207,096.90 to $6,661,512.14. Revenue for the year 1795 was estimated at $7,172,425,38. The government was operating in the black, for current expenditure was $5,481,843.84, and the excess of revenue was $1,070,456.90. The employees of the Treasury, who always far outnumbered those of War and State, had grown to a total of 570, principally engaged in the Philadelphia offices and in the customs service. The intrinsic importance of Treasury functions and its personnel stationed in all parts of the country had given Hamilton patronage that strengthened the Federalist party which he led.

His last major report to Congress, given in January 1795, was a legacy from his experience and a trust that his tested policies would be continued. The emphasis was on means of extinguishing the entire debt of some $76 million without resort to new sources of revenue. He hoped that the lawmakers would act on what the President (in Hamilton's words) had charged at the opening of Congress a month earlier—that the nation should redeem present debt and avoid accumulating more.

The report was received immediately in both houses, in the lower on what the disgusted Madison believed was a prearranged motion of Boudinot, "the ready agent of all such sycophantic jobs." Hamilton's proposals were more detailed than those contained in a House committee report on debt redemption, which was then being vigorously debated. William Loughton Smith and Fisher Ames were the Federalist defenders; Nicholas, Findley, Venable, and others were the Republican opponents. The critics were at a disadvantage, for here were "the patrons . . . of certificate nobility," the cherishers of public debt for their vile purposes, urging that it be wiped out.

Hamilton presented ten propositions for completing the fiscal system; if followed, every obligation, deferred and accruing, would be met. He luminously explained each measure.

First on his list was the commencement of annual appropriations to pay interest and principal of the unsubscribed debt. This had been Hamilton's solemn promise when funding was broached. He now warded off the antagonism of those who had come into his scheme and had converted their holdings at some sacrifice of original terms but on conditions that seemed good to them. They should not now cavil at the delayed satisfaction of those who stood on their undoubted right to receive in full what had been initially stipulated. A related recommendation was that the federal government should assume responsibility for interest and principal of the new emission bills of credit, those that took the place of the old continental currency at the rate of 40 to 1; holders should no longer have to rely on faith of the issuing states.

A little more stock should be offered as inducement to convert foreign into domestic debt. This would eliminate transfer problems and bolster public credit. This credit could be rendred immortal by increasing the sinking fund and "contracting with lenders that the fund would be inviolable." Thus the existing debt could be discharged in thirty years. No new debt should be created without the government at the same time providing means of redemption. Without this, "the public debt swells until its magnitude becomes enormous, and the burthens of the people gradually increase, till their weight becomes intolerable. Of such a state of things, great disorders in the whole political economy . . . are a natural offspring." Hamilton called down imprecations on any who would raid the sinking fund; no emergency authorized diverting it from its dedicated objects.

He ended by declaring that government was not at liberty to tax its own funds or to sequester them in time of war, either of which actions would violate the commitment to the lender. He used words that have colored his reputation as finance minister: "The true definition of public credit is a *property subsisting in the faith of the Government. Its essence is promise.*" No compulsory modification not provided for in the instrument was permissible. This was "a principle . . . most sacred." Any temporary gain from wronging a few creditors would produce vastly larger losses, for "Credit is an *entire* thing. Every part of it has the nicest sympathy with every other part; wound one limb, and the whole tree shrinks and decays." Preserve public credit and private capital will not be wanting.

Critical features of the bill embodying Hamilton's plan were attacked in the House by Giles and others and were defended by Sedgwick and William L. Smith; King was chief supporter in the Senate. The measure passed both branches of the legislature; it carried Hamilton's objects, with the exception of the provision for unsubscribed debt and new tenor bills. Hamilton, already out of the Treasury, was humiliated and angry at the omission of non-subscribers. He begged Sedgwick and King to retrieve the country's pledge. He was "tortured" by the discrimination. "The . . . abominable assassination of the national honor . . . respecting the unsubscribed debt . . . haunts me every step I take, and afflicts me more than I can express." King should cancel Burr's "false and horrid . . . subtleties" which reproached the public character. Fisher Ames agreed that failure to embrace the small unsubscribed debt was regrettable, but he felt that it was a minor fault in the crowning federal measure. Nevertheless, Hamilton retired "full of the horrors, on this account."

To the last moment Hamilton was busy for his department's welfare. On his hearty recommendation, the President would appoint Wolcott as Secretary of the Treasury. For the replacement of Wolcott as Comptroller, Hamilton urged the fitness of Edward Carrington. The Mint could not flourish under part-time direction, and it should be transferred from the State Department to the Treasury. The Post Office, on the other hand, had primarily to do with communications and should be moved from Treasury to State. One of Hamilton's last formal acts was "the expression of the high sense I continue to entertain of the fidelity and ability with which" the firm of Dutch bankers "have uniformly served the United States." Then he sent in his formal resignation. It brought from the President the top testimonial in American history: "In every relation," said Washington, "which you have borne to me I have found that my confidence in your talents, exertions, and integrity, has been well placed. I the more freely render this testimony of my approbation, because I speak from opportunities of information which cannot deceive me."

Chapter 18

LAW PRACTICE AND FAMOUS FAREWELL

After more than five years Hamilton could leave the Treasury because, he said, his object "of establishing public credit, and introducing order into the finances" had been accomplished. With help from friendly quarters he had been the main mover in the many-sided transformation of his country in a few years. After repeated investigation, his conduct in office had been vindicated and praised. Not simply the Treasury, but the national authority had been served by supression of the "Whiskey Insurrection." The Common Council of New York granted Hamilton the freedom of the city. Henry Van Schaack, who was sorry to see Hamilton go, wrote to Sedgwick what was surely the opinion of Federalists: "It is to that mans Talents in a great measure" that America "owes its progressive felicity." It was to be expected that Republicans would exult, as did Fulwar Skipwith to Monroe—"Forced by the impending displeasure of the freemen of the United States . . . Hamilton is about to give in his resignation."

After John Jay quit the Supreme Court to become governor of New York, William Bradford wrote Hamilton, "I wish to heaven you would permit me to name you chief justice." He was "afraid that department, as it relates neither to War, finance nor negociation [sic], has no charms for you: and yet when one considers how important it is, where [the Justices] have the power of paralyzing the measures of the government by declaring a law unconstitutional, it is not to be trusted to men who are to be scared by popular clamor." If Hamilton had been proposed for Chief Justice he would doubtless have been approved by President and Senate. In appropriate decisions he would have favored full constitutional scope for the central government. Removed from party politics, he would not have committed the error of attacking President John Adams. He would hardly have been called back from judicial robes to military uniform for the unprofitable interval of preparation against war with France. And he would not have been challenged and killed by Aaron Burr.

However, Hamilton was destined for action. As Bradford observed on receiving Hamilton's polite refusal, "You were made for a Statesman, & politics will never be out of your head." He did consent to join Bradford as special counsel in defense of the carriage tax before the Supreme Court.

Hamilton responded to Wolcott's frequent applications with advice on puzzling problems. He wanted to help his successor, and he felt a continuing responsibility for the credit of the country. For example, when seizure by the belligerents of American vessels in the West India trade blocked receipt of specie, he told Wolcott that the government had to preserve credit at home. So long as interest was paid on foreign obligations, disturbances of the times would excuse delays in paying principal abroad. Foreign credit depended upon keeping domestic credit sound. We should pay foreign debts with proceeds of our commodities consigned to French and Dutch agents for that specific purpose. Hamilton closed his letter

with, "If any thing further occurs you shall have it. Write me
as freely as you please."

Wolcott imparted that "The public affairs are . . . in a critical state. I do not clearly see how those of the treasury are to
be managed." Hamilton's suggestions ran from the fiscal into
the political, and thus his policy proposals were given to the
Cabinet with Washington's ready acceptance. The President
usually queried Hamilton with letters in his own hand,
marked "Private." Once, when he was to be absent, he instructed the Secretary of State (Randolph) to be guided by
Hamilton's advice on a critical point in closing Jay's Treaty.
While Hamilton was accused of conceding too much to the
British in the treaty, in fact he was willing to forfeit it entirely
if certain of our plain rights were refused.

Washington wrote Hamilton, "Although you are not in the
administration—a thing I sincerely regret—I must, nevertheless, (knowing how intimately acquainted you are with all the
concerns of this country) request . . . of you to note down
such occurrences as . . . are proper subjects for communication to Congress at their next session." Hamilton
promised items for the President's message, and he ended, "I
beg, Sir, that you will at no time have any scruples about commanding me. I shall always with pleasure comply." The President's need for Hamilton's counsel on grave matters of state
was the greater because the original Cabinet had dissolved—
Jefferson had resigned before Hamilton, Knox more recently,
and Randolph had quit as Secretary of State under charges.
The able Bradford, brought in as Attorney General, had died
in August 1795. Pickering was competent as Secretary of War.
"What am I to do for a Secretary of State?" the President asked
Hamilton. Four eligibles (Paterson, Johnson of Maryland,
C. C. Pinckney, and Patrick Henry) had declined the post.
Would Hamilton sound out Rufus King? John Marshall chose
not to be Attorney General. Hamilton replied that King did
not make himself available, then suggested others with neces-

sary reservations. Samuel Dexter or Christopher Gore would be good for Attorney General.

The President was placed in a delicate position, in both a personal and political way, by the arrival in America in October 1795 of George Washington Lafayette with his tutor, M. Frestel. The President wished to welcome his namesake to his protection, but what would be the effect in France now the Marquis was imprisoned as a foe of the Revolution? Hamilton acted for Washington. He kept the visitors in a rural retreat for six months, then sent them to the President with a frank explanation for the delay. The situation was further complicated by the arrival of Dr. Justus Erich Bollman, who had almost contrived the escape of Lafayette from Olmütz. Bollman and young Lafayette pressed on Washington a renewal of the attempt. The President could countenance nothing secret, but wrote his appeal, "as a *private person*," to the Emperor of Austria to free the Marquis if he would come to America.

On leaving the Treasury the last day of January 1795 Hamilton did not at once resume law practice, but visited the Schuylers at Albany for two months or more. However, as soon as it was rumored that he would resign his public office, litigants applied to engage his legal services, and in the interval of his stay at Albany more sought his help. His old friend Judge Richard Peters furnished a client and assured him that "as to money . . . you will pick that up fast." Robert Troup, who had taken over pending cases when Hamilton entered the Treasury, and who should have known better, lamented that "the hard earned profits of the law will wear you out, and leave a net revenue at the end of ten years that will not maintain a family."

This warning prefaced Troup's invitation to Hamilton to join him, and, possibly, John Jay, in a speculation with English and Dutch capitalists in several million acres of land in Ontario County, New York. Soon he offered Hamilton a retainer of £100. It is not clear how Hamilton and Jay were to profit;

their legal fees would be limited, and their prestige was not
the object of the enterprisers, as their part in the venture was
not to be publicly known. In any event, Hamilton declined the
offer, resolved, as Troup said, "to be poor." Hamilton did own
western lands, but not in this tract; they yielded nothing in
his lifetime.

About this time, low in health and with special reason for
arranging his affairs (as will appear below) he made Troup his
executor. His debts probably exceeded his property on leaving
the Treasury. His chief creditor was his brother-in-law, John
Barker Church, to the extent of £5000; he owed others small
sums. In a postscript he called Troup's attention to "my leather
trunk," which contained "a bundle inscribed thus—

I R
To be forwarded to Oliver Wolcott, Junr Esq.
I entreat this may be early done by a careful hand."

Surely these were the papers relating to James Reynolds ("I"
for "J"), of which only Wolcott, among his friends, had prior
knowledge.

Hamilton's law practice was active and lucrative from the
moment of his re-entry into private life. He was often associated in cases with Troup, Harison, Brockholst Livingston,
and Aaron Burr. He seems to have had no law partner; Baltha-
zar DeHeart was his confidential office manager. When he let
his practice lapse for the better part of two years to become
Inspector General, he sacrificed large professional fees. For example, Richard Stockton's clients wanted Hamilton to argue an
important equity cause in Circuit Court in which they were
complainants. Stockton wrote, "I need not tell you that they
have great reliance on the aid they are to receive of you, and
that the compensation you shall deem adequate will be ready"
if Hamilton agreed. By this time Hamilton was accounted
leader of the New York bar.

A principal commercial suit in which Hamilton was counsel was that of *LeGuen v. Gouverneur and Kemble,* which extended from 1796–1800. The case involved the sale and export to Europe of 600 bales of cotton and 12,000 pounds of indigo by Gouverneur and Kemble as agents for LeGuen; the claim was for $120,000. Counsel with Hamilton for LeGuen were Richard Harison and Aaron Burr; opposed were Gouverneur Morris, Brockholst Livingston, and Robert Troup. Hamilton and his colleagues at length won for LeGuen in the New York Court of Errors. Hamilton drew commendation for refusing more than a moderate fee.

Hamilton took few criminal cases. The one best remembered was his defense, together with Aaron Burr and Brockholst Livingston, of Levi Weeks against the charge of murdering Gulielma Sands. The two were fellow lodgers at a boardinghouse on upper Greenwich Street. About 8 o'clock of the evening of December 22, 1799, Gulielma went out on an unexplained errand. She did not return. Some days later the muff she carried was found near or in a public well in Lispenard's meadow (now roughly the area east of the Manhattan entrance to the Holland tunnel). It was a while after that before the well was probed and her body recovered. In the interval of the girl's disappearance suspicion mounted against Weeks, to whom she had said she was engaged to be married.

Excitement was busily fed by unsupported accusations made by acquaintances of Gulielma—and by rumor—not to speak of the exhibit of the body to public gaze in the street. When Weeks was brought to trial in the spring of 1800 only part of the eager crowd gained the courtroom. The hearing continued for forty-one hours with one adjournment of eight and a half hours to permit all concerned to get some sleep. The prominence of the case may have drawn Hamilton into it, as it did Burr and Livingston, but friendship must have played a part. John H. McComb, the architect who was soon to design Hamilton's house in Harlem, and McComb's associate, Ezra

Weeks, the builder, were witnesses. Levi Weeks, the accused, was foreman in the carpenter shop of his brother Ezra.

Levi was prosecuted by Cadwalader Colden, Assistant Attorney General of New York, grandson of the colonial lieutenant governor. Aside from popular clamor against Weeks, Colden had only circumstantial evidence to present, and that exceedingly thin. The defense offered a score of witnesses who testified to young Weeks's excellent character. Gulielma was variously described as of a cheerful or melancholy disposition, lively or prone to threats of suicide, given to mysterious night outings, and fond of laudanum. Complaints by today's New Yorkers against thin partitions between apartments are nothing new: the party wall between the lodginghouse and the dwelling next door was made of boards, lathed and plastered on each side. The court allowed testimony of the estimable neighbor: he said that he had been disturbed by the creaking of the bed on the other side of the partition, in which, it was implied, Gulielma and a male companion—not Weeks—were furiously making love.

Hamilton's son, in his account of the trial, gave his father a dramatic role in questioning one witness, Croucher, who had been persistent in generating rumors against the prisoner. Hamilton, so the story went, placed candles at either cheek of Croucher and called on the jurors to observe his countenance intensely. He all but accused Croucher as the murderer. Of this there is nothing in the three published accounts of the trial (all sensational), and, in fact, what parts of the examination were conducted by Hamilton is not told. In the end, at three o'clock in the morning, the jurors awakened themselves enough to hear the charge of the judge, which was virtually a direction to acquit Weeks. This they did five minutes after leaving the box.

Hamilton drew wills and agreements involving institutions which have survived into the present—and have withstood efforts to alter them. One was the will of a Captain Robert Richard Randall, leaving properties in what is now the Washington Square area of Manhattan to a home for retired mariners. It was unsuccessfully contested up to the Supreme Court, with Daniel Webster of counsel. With Richard Harison and Robert Troup, in 1797 and later, Hamilton gave the opinion for erecting St. Mark's in the Bowery as a parish separate from Trinity, not contemplated in the charter of the latter. This too has resisted reversal.

Reference has been made to Hamilton's argument in the carriage tax case before the Supreme Court, in spite of his rule not to practice there. After earlier advocacy, he recommended the law of 1794, which placed taxes on pleasure vehicles from $10 down to $1.00. Madison opposed the tax because it was direct, not apportioned according to population, as required by the Constitution. Daniel Hylton of Virginia, inspired politically as much as monetarily, brought suit. The Circuit Court was equally divided.

Hamilton, with Attorney General Charles Lee (Bradford had died), was opposed by Alexander Campbell, attorney of the Virginia District, and Jared Ingersoll, Attorney General of Pennsylvania. Hamilton found no reliable distinction between direct and indirect taxes, and he regretted the inclusion of terms so vague in the Constitution. However, the framers of the document had intended that Congress should have power "over every species of taxable property, except exports." The court should be governed by the interpretation of the English law (from which our jurisprudence derived) that a tax on carriages was indirect, a means of measuring capacity to contribute to public revenue. As with the tax on ship tonnage, the tax on carriages was lawful so long as it was uniform. The Court agreed. Hamilton was paid by the government $500 for his fortnight's work on the case. Many federal taxes were justified on Hamilton's rule until the income tax, a century later, required a constitutional amendment.

At the height of the controversy over Jay's Treaty Hamilton

challenged Commodore James Nicholson, father-in-law of Albert Gallatin and active in Republican politics, to a duel. The episode is worth recounting because it anticipated in several respects the duel with Burr, and was symptomatic of the overcharged political atmosphere of New York in 1795. Fourteen messages, all exchanged within a week, reveal that Hamilton and his Federalist friend, Josiah Ogden Hoffman, encountered the commodore on the street or in some other public place. Commodore Nicholson and Hoffman had commenced a quarrel in which Hamilton intervened as peacemaker, only to be repulsed by Nicholson. Nicholson, according to Hamilton, replied "harshly . . . that he [Hamilton] was not the man to prevent his quarrelling[,] called him an Abettor of Tories and . . . Mr Hamilton would not pursue the affair for he had declined an interview upon a former occasion." It was this last which Hamilton resented; Nicholson afterward did not remember the slur on Hamilton's honor.

Hamilton promptly sent Nicholas Fish, one of his seconds (Rufus King was the other), to Nicholson with a challenge for a week hence at Paulus Hook, New Jersey. The day was remote because Hamilton must first attend to trusts for clients, yet the commodore wished the meeting to be the very next morning, for Fish's visit had alarmed the Nicholson family, which might interfere. Hamilton, in his reply, opened the way for an explanation by Nicholson. But Nicholson was more than ever fearful that the impending duel would be publicized and stopped. That afternoon he was visited by a woman of mutual acquaintance who repeatedly tried to get Mrs. Nicholson into the garden privately. To prevent confidences the commodore ushered her home. The unnamed friend may have been Mrs. Hoffman, anxious to prevent a duel of which her husband was the innocent cause.

Both Hamilton and Nicholson denied initiating a peace move. Friends of both, "with nothing but honourable intentions on both sides," were doubtless proposing an agreement.

It seems that Udny Hay, an outsider but possibly acting for DeWitt Clinton, the commodore's second, began the armistice talks with Fish. Soon the cast was enlarged to include Brockholst Livingston as a second for Nicholson and Rufus King as the same for Hamilton. These friends surely were active in composing the difference.

However, the prospect of bullets was real enough to prompt Hamilton to make his will. He wished he could give a preference, in distribution of his small estate, to drafts for $700 drawn on him by his father in the West Indies, "lest they should return upon him and increase his distress." He declined to do so because a "voluntary engagement" should not be put ahead of other commitments.

Fortunately for sanity, on the eve of the appointed encounter near Paulus Hook the commodore signed an apology drafted by Hamilton. It read in part, "as to the suggestion alleged to have been made by Mr Nicholson namely that Mr Hamilton had declined a former interview he does not recollect . . . having made it neither did he intend the imputation which it would seem to imply and that if he did make the suggestion he regrets the pain which it must have occasioned to Mr Hamilton." All of the seconds witnessed the signature and put their names to their own statement that the "controversy . . . has been settled in a satisfactory and honorable way to both the parties."

This had been a private spat between political protagonists. The backgronund of friction between adherents of Great Britain and of France in the war raging in Europe gave President Washington alarm. All along he had sought to keep the peace at home and in our foreign relations. His most famous expression of this hope was in his Farewell Address to his countrymen. This celebrated document was penned mostly by Hamilton, using a framework of topics supplied by Washington plus some of Hamilton's own.

When Washington projected the Farewell Address in 1792

Hamilton had no part in it; on the contrary, he begged the President to accept a second term in office. Madison was the collaborator, but his changes in Washington's draft were merely verbal, and on the side of caution. Madison was out of sympathy with Washington's policies, and at first he opposed his re-election. Of course as the President remained in office nothing came of the farewell at that time.

In 1796 Washington returned to the project of a valedictory, and he asked Hamilton's aid. Would Hamilton please revise the Washington-Madison draft, and also prepare a new address based on Washington's substantive recommendations? The President at first thought of including a reproof to Madison as a defamer of the administration, one who well knew that Washington yearned for retirement, not for unconstitutional power. Fortunately, this personal reference was abandoned in a paper which was more loftily pitched.

Hamilton felt he could do nothing with Madison's handiwork. He submitted his own clothing of Washington's ideas with a development of additional headings. Hamilton wrote with sincerity, with perfect knowledge of Washington's intentions, and with eagerness, under such auspices, to submit guidance for his country. In offering his first draft he observed to the President that it had been his object "to render this act importantly and lastingly useful, and . . . to embrace such reflections . . . as will wear well, progress in approbation with time, and redound to future reputation."

Then he did make a try at revision of Madison's draft, but it was discarded. John Jay, at the President's request, had a small advisory part in the final form of the Address, but he wrote none of it.

Subsequent generations forgot the domestic dissensions and foreign perplexities which informed the President's rich advice, but were enduringly impressed by the admonitions of harmony at home and goodwill toward, but not permanent alliances with, foreign nations. "It is our true policy to steer clear of . . . inveterate antipathies against particular Nations, and passionate attachments for others." A hundred and fifty years later many in America, including those in highest office, were ready to discard the advice of patriots of the eighteenth century. A closer knit world, they declared, compelled this country to entertain "inveterate antipathies against particular Nations" and cherish "passionate attachments for others," making political and military alliances with the latter amidst the "cold war." In the sequel, our massive and inconclusive military intervention in Southeast Asia returned Americans' thoughts to the wisdom of their fathers, who had not had the benefit of knowledge of intercontinental missiles.

A subordinate question is the pertinence for later days of Hamilton's plea in the Address, "Cherish public Credit as a means of strength and security . . . use it as little as possible. . . . Avoid the accumulation of debt . . . not transferring to posterity the burthen which we ought to bear ourselves." Hamilton valued public debt as a bond of union while the nation was weak, but strove to extinguish that debt as we were able to do so. It may be that modern exigencies make deficit financing inevitable and at times desirable, but doubtless Hamilton would not have approved of devaluation of the currency as a means of meeting inflation.

The Farewell Address, after careful revisions by Hamilton and Washington, was presented, and it was speedily and generally acclaimed by the country. "The enemies of the government," James McHenry reported to Washington, showed a sullenness and uneasiness "that marked . . . chagreen [*sic*] . . . at the impression it was calculated to make on the public mind." William Vans Murray, American ambassador at The Hague, in a just estimate of the Address, said that Washington's "death will give it a sanctity that nothing but the greatest virtue can bestow."

After Hamilton's death, his wife and son wished to procure the papers that confirmed her knowledge of her husband's

agency in composition of the Farewell Address. These proofs
were principally in a packet of manuscripts deposited by
Nathaniel Pendleton, one of Hamilton's executors, with Rufus
King. Pendleton's "object in their delivery to me," said King,
"was to prevent their falling into the hands of the General's
family," for he knew that "Mrs. Hamilton [would] endeavor to
show that General Hamilton, not George Washington, was the
author . . . of the farewell address. . . . Judge Pendleton . . .
concluded that public opinion, upon this subject should not
be disturbed." Other friends of both Washington and Hamilton, including Richard Peters, John Jay, and John Marshall,
deplored or resisted disclosure that would take off from the
credit of Washington. Peters would not tell what he called
"mischievous Truths."

When Mrs. Hamilton's suit against Rufus King to retrieve
the papers belonging to her husband's estate did not succeed,
she recorded Hamilton's obedience to Washington's request.
The President had written Hamilton in May 1796, explaining
his motives for *"my draft* of the valedictory Address," and
directing, "If you form one anew, it will, of course, assume
such a shape as you may be disposed to give it, predicated
upon the Sentiments contained in the enclosed Paper."

John Marshall, writing to Bushrod Washington, was sure
that Hamilton did not preserve the evidences of his part in the
Address in order to detract from the fame of George Washington. All that is known about Hamilton's writing for others at-
tests to that view. Nor was Marshall correct in fearing that
Mrs. Hamilton would violate her husband's confidence. When
she was nearly ninety years old and living in Washington,
happening to be in the Capitol, she called on the Librarian of
Congress and told him how Hamilton, in preference to revis-
ing Madison's draft, undertook "to prepare a different one."
She reiterated that this was "a secret, about my husband, and
you must not tell it until I am gone."

John Beckley, the peddler of political gossip, anticipating

the election of 1796, could hardly credit a report that Hamilton conceded "there may be a state of things" favoring the choice of Jefferson without opposition. Beckley supplied what he supposed to be Hamilton's reasoning. The Southern states would never consent to our declaring war on France. If France declared war on us, which the Federalists believed inevitable, "Mr. J's influence could alone preserve the Union, and produce a favorable termination of the breech." Beckley dismissed this as too magnanimous. "Hamilton himself industriously propagates that Adams and pinckney are [the Federalists'] choice." But Beckley conjectured a different event. Caleb Strong and George Cabot might be electors in Massachusetts and carry that state for Hamilton. Rhode Island, Vermont, Connecticut, New York, New Jersey, and Maryland would follow unanimously.

John Adams, some years after Hamilton's death, said that one party was reconciled to Washington's departure from the presidency "because they believed it a step towards the introduction of Mr Jefferson, and the other because they thought it an Advance toward the election of Mr Hamilton who was their ultimate Object." Adams, characteristically, observed that "As both parties despaired of obtaining their Favourite, Adams was brought in by a miserable Majority of one or two votes, with the deliberate intention to sacrifice him at the next election." He added, with commendable candor, that if Hamilton's supporters had wished to make their idol "an hereditary executive," they never mentioned such an idea to Adams.

Chapter 19

MARIA REYNOLDS

In July of 1791 a young woman called to see Hamilton at his home in Philadelphia. It was a private meeting. She explained that she was from New York, a sister (sister-in-law) of Mr. G. Livingston. Her husband, James Reynolds, had left her for another woman. Would Hamilton furnish her with the means to return to her friends in New York? He had not the money at the moment but that evening took a bank note to her address near by. She received him at the head of the stairs and ushered him into her bedroom, where, after some conversation, "it was quickly apparent that other than pecuniary consolation would be acceptable."

Thus commenced a liaison which continued for a year or more. Shortly after the first meeting Mrs. Hamilton and her children went on a visit to the Schuylers at Albany. In the family's absence most of the assignations were at Hamilton's home, others at Maria Reynolds's lodgings or perhaps at an inn. Soon she told him that her husband wished to return to her, and Hamilton encouraged the reconciliation, without, however, dropping his relations with her. She informed him that Reynolds could give information of connivance in the Treasury staff in speculation.

Hamilton sent for Reynolds who declared that William Duer had given him a list of claims against the government which he (Reynolds) had used in speculation. Hamilton's passions dictated keeping Reynolds friendly, so he hinted at finding public employment for him. Further knowledge of Reynolds's character forbade giving him a clerkship in the Treasury. When Hamilton suspected a collusion between husband and wife to keep up the intrigue, Hamilton wanted to end it, but this provoked in Maria such "agonizing distress" that he yielded to her entreaties. "My sensibility," said Hamilton, "perhaps my vanity, admitted the possibility of a real fondness; and led me to adopt the plan of a gradual discontinuance . . . as least calculated to give pain, if a real partiality existed." Maria readily made a good impression. Twenty-three, "her innocent Countenance appeared to show an innocent Heart"—this from an acquaintance who later professed himself undeceived. Her family connections entitled her to ask help not only from Hamilton, but also from Governor Mifflin, Alexander J. Dallas, and Jeremiah Wadsworth, all of whom softened to her appeal. She must have been attractive, or an intrigue with her would not have been started, much less kept up at obvious risk.

In mid-December 1791 Maria notified Hamilton that her husband had found them out. At the same moment Reynolds wrote him, demanding satisfaction. In personal interviews and letters, Reynolds, after much bluster, allowed that his wounded honor would be comforted by a payment of $1000. Reynolds would take himself and his young daughter off, leaving his alienated wife to Hamilton's attentions. Hamilton paid the blackmail in two installments; Reynolds receipted with the mocking words "in full of all demands."

Reynolds remained on the scene, begging Hamilton to renew his visits to Maria. She reinforced with her supplications: "I have kept my Bed those tow dayes and now rise from my pillow which your Neglect has filled with the sharpest thorns. . . . I only do it to Ease a heart which is ready Burst with Greef[.] I can neither Eat or sleep[.] I have Been on the point of doing the most horrid acts. . . . I feel as If I should not contennue long and all the wish I have Is to see you once more . . . for God sake be not so voed of all humanity as to deni me this Last request." Though it be midnight, she would welcome him. Two days later she learned from Reynolds that Hamilton had deserted her from choice. "I scarce knew how to beleeve my senses and if my seturation was insupportable before I heard this it was now more so . . . if my dear freend has the Least Esteeme for the unhappy Maria whos greateest fault is Loveing him he will come as soon as he will get this. . . . I shal be Lone as Mr. is going to sup with a friend."

Now was the moment for Hamilton to resist or be fetched into deeper trouble than blackmail. He responded both to Maria's beseechings and to her husband's requisition for "loans." Reynolds affected to be humiliated because Hamilton entered by the back way. Was he a person of such bad character (a procurer for his wife!) that Hamilton was ashamed to be seen at his house? Then come no more. Hamilton was by now glad to stay away, though he was beset by fresh levies on one excuse and another through August 1792. He paid where he could lest his adulterous affair be disclosed to Mrs. Hamilton or others. Reynolds preserved Hamilton's notes to him, though they were in a disguised hand, unsigned, and supplemented his collection by scraps perhaps secured from the wastebasket in Hamilton's office. All were to figure in accusations later.

The story moved into a more painful phase. In early November 1792, Oliver Wolcott, as Comptroller of the Treasury, prosecuted Reynolds and his confederate Jacob Clingman. The charge was suborning perjury; Reynolds and Clingman wanted to obtain letters of administration upon the estate of a claimant against the United States who was still living. They plotted to secure a payment from the government not due them. Clingman was arrested first; he begged Henry Seckel, a Philadelphia merchant for whom he was formerly bookkeeper, to bring Reynolds, who would help him. Thereat Reynolds also was arrested.

Hamilton promptly had callers sent by Reynolds. Seckel brought a letter which Hamilton refused to receive; he warned Seckel not to involve himself in Reynolds's crime. Wolcott reported a threat of Reynolds, made in prison, that he could "make disclosures injurious to the character of some head of a Department." Hamilton opposed any steps to liberate Reynolds until he explained this threat. Clingman turned to another former employer, Frederick A. Muhlenberg, lately Speaker of the House, for aid. Muhlenberg and Aaron Burr applied to Hamilton and Wolcott; they both declined to intercede. Later Wolcott suggested that Reynolds be excused from prosecution if he made restitution, surrendered his list of claimants, and revealed from whom he got them. (His informant turned out to be a clerk in the Treasury, not Duer at all). Meantime Jeremiah Wadsworth, at Maria's request, had appeared on Reynolds's behalf—during the war Reynolds's father had been under Wadsworth in the commissary department. In December Clingman also accepted Wolcott's conditions, and he and Reynolds were dismissed.

In the weeks that Wadsworth was in touch with him Clingman frequently hinted that Reynolds had it in his power to injure the Secretary of the Treasury, that Hamilton had advanced money to Reynolds as his agent in improper speculation. Muhlenberg shared this report of official corruption with two fellow Republican (Antifederalist) members of Congress, James Monroe of the Senate and Abraham Venable of the House. Reynolds refused to enlarge on his insinuations until freed from prison that night. Lest he fail to keep a promised appointment next morning, Muhlenberg and Monroe hied them to his house to catch him as he returned from jail.

Finding only Mrs. Reynolds, they plied her with questions. Yes, she, at Hamilton's wish, had burned letters from him to her husband. However, Clingman had others of which Muhlenberg and Monroe possessed themselves. She showed them two letters offering to aid her, one signed with Hamilton's name. Thus munitioned, Monroe and Venable thought of laying the matter before the President at once, but were willing to hear Hamilton's story first. When they broached their suspicion of an improper financial connection between him and Reynolds, Hamilton was for ejecting them from his office at once. He retreated when they declared that they did not take the fact as established, but showed him notes which he acknowledged he had written in a disguised hand. He would remove their imputations of malfeasance in the Treasury if they would come to his home that evening. Hamilton revealed his intrigue with Mrs. Reynolds to Wolcott and engaged him to be present at the audience with the Congressmen.

At Hamilton's home that night his inquisitors exhibited their reports from the Reynolds pair and Clingman, and Hamilton's missives. He heard them through, then offered his proofs that their mistrust related to his private lapse with Maria and in no way indicated official misconduct. Before Hamilton finished reading, Venable, and perhaps Muhlenberg, declared that they had heard enough to convince them of his innocence, but Hamilton insisted on completing his disproof. "The result," Hamilton wrote, "was a full and unequivocal acknowledgment on the part of the three gentlemen of perfect satisfaction with the explanation and expressions of regret at the . . . embarrassment which had been occasioned to me. Mr. Muhlenberg and Mr. Venable, in particular, manifested a degree of sensibility on the occasion. Mr. Monroe was more cold but entirely explicit."

Hamilton asked his visitors for copies of the papers they had, and begged that the originals be not returned to the Reynolds pair and Clingman so that there would be no further attempt to use them to his defamation. Monroe had all of the papers, sent copies, and would keep the originals safe.

Soon after this episode Hamilton, in a veiled way, expressed compunction for his adultery in a piece in Fenno's paper. He was urging American neutrality in the expected war between France and Britain."A . . . virtuous Citizen," he wrote, "will regard his own country as a wife, to whom he is bound to be exclusively faithful and affectionate; and he will watch . . . every propensity of his heart to wander towards a foreign country, which he will regard as a mistress that may pervert his fidelity."

Hamilton's indiscretion was not buried in oblivion. Five years later it was publicized, with damaging distortion, in James T. Callender's *American Annual Register, or Historical Memoirs of the United States, for the Year 1796.* It was advertized to contain "singular and authentic papers respecting Mr. Alexander Hamilton." The fifth installment recited the suspicions of Muhlenberg, Monroe, and Venable that Hamilton, while Secretary of the Treasury, had speculated in the funds, and that he had oppressed Reynolds, his agent, in order to prevent disclosure. This Hamilton at once denied in a letter to Fenno's *Gazette.* This was the type of prejudicial tale that a man in public life could expect. The sixth installment ploughed deeper and was far more injurious. Callender charged that Hamilton's explanation to the Congressmen was false. The letters and receipts did not have to do with an amour with Mrs. Reynolds; but betrayed Hamilton's guilty connection with her husband. "So much correspondence," Callender declared, "could not refer exclusively to wenching." The exchanges bespoke betrayal of public trust and tokened Mrs. Reynolds's "innocence in the clearest stile."

Political vindictiveness rather than zeal for purity in the

Treasury inspired Callender's alleged exposure. The "immediate motive in the publication of these papers," he confessed, was to discredit Hamilton, whom he held responsible for the recall of Monroe from his post of United States minister to France. Not content with the accusation of malfeasance in the Treasury, Callender raked Hamilton fore and aft for a list of misdeeds.

Hamilton's reply was that Callender's calumnies would not have been worth notice except that he called to witness men of position in the nation. Hamilton applied to the three members of Congress who were cited by Callender to repeat their assurances of their belief in his official integrity and to deny Callender's arraignment. Appearance of the papers in print proved infidelity somewhere. In his reply he included a copy of the exculpation they had given him in 1792.

The next day he declared in Fenno's paper that the explanation of the letters paraded by Callender "is simply this—They were the contrivance of two . . . profligate men . . . to obtain their liberation from imprisonment for a serious crime by the *favor of party spirit.*" Two of the three Congressmen to whom they had turned for rescue were Hamilton's *known political opponents.* All three, Wolcott a witness, had agreed the charges were trumped up.

He might have let this disclaimer suffice. Friends urged him to go no further, and he had proclaimed that the public men whose names seemed to sanction the charges had testified to his innocence. More would see and credit his denial than would ever read Callender's pamphlets. He need not have confessed his intrigue with Mrs. Reynolds, supported by documents, thus causing pain to his family.

But he felt that full disclosure with proofs of his private fault was preferable to resting under a charge of misconduct in office. Also his anger was cumulative. He had suffered other attacks on his public character through the years. He had been vindicated by Congress before he left the Treasury. Now, two years later, new accusers had disavowed their suspicions, but his confidence in their promised future silence had been betrayed. This was too much; he would lash out at his tormentors. He announced in his letter to Fenno his "intention shortly to place the subject more precisely before the public."

He was freshly spurred to this by taunts from Callender in response to Hamilton's first brief denial of the indictment. Callender, in close conjunction with Monroe, sought to free the three legislators from Hamilton's conviction that they had rallied to Reynolds from party motives. If Hamilton's "penitential tale of . . . depravity" with Mrs. Reynolds could be believed, it did not explain dealings with her husband. Callender practically called Hamilton a liar, and repeated that he, Hamilton, had been anxious to keep the incriminating papers from the eyes of the President. Hamilton had best publish his extensive defense, as now "the public . . . have . . . some unlucky doubts."

Muhlenberg and Venable, writing from Philadelphia, at once confirmed their earlier exculpation of Hamilton. Monroe had just come from Philadelphia to New York, and Hamilton and his brother-in-law, John Barker Church, called on him at his lodgings. They found Monroe's political friend, David Gelston, present by arrangement. Hamilton, much agitated, demanded to know how, contrary to promise, the papers now came to be published. Monroe vouchsafed that he had "sealed up his copy of the papers . . . and . . . delivered them to his friend in Virginia—he . . . knew nothing of their publication until he arrived at Philada from Europe and was sorry to find they were published."

Hamilton angrily taxed Monroe with not having given him an earlier reply. Monroe explained that he had wanted to make a joint statement with Muhlenberg and Venable but had not time to meet them before leaving Philadelphia. Church exhibited Callender's pamphlets as a reproach to Monroe, who offered to give Hamilton his individual certificate then and there. He rehearsed his connection with the business, ending with his certainty "that the packet of papers . . . remained sealed with his friend in Virginia."

Hamilton branded this representation "totally false . . . upon which the Gentlemen both instantly rose Colo M. . . . saying do you say I represented falsely you are a Scoundrel. Colo H. Said I will meet you like a Gentleman Colo M said I am ready get your pistols." This is Gelston's account. He and Church separated the disputants and calmed them. It was agreed that Monroe, on early return to Philadelphia, would make a further joint reply with Muhlenberg and Venable. Hamilton would go to Philadelphia to conclude the controversy.

Hamilton was followed to Philadelphia by news of the perfect confidence of his wife, who was eight months' pregnant. She had read the newspaper with Callender's most recent thrust, but, Church reported, "it makes not the least Impression on her, only that she considers the whole knot of those opposed to you to be [scoundrels? scratched out]."

In the interval of Monroe's journey back to Philadelphia, Hamilton read in the next installment of Callender's *History* a document which had not been published before. Under the date of December 16, 1792, the three legislators recorded their visit to Hamilton's home, his confession of his intrigue with Mrs. Reynolds, his explanation that his payments to the husband were blackmail. The three concluded, "We left him under an impression, our suspicions were removed."

This was equivocal on the essential point, but more hurtful was an appended paragraph of a fortnight later, signed by Monroe alone. He reported having had a conversation that evening with Clingman, who had called on him to contradict the certificate of the Congressmen freeing Hamilton of any suspicion of guilt in his public capacity. "He . . . observed to me, that he communicated the same to Mrs. Reynolds [that is, the explanation of a liaison with her], who *appeared much shocked at it,* and *wept immoderately.* That she denied the imputation . . . it had been a fabrication of colonel Hamilton, and that her husband had joined in it, *who had told her so,* and *that he* [Reynolds] had given him [Hamilton] receipts for money and written letters, so *as to give countenance to the pretence."* Clingman "was of opinion she was innocent."

Hamilton, furious, reproached Monroe: ". . . you imply that your suspicions are still alive. And as nothing appears to have shaken your original conviction but the wretched tale of Clingman, which you have thought fit to record, it follows that you . . . attach . . . weight to that communication. . . . The result . . . is that you have been and are actuated by motives toward me malignant and dishonorable." Just how Clingman knew of Hamilton's defense against the suspicions of the legislators does not appear.

Monroe partly conceded to Hamilton's complaint. "I never intended," he declared, "to convey an opinion" on Clingman's statement, nor did his note of it "convey any opinion of my own." He simply recorded a further item in the episode, on the credit of Clingman only. Monroe's companions, he said, should also have signed the minute. However, he refused to state "that this communication made no impression on my mind." It did not absolutely change his opinion, or he would have acted on it.

Callender's publication of Monroe's partial retraction of his faith in Hamilton's innocence of official wrongdoing led to a long and lively correspondence. As Monroe stuck to his position, it threatened to bring on a duel. It firmed Hamilton's resolve to spell out the whole affair for the public.

In his stay in Philadelphia, Hamilton, with Wolcott's help, busily collected supporting documents, which he appended to his pamphlet, published August 31, 1797. One needs to disregard the unobtrusive title to experience the excitement of the contents. The tract was called *Observations on Certain Documents, Contained in No. V and VI of "The History of the United*

States for the Year 1796," in which the Charge of Speculation
against Alexander Hamilton, late Secretary of the Treasury, is
Fully Refuted. Written by himself.

He began by striking back at his Jacobin enemies who practiced reiterated slander despite formal congressional disproof.
In this connection he included two recent, friendly letters of
Jefferson to A. G. Fraunces, who had been dismissed from a
Treasury clerkship and had plotted to undermine Hamilton's
reputation. The "system of defamation" had reached its vilest
in Callender's present falsehoods. The charge was improper
speculation with Reynolds. "My real crime is an amorous connection with his wife . . . with his connivance, if not originally brought on by . . . husband and wife . . . to extort
money from me." The very documents on which his accusers
relied refuted their charge. What head of the money department of the nation, with access to millions, if corrupt, would
have confined himself to petty peculations with obscure crimi-
nals as his agents? He recited his affair with Mrs. Reynolds,
supported by letters from her and her husband, which left no
doubt that his notes to Reynolds pertained to the blackmail
levied on him, not to speculation. The letters of the Reynolds
pair, which Callender did not have, showed that the husband
was a despicable villain and the wife was as susceptible or
sinister as one chose to read her. Hamilton pinned Monroe for
his conduct throughout.

Those closest to the event, whatever their attitude, agreed
that it was John Beckley whose clerk had copied the papers for
Muhlenberg and Venable, and who was believed to have retained copies himself. Beckley was all along a traducer of
Hamilton, and was not in need of additional souring against
the Federalists because of his recent failure of re-election as
Clerk of the House of Representatives.

Callender declared that Hamilton had forged Maria Reynolds's letters to him, purposely falling into errors of spelling,
punctuation, and capitals, but that he had been unable to hide

an elegance of expression that did not belong to "an illiterate writer." (The accusation has been repeated by Julian Boyd at this late day, in his definitive edition of Jefferson's papers.) In assembling materials for his pamphlet Hamilton himself told Jeremiah Wadsworth "I am somewhat embarrassed to prove Mrs. Reynold's hand writing." As Wadsworth had probably received notes from her when she had applied for his assistance, would he be able to certify that her letter which Hamilton enclosed was in the same hand? Hamilton appended to his pamphlet the sworn deposition of Mary Williams, a Philadelphia boarding house keeper, that she was familiar with Maria Reynolds's handwriting and that she endorsed as genuine the letters which Hamilton had shown her and afterward had printed. Further, Hamilton was careful in his pamphlet to call attention to his deposit of "all the original papers which are contained in the appendix to this narrative" with William Bingham, and he said that any gentleman was invited to peruse them. Two months after Hamilton's pamphlet appeared, Callender, in a two-faced letter, applied to him for an order "to inspect the papers lodged with Mr. Bingham;" if he thought them genuine he was ready to retract his allegation of their having been concocted by Hamilton. Hamilton endorsed Callender's letter "Impudent Experiment No *Notice.*" As to the feeling with which Maria could infuse her letters, Richard Folwell, a printer who knew her well (and who was not connected with Hamilton), spoke of receiving from her "a very pathetic Letter . . . it would move any one almost to serve her, that was not perfectly acquainted with her Character."

Aside from Maria's letters, in whosoever's hand, the pettiness of the speculation alleged, and with such a profligate confederate as Reynolds, was conclusive of Hamilton's innocence.

In the personal controversy between Hamilton and Monroe, as it approached armed encounter, Major William Jackson acted as Hamilton's friend and Aaron Burr as Monroe's. The thing dragged on for months, as Monroe needed time to pre-

pare his vindication of his mission in France. Whether a frank
challenge was issued, and if so by whom, is not clear. In the
end Burr composed the quarrel, though Monroe rested under
Hamilton's charge that he had shown himself "dishonorable."

A footnote is Mrs. Hamilton's permanent resentment of
Monroe's actions. Long afterward, Monroe called on her; she
was barely persuaded to see him (this by a nephew who was
with her), and she did not ask him to sit down. It was many
years, he said, since they had met, they were both nearing the
grave, when past differences could be forgiven. "She answered, still standing, and looking at him, 'Mr. Monroe, if you
have come to tell me that you repent, that you are sorry, *very*
sorry, for . . . the slanders . . . you circulated against my
dear husband . . . I understand it. But, otherwise, no lapse of
time, no nearness to the grave, makes any difference.' "
Whereat Monroe took his leave.

As the original documents in the case have never been
found, it is likely that Bingham returned them to Hamilton
and that after his death Mrs. Hamilton destroyed them. The
Hamilton family tried to buy up the edition of Hamilton's
pamphlet.

While his enemies from time to time had sport in reverting
to his illicit affair with Maria Reynolds, there is no evidence
that his self-revealed fault lowered the esteem in which he was
held by his contemporaries.

Aaron Burr got Maria a divorce from Reynolds on the
ground of his(!) adultery; then she married Clingman a half-
hour before the divorce was effective.

Chapter 20

ABORTIVE INTERLUDE

The interval in Hamilton's life which he could best have spared was that of 1798–1800, when he prepared for expected war with France. The waste of his time and talents was worse because he sought the assignment and was willing to shoulder aside excellent officers much senior to him in age and rank in the old army. George Washington consented to be Commander in Chief, with the condition that he would not come out of his retirement and take the field unless this country were actually invaded. President John Adams had no wish to name Hamilton among the major generals, but would place him at best third after Knox and Charles Cotesworth Pinckney. Washington threatened to decline to serve unless Hamilton was given precedence, as next under himself. This alienated General Knox, who eliminated himself, though General Pinckney gracefully accepted appointment subordinate to Hamilton. On Hamilton fell the immediate responsibility for recruiting twelve additional active regiments and forming plans for calling up a provisional force of 50,000 militia.

French spoliations on our neutral shipping, insults to our

envoys, and subjugation of successive European states excited Hamilton to the conviction that the Directory was a menace to western civilization. In fervid writings he looked "upon the Question before the Public as nothing less than whether we shall maintain our Independence." Congress should provide more troops, ten ships of the line, defense of principal ports, suspend treaties with France, and borrow in anticipation of new tax revenues. All this he did not think "will lead to general rupture." The election "is between tame surrender of our rights or a state of mitigated hostility."

When Pinckney was repelled by the French government "with circumstances of indignity" Hamilton urged on his friends in the Cabinet his program of preparing for war while continuing to press negotiation. Congress should be called in special session to dispatch a three-man commission to France; his choices were Pinckney, George Cabot, and Jefferson or Madison.

Hamilton relied on the belligerence of President Adams against France. Adams expressed his hostility to Congress after our three envoys were insulted by a demand for a bribe. He fell in with Grenville's promotion of a British-American military alliance. Britain would supply the navy, which would welcome American seamen; the United States would wrest Louisiana and Florida from Spain. St. Domingo would pass to British possession. Robert Liston, the British minister here, reported Adams's reaction: he "conceived it to be the interest of this country as well as that of Great Britain to . . . concert plans of operation, for the joint conduct of the war against France . . . if it depended upon him, he would enter into the engagements . . . without scruple and without loss of time." But he was obliged to wait for approval, on which the people were deliberating. Adams, in response to patriotic addresses, sought "to enflame . . . animosity against the French Republick." Adams's ardor cooled, however, with outcries against the administration and hints of peace from Elbridge Gerry, then in Paris.

The Federalists, in enforcing the Alien and Sedition Acts, were harsher than Hamilton approved. Dissent must not be erected into division. "Let us not established a tyranny," he begged Wolcott. "Energy is a very different thing from violence." Foreigners should not be expelled indiscriminately. Still, the degree to which he accepted the laws against supposed subversion was not to his credit.

Hamilton's efforts at mobilization, actual and prospective, were hampered. Urgency of warlike preparation was lacking because peace negotiations were proceeding. Except for the narrow mandate of Congress, Hamilton had to refer measures to President Adams, to whom, on account of mutual dislike, he had no personal access. The pro-French party opposed the defense policy and declared that the purpose of the augmented army, in conjunction with the Alien and Sedition Acts, was to repress protest at home more than to meet foreign attack which did not materialize. Adams was resentful of Hamilton's unofficial dominance of his Cabinet. Semi-isolated politically, his pride hurt, President Adams took no pains against capricious exercise of his undoubted authority.

The existing skeleton army on which the expanded force was to be based was dispersed and ill administered. Hamilton felt obliged to confide to Washington that "McHenry is wholly insufficient for his place [Secretary of War] with the additional misfortune, of not having the least suspicion of the fact." But McHenry was an old and good friend and could not be replaced. Hamilton volunteered to take certain duties off McHenry's hands, but without result. Hamilton told Washington, "I more and more . . . apprehend that obstacles of a very peculiar kind stand in the way of an efficient and successful management." He tapered off his law practice until his income from that source shrank to half the usual, yet his army pay was not authorized for weeks after he was in uniform and then amounted to only a fourth of what he had earned from clients.

He busied himself to bring system to the scattered posts, requiring that reports be made directly to him, not to the Secretary of War. Along with more important matters this involved him in fatiguing, petty detail which should have been the care of assistants whom he did not have. More congenial was supervision of erection of defenses of New York harbor. He worked with Aaron Burr on this assignment, the last instance of their association before the election of 1800, which signaled commencement of their bitter enmity.

Hamilton, de facto head of the army, such as it was, besides casting covetous eyes on Florida and Louisiana, responded to the project of a cooperation between the United States and Britain to liberate Spain's South American colonies. This had long been the ambition of Francisco de Miranda, the Venezuelan revolutionary patriot with whom Hamilton was in touch from time to time. The Spanish colonies were to be guaranteed their independence by the liberating powers, which would share equally in the trade benefits. Hamilton was stimulated to his filibustering enterprise no more by Miranda than by Rufus King, the American minister to England. He wrote to King, "I wish it much to be undertaken, but I should be glad that the principal agency be in the United States," which should furnish the whole land force. "The command in this case would . . . naturally fall upon me, and I hope I shall disappoint no favorable anticipation." This was going much beyond defense of the United States; it was symptomatic of the emotional state into which Hamilton had worked himself. However, he would do nothing of this sort unless ordered to do so by the United States government. Some have said that his disappointment at the peaceful settlement with France was the keener because he must relinquish imperialist ambitions. In any event, he sanctioned the accommodation with France.

Strangely, Hamilton showed faith in James Wilkinson, his subordinate in the southwest, and recommended his promotion to major general. Early in the Revolution Wilkinson had disparaged Washington and Hamilton. As American commander on the frontier he did not scruple to take pay from

Spain. For once McHenry was able to give Hamilton good advice. He cautioned that Wilkinson did not deserve the confidence of government so long as he was guilty of divided allegiance. McHenry begged Hamilton to "avoid saying any thing to him which would induce him to imagine government had in view any hostile project . . . against any of the possessions of Spain. I require this caution on good grounds."

Fear of giving military authority to subversive individuals or groups possessed the administration, and, indeed, Congress, as is indicated by the Alien and Sedition Acts. Recruits to the army, especially officers appointed, should be loyal. Those unsympathetic with the preparedness mobilization stigmatized the "Pretorian Bands" designed for "Party Persecution." Several men who were nominated were refused approval by the Senate because they were "anti-federal," "nobody," "opposed to the government and of French principles," and so on. Hamilton regretted the rejection of Caleb Gibbs, who had commanded Washington's bodyguard during the Revolution and who was eligible as colonel of a Massachusetts regiment.

Hamilton insisted on soldiers faithful to the government, but not necessarily Federalists. Nor did he balk at including worthy foreigners. He recommended his friend Major Louis Tousard for the critical post of inspector of artillery. Tousard had earned trust by his one-man attack on a cannon in the battle of Rhode Island, in which he had lost an arm. President Adams at first objected to commissioning Tousard, because "an angel with the name & tongue of a Frenchman would not in a French war have the confidence of this nation." A friend of Tousard remarked that Hamilton had none of those "prejudices which . . . exist in the fountain of Power."

Aaron Burr offered to serve as a brigadier, and Adams was eager to have him. But Washington refused because, though he knew Burr was brave, he held him to be an intriguer; Hamilton's opinion was similarly unfavorable. Adams's postscript to the incident was that Washington "had compelled me to promote, over the heads of Lincoln, Gates, Clinton, Knox, and . . . Pinckney, one of his own triumvirate, the most restless, impatient, artful, indefatigable and unprincipled intriguer in the United States, if not in the world, to be second in command under himself, and now dreaded an intriguer in a poor brigadier!"

Recruiting of the additional regiments lagged; Hamilton had only one clerical assistant, his nephew, Captain Philip Church, and the Secretary of War had difficulty in meeting the unusual demands on his office. Progress was slowed because the clothing contractors did not deliver the necessary uniforms. Hamilton must have winced under General Washington's remonstrance of February 25, 1799: "If the augmented force was not intended as an interrorem [*sic*] measure, the delay in recruiting it, is unaccountable, and baffles all conjecture. . . . The . . . enthusiasm . . . excited by the Publication of the Dispatches of our Commissioners at Paris (which gave birth to the Law authorizing . . . the twelve Regiments &c) are evaporated. It is now no more, and if this dull season, when men are idle . . . and . . . might be induced to enlist, is suffered to pass away also, we shall . . . set out as a forlorn hope, to execute this business." That very day President Adams nominated the new commission to France, which further sapped military ardor. A month later Washington spoke not of the army, but "more properly of the embryo one, for I do not perceive . . . that we are likely to move beyond this."

Hamilton reported to Washington his hope "that in the summer and fall the army will be at its complement." Nine hundred tailors were turning out uniforms; hired civilian fifers and drummers were rallying to the colors.

An impediment was the "rebellion," in Northampton and contiguous counties of Pennsylvania, known by the name of John Fries, who roused the German farmers against the taxes on lands and houses levied to support the threatened war with

France. The President issued his proclamation against "combinations to defeat the execution of the Laws"; he was determined to call out the military to aid the marshal. The insurrection had been allowed to run on too long, and it might incite similar resistance elsewhere. Wolcott lamented to Hamilton that all at the capital was "languor & indecision," as "we have no Prest here . . . The Governor is habitually intoxicated every day & most commonly every forenoon." To counteract the government's feeble measures, Hamilton ordered to the scene in Pennsylvania an advance detachment of one hundred from the garrison at Fort Jay, New York. Brigadier General William Macpherson followed with 240 horse and two companies of artillery. Hamilton, dispatching ample correction, reverted to his precedent in the whiskey rising of five years before. He counseled the Secretary of War: "Beware of magnifying a riot into an insurrection by employing in the first instance an inadequate force. . . . Whenever the Government appears in arms it ought to appear like a *Hercules,* and inspire respect by the display of strength," though judgment should be used, of course.

A month later Macpherson reported to Hamilton that order was restored, but regulars should remain in Reading, Allentown, and Easton. Actually the danger had been exaggerated by those, Hamilton included, whose fears were stirred by international and party tension. Hamilton held it against Adams that he pardoned Fries, who had been condemned to death.

Pickering, the Secretary of State, asked Hamilton to outline a scheme of government for San Domingo in case Toussaint, who had rebelled against French rule, declared the island independent. The gain to United States commerce was the object. Hamilton's friend from boyhood, Dr. Edward Stevens, was about to go to San Domingo as United States consul-general. The plan Hamilton proposed reflected the prevailing violence and the complete inexperience of self-government of the people. He recommended a strict military autocracy. His

political foes in America who called him "Little Mars," would
have descanted on his sway of the sword had they known of
it.

When it appeared that the regiments he was recruiting
might be disbanded in consequence of peace diplomacy,
Hamilton nonetheless formed plans for future use of the nation's army. He reworked Steuben's regulations for the infantry, submitted the portion governing regimental maneuvers to
General Pinckney for review, and committed directions for the
cavalry and artillery to Brigadier General William Washington
and Lieutenant John DeBarth Walbach.

Hamilton also promoted the establishment of a training
school for officers, often urged by Washington, which became
the United States Military Academy at West Point. The smaller
the standing army, the greater the need for its efficiency.
"Since it is agreed," he wrote to the Secretary of War, "that we
are not to keep on foot numerous forces instructed and disciplined, military science in its various branches ought to be
cultivated . . . in proper Nurseries . . . ready to be imparted
and diffused. . . . This will be to substitute the elements of an
army to the thing itself," so the forces could be expanded in
emergencies.

The academy should have a fundamental school in which all
students spent two years learning mathematics, mechanics,
geography, and tactics. Then followed a period in one of four
specialized branches—artillery and engineering (two years),
cavalry, navy (one year each). The site should permit of an artillery range and be on navigable water suitable for ship construction. A cannon foundry and small arms manufactory,
operated by army detachments, would furnish object lessons
for the students. Hamilton sent his outline to Washington for
his suggestions, and, in the last letter he ever wrote, two days
before his death, the General gave the project his warm approval.

In March 1800 the joint efforts of Hamilton and McHenry

produced "A Bill for Establishing a Military Academy, and for better organizing the corps of Artillerists and Engineers." It was twice read in the House and scheduled for the Committee of the Whole, but got no further then. However, Hamilton secured the promotion of Louis Tousard to lieutenant colonel and inspector of artillery, and he became, in effect, the first director of the limited military academy founded by law at West Point in 1802.

The creative period of Federalist administration called out Hamilton's finest efforts. He began urging a strong national government a number of years before Washington was inaugurated, so that his active service in this behalf extended over more than a decade. When rescue from the backwash of the Revolution was accomplished, internal dissension followed. Developing popular protest against Federalist policies was to reach its crest with Jefferson's election to the presidency. By the same token, Hamilton's role waned after, say, the negotiation of Jay's Treaty. His always cordial cooperation with Washington, virtually as minister without portfolio, was succeeded by his suspicion of President John Adams and his secret influence on the members of Adams's Cabinet.

Party conflict was not Hamilton's forte. As Federalist leader he engaged in it of necessity, but he did not know how, by concessions and compromises, to keep his followers in power. Instead, he became overwrought, embittered, and ended by giving his own party its mortal wound. He was first-rate as a statesman, a failure as a politician. His faults as party manager bespoke a decline in his own capacities. His judgment suffered; he no longer saw problems in true proportion; his vision was skewed. This was not a constant disability; he could jerk back to reality and for an interval manifest his abiding talents. Thus his lamentable attack on John Adams in the election of 1800 was closely followed by his splendid espousal of Jefferson in preference to Aaron Burr.

Toward the end of his career he realized that he had ne-

glected to form a Federalist bond with the mass of the people.
He had been too busy devising measures *for* the people to
propose progress *with* them. By the time he came to act on this
policy it was too late, for Jefferson, long in the field, had attracted the people's support. Hamilton's tardy plan for Federalist revival was given to Jonathan Dayton, a member of the
House, in 1799. Hamilton urged "Establishments which will
extend the influence and promote the popularity of the Government." Such would be more conveniently located justices
of the peace. "The improvement of the roads would be a measure universally popular." He recommended a "national system" of turnpikes and canals that would extend the services of
government; this anticipated by a decade Gallatin's report on
internal improvements. Premiums for improvements in agriculture and inventions in the mechanic arts would "speak
powerfully to the . . . interests of those classes of men to
whom the benefits derived from the Government have been
heretofore . . . least manifest."

These were the ameliorative features of his program. The
others leaned toward repression—a somewhat enlarged standing army, calls on militia to put down insurrections, and
"Laws for restraining and punishing incendiary and seditious
practices." Probably the Kentucky and Virginia resolution of
1798 prompted Hamilton's response: "The subdivision of the
great states is indispensable to the security of the General
Government and . . . of the Union." They should be frac-
tioned to permit republican administration.

In consequence of assurances from Talleyrand, President
Adams nominated new commissioners to compose differences
with France. Hamilton wrote Lafayette that he hoped the mis-
understandings would be banished. It was "in the power of
France, by reparation to our merchants . . . and the stipula-
tion of justice in the future, to put an end to the controversy."
Hamilton shared the astonishment of the Federalists in
Congress that Adams responded to the French overture with-

out consultation. The lawmakers did persuade the President to place Chief Justice Ellsworth and Governor William R. Davie of North Carolina with William Vans Murray in the delegation to Paris.

A year later, in his pamphlet attack, Hamilton blamed Adams, not for renewing his peace effort, but merely for the manner of it, on his sole responsibility, and for intending to rely on Murray alone. This was a censure which Hamilton should have omitted, for he agreed with the result of Adams's action. Hamilton did not deserve the slap of the Democratic *Aurora*, that when President Adams "saves his country from a ruinous war, the dogs of faction are let loose, the old jockey gives the haloo, and the whole pack yelp in chorus." Adams's own indictment may have applied to some Federalists, but not to Hamilton. Reflecting on the split in Federalist ranks, he declared that "the British faction was determined to have a war with France, and Alexander Hamilton at the head of the army, and then President of the United States. Peace with France was . . . treason against their . . . reasons of state. . . . No wonder they hate the author of their defeat."

Hamilton would have done better to overlook the annoying inconsistencies of Adams in the light of his signal, unaided success in preventing war with France. Hamilton himself had been chiefly reponsible for avoiding war with Great Britain earlier. Adams's stroke was more difficult. The United States was now stronger, she was smarting under repeated French insult to our envoys, naval fights were actually occurring, and vast territory might fall to this country in event of victory. Adams had a right to pride himself on "a peace that . . . accomplished a predominant wish of my heart . . . which was to place our relations with France and Great Britain upon a footing of . . . impartiality; that we might be able to preserve . . . neutrality in all the wars of Europe."

The death of Washington, after the briefest illness, in December 1799 was a blow to Hamilton personally as well as a political blow worse than was suffered by any other man. Washington had been his patron in war and peace. It is doubtful whether Hamilton could have made his impress without Washington as sponsor. He wrote to Tobias Lear, "I have been much indebted to the kindness of the General, and he was an Aegis very essential to me." Washington's death closed the Federalist era. Hamilton wrote in a gloomy mood to Rufus King: "Our measures . . . are too much the effect of momentary impulse. Vanity and jealousy exclude all counsel. Passion wrests the helm from reason. The irreparable loss of an inestimable man removes a control which was felt, and was very salutary." While Hamilton was Washington's coadjutor, both were strengthened by their alliance. Hamilton, more than any other man, was Washington's heir, but he could not rule the storm that arose. Indeed, by ill judgment he helped get up the wind. However, it was only a matter of time before the Federalists who had guided the country in its first dozen years would be supplanted by popular forces.

After Washington's death several military men addressed Hamilton as Commander in Chief, and in fact he acted as such. He was not so designated, probably because President Adams heartily disliked him, and the auxiliary army would soon be disbanded. By mid-February of 1800 Congress had forbidden further enlistment, and a month later the President was authorized to discharge all of the added force except dragoons, engineers, and artillery. The troops thus to be dismissed had not reached half the full complement, which was to have been 8448. Some regiments had few men, and many had deserted from those with more. Companies were unequal; some had more than fifty men, others fewer than thirty, and one company had only a lieutenant and a drummer. Adjutant William North had recommended that new officers be put in command of the fort in New York harbor, as discipline of the garrison was neglected and "nothing is in a situation to meet the attack of a privateer of 10 Guns."

Had recruiting continued, perhaps the regiments would have been filled. And it may be that the gesture of increasing the army had some effect in bringing France to terms. But as matters stood after two years of preparation, the result was not creditable to the Inspector General. He directed that old regiments be recruited from those to be dissolved, thanked the discharged soldiers in the name of the President and himself, and made sure that they received their pay in full, including three months' dismissal wages. The war office itself was vacant because McHenry had incurred the President's distrust; Stoddert, Secretary of the Navy, took over McHenry's duties. On July 1, 1800, Hamilton quit his headquarters in New York, ended his military service, and submitted his accounts.

Hamilton's two years of effort for defense against France, invited by himself, was largely abortive. By interrupting his law practice he had sacrificed three-fourths of his income. The whole experience was fretful and frittering. He would have done well to take a vacation to restore him to a calm view. Instead, with the national election four months away, he posted to New England to discover Federalist sentiment in that quarter, plunged into vehement political correspondence, and invited the destruction of his party. His friend William North tried to check him as he put off his uniform and re-entered the political arena. "To you . . . all eyes look. . . . Your head is always right, I would, your heart was a little less susceptible" and apt "to carry you out of the direct path."

Hamilton set about marshaling his forces. He instructed Sedgwick, in Congress, to have the Federalists there come to "a solemn concert . . . to support *Adams* and [Charles Cotesworth] *Pinckney* equally." This "is the only thing that can possibly save us from the fangs of *Jefferson.*"

The Federalists were defeated in elections to the state legislature in New York City and near-by parts. This unprecedented setback on home ground pitched Hamilton into a reprehensible proposal to Governor Jay. An Antifederalist majority in the incoming legislature would choose electors who would make Jefferson President. To preserve the helm of state from "an atheist in religion, . . . a fanatic in politics," the Governor should call the existing legislature into special session. The purpose would be to change the law, to take the choice of electors away from the new legislature and give it to the people voting in districts. Here Hamilton was scheming to subvert the manifest intention of the voters. If the Jeffersonians had tried such a trick he would have cried to heaven against it. Governor Jay endorsed Hamilton's letter, "Proposing a measure for party purposes which it would not become me to adopt."

Hamilton received disquieting news from New England. Samuel Dexter feared that if Federalists voted for Adams and Pinckney equally, Pinckney might be the choice of the country; Adams's supporters would be disgusted, and the Federalist party would crumble. Throughout the Union there were enough Federalist electors to permit those of New England to throw away a few votes to ensure the success of Adams. By this time President Adams had declared war on Hamilton's following by dismissing Pickering and McHenry from his Cabinet. Hamilton rejoined with equal hostility: "I will never more be responsible for [Adams] by my direct support, even though the consequence should be the election of *Jefferson*. If we must have an *enemy* at the head of the government, let it be one whom we can oppose, . . . who will not involve our party in the disgrace of his . . . bad measures." If New England would support Pinckney equally with Adams, Hamilton would espouse Adams with Pinckney, but it was plain that his hopes rode with Pinckney.

Hamilton visited Massachusetts, New Hampshire, and Rhode Island, where the preference of Federalists for Adams, as Hamilton saw it, endangered the coming election. He came away with the report that "the greatest number of strong minded men" rated Pinckney the equal of or superior to

Adams. However, the majority of the Federalist leaders of the second class were so attached to Adams that they would withhold votes from Pinckney. He confessed to James A. Bayard, influential Federalist in the House, "There seems to be too much probability that Jefferson or Burr will be President. The latter is intriguing with all his might," hoping "he will overtop his friend Jefferson." If elected, "Burr will certainly attempt to reform the government *à la Buonaparte*. He is as unprincipled and dangerous a man as any country can boast—as true a Catiline as ever met in midnight conclave."

Nevertheless, Hamilton would reinforce his plea to the lesser Federalists of the Eastern states with a written statement "of the facts which denote unfitness in Mr. Adams." He applied to Wolcott, who was still in Adams's Cabinet, and to Pickering, recently dismissed, for illustrative materials. His impropriety in asking them to betray confidence seemed not to bother him, nor did he flinch in the end from exposing the two as tale-bearers in a public letter.

George Cabot and Fisher Ames, "high Federalists" of Massachusetts, shared Hamilton's distrust of Adams, but warned against the danger—the folly, they should have said—of discrediting the titular head of the party when he was running for re-election. This would split the Federalists, when unity was more than ever necessary. Therefore, after demonstrating Adams's defects, Hamilton must urge Federalists to vote for him, otherwise Adams's devoted friends would not hold to the agreement to vote for Pinckney also. This committed Hamilton to a glaring contradiction of counsel—tearing Adams down, then re-erecting him as candidate. Cabot and Ames begged further that Hamilton not sign his letter. It would be hard enough to conceal his authorship. If he acknowledged his attack on President Adams he would deliver his party to the enemy.

Chapter 21

FURY FOR ADAMS, FAVOR FOR JEFFERSON

Except for his tangle with Aaron Burr, Hamilton's political attack on President John Adams was his worst mistake. It contributed to the sinking of the Federalist party, which Hamilton had led, and it ushered his enemies into office. John Quincy Adams, looking backward a quarter-century later, was sure that Hamilton had rejected his father for a second term because President Adams had thwarted Hamilton's political ambition. "Hamilton's system of policy looked to a war with France, and a large army, of which he was to be the head." The "conflict between a French war and a pacific mission was the immediate cause of that schism in the Federal party which accomplished their political ruin and the fall of my father's administration." The mission prepared the way for the Louisiana Purchase and averted war with France, "and this abortion of the army of fifty thousand men, was the cause of the inextinguishable hatred of Hamilton and Pickering to my father."

This filial explanation is questionable. Hamilton agreed that peace with France was wise; the army would never have reached fifty thousand, it was actually one-tenth of that when disbanded. John Adams and Hamilton were of different temperaments and experience in the national government. Hamilton, younger than Adams by twenty years, was friendly; he penetrated the dignity of Washington. Adams was distant, vain, self-conscious, piqued at any slight. As Vice President for two terms under Washington he had felt humiliated in his inactive office. Hamilton, by contrast, in these years was the most enterprising and, except for the President, the most responsible member of the administration. On Washington's retirement many Federalists, Hamilton especially, preferred as his successor Thomas Pinckney, former minister to England and negotiator of the popular treaty with Spain. Adams was furious that the Federalists did not give him their entire support in 1796.

Adams's subordinate position in Federalist allegiance was evident in his own Cabinet ministers; they were inherited from Washington's presidency, had been recommended by Hamilton, and did Hamilton's bidding. This was the more natural because President Adams, at every opportunity, quit the capital for his ancestral home at Braintree, Massachusetts, three hundred horsedrawn miles away, where he might remain for months, unavailable for important decisions.

The title of Hamilton's pamphlet was *Letter from Alexander Hamilton Concerning the Public Conduct and Character of John Adams, Esq., President of the United States* (New York, 1800). He began by declaring his early admiration of Adams, then passed to his later disillusionment. In the end Hamilton found Adams "a man of an imagination sublimated and eccentric; propitious neither to the regular display of sound judgment, nor to steady perseverance in a systematic plan of conduct; and . . . to this defect are added the unfortunate foibles of a vanity without bounds, and a jealousy capable of discoloring every object." At other points Hamilton spoke of "the disgust-

ing egotism, the distempered jealousy, and the ungovernable
indiscretion of [his] temper"; "he is often liable to paroxysms
of anger, which deprive him of self-command, and produce
very outrageous behavior to those who approach him;" many
distinguished persons "have been humiliated by . . . these
gusts of passion." The President's conduct "has sunk the tone
of the public mind—it has impaired the confidence of the
friends of the Government in the Executive Chief—it has distracted public opinion—it has unnerved the public councils—
it has sown the seeds of discord at home, and lowered the reputation of the government abroad."

Hamilton did not have to emphasize his censure of Adams's
complaint that in the first national election Adams had not
been allowed an even chance with Washington. A few votes
had been deliberately diverted to others to ensure that Washington, the supreme man, would be President. How could
Adams be so blind to the desire of the country? Yet Adams
was furious later, when many Federalists, and Hamilton particularly, urged equal electoral votes for Adams and Thomas
Pinckney. Hamilton went to lengths in his pamphlet to defend
Pinckney against Adams's abuse of him.

Hamilton next brought on the boards Adams's actions in the
controversy with France. After the refusal to receive Charles
Cotesworth Pinckney as our minister, and the demand for a
bribe from our first commission of three, Adams would not be
budged from his rage. It was suggested to him that if France
retracted and sent a minister to this country he should be
treated in the spirit of accommodation. Adams's answer was
"That if France should send a minister to-morrow, he would
order him back the day after." However, "In less than forty-
eight hours from this extraordinary sally, the mind of Mr.
Adams underwent a total revolution;" not only would he accept a minister from France, but he would send one to Paris if
assured of his respectful treatment. Hamilton charged that this

last went too far; it sacrificed our honor and the advantage of negotiating on our own ground.

The next scene was not more to Adams's credit, as Hamilton saw it. Adams had accepted the informal overture through Murray, our minister at The Hague, and without consultation with our Secretary of State he had nominated Murray as envoy to France. He was persuaded to add Ellsworth and Davie to make up a commission of three, but they were not to leave the United States until fuller assurance was had from France. Hardly was this done when another revolution in the Directory dictated renewed delay here. Adams agreed to this, then, bypassing his Cabinet, he dispatched the envoys instanter. Sometimes Adams forecast that the mission would demonstrate the necessity of war with France; more often he expected peace to result. At the time Hamilton wrote, the adjustment with France (by the Convention of Montefontaine, September 30, 1800) was not known in America.

Hamilton contradicted the charge of President Adams that Hamilton had gone to Trenton to conspire with his friends in the Cabinet to counteract the President's policy toward France. Hamilton had been at Trenton to meet General Wilkinson on military matters; he had had no advance notion of Adams's visit.

Hamilton intended to show the trifling reasons President Adams gave for dismissing Secretaries Pickering and McHenry. However, the abrupt dropping of them followed a long period of neglect of their advice and resentment on their part of the President's imperious manner. The narrative of their exit from the Cabinet unmistakably reveals their confidences with Hamilton.

Adams had freely declared that John Fries and others, if found guilty of defying the revenue laws, could expect no leniency from him. His surprising pardon of those under death sentence was taken by Hamilton to mean that he had made "Some system of concession to his political enemies." Hamilton condemned the sudden forgiveness because Fries's rebellion came on top of the Whiskey Insurrection, also a resistance to the national government.

After calling over the list of Adams's alleged offenses against the public, Hamilton confessed his "personal dissatisfaction" with the President. This was chiefly because of Adams's "virulent abuse" of Hamilton "as the leader of a British faction," an arraignment which he undertook to disprove.

Having dwelt elaborately on Adams's "unfitness for the station of Chief Magistrate," Hamilton was yet "resolved not to advise the withholding from him a single vote." He justified this inconsistency by avowing his loyalty to the caucus agreement by which pro-Adams and pro-Pinckney Federalists would support the two candidates equally. This tactic would "increase the probability of excluding a third candidate [Jefferson], of whose unfitness all sincere Federalists are convinced."

He promised to circulate his tract "within narrow limits" and "in such a manner as will not be likely to deprive Mr. Adams of a single vote." To what leaders he would send it for private perusal is not clear, but it is evident from his own words that he knew it would in fact become public property. In the hands of Aaron Burr it was a precious Antifederalist campaign document, picturing Adams wounded in the house of his friends. The printer, who owned the copyright, added to the issues of the damaging pamphlet.

Hamilton notified Pickering, who had buried himself deep in the western woods, that "The press teems with replies, and I may . . . think it expedient to publish a second time" with new anecdotes of Adams's unworthiness. Adams men were swift in rebuttal; Democrats exulted in the disservice Hamilton had done his party and himself; friends found him showing the same vanity that he charged against Adams.

A lusty rejoinder came from James Cheetham, who was to all Federalists a prime "disorganizer." He observed that the struggle between England and France had set the pattern of political convulsion in America. Hamilton was "the zealous friend of monarchical government, . . . a dangerous character under any republican system . . . whose power, if equal to his will, would bestride the world." Praising Jefferson, Cheetham made ungenerous use of Hamilton's confession of his intrigue with Maria Reynolds.

Noah Webster, who was long loyal to Hamilton's principles, also replied. He signed himself "Federalist." He extolled Hamilton's earlier service in preserving party harmony. But, he said, President Adams had restrained the New Yorker's influence "and [had] called into *open* opposition, the *secret* enmity which . . . long rankled" in Hamilton's breast. The President's mission to France removed every pretext for a permanent armed force, hence "the deep chagrin and disappointment of a military character" devoted to that ambition. It was Hamilton's fault that his party was divided; he would be the culprit if an Antifederalist became President.

Another critic (William Pinkney?) would "discover the black blood that eddies round [Hamilton's] heart." If the Jeffersonians succeeded in the election, blame must be laid to Hamilton's "malice of disappointed ambition, animated with the hope of speedy resuscitation" should C. C. Pinckney become President. *A Vindication of the Character and Conduct of John Adams* (the author is unknown, but he was a New Yorker) inquired, since Hamilton refused to divert a single vote from Adams, "Why . . . in the name of common sense, was this extraordinary performance published at this critical moment?" Many Federalists would fear internal dissension were either Adams or Pinckney elected; they would prefer Jefferson for harmony in the government. Hamilton, "the statesman, the patriot, the polar star of Federalism. . . . When he wakes from his delusion, how will he . . . bear the yell of Jacobinic triumph that shall hail a Democratic President!" Oliver Wolcott was resigned to the split in Federalist ranks. Before the results of the election were known, he forecast that "the division will . . . continue & all attempts to reconcile it will be fruitless."

Had Hamilton made no difficulty about the candidacy of Adams for a second term, had he effaced himself where he found Adams antagonistic, Adams would probably have been defeated anyhow. Jefferson did not upset the national applecart. He began his administration with the Louisiana Purchase, which was in the Federalist spirit. He conformed to several Federalist tenets. America's condition was mostly determined by fortunes in Europe, not here. Anyhow, John Marshall, as Chief Justice, cherished central authority. The Federalists' work was measurably done. Continued in power for another term, they might have further offended against liberty, as in the Alien and Sedition Acts. In a dozen years they had supplied the material basis for a more democratic government. Now it was time for the new dispensation.

In 1800, when Jefferson and Burr had an equal number of electoral votes and the choice was thrown into the House of Representatives, most Federalists preferred Burr. Jefferson they had long feared as prime public enemy, while Burr was less known but was supposed to be more amenable to Federalist persuasions. Harrison Gray Otis, in the House, referred to Hamilton the question whether the Federalists should enter into a negotiation with Burr, perhaps bringing him to Washington for the purpose; he added that "few of us have a personal acquaintance with Mr. Burr." He begged Hamilton, from his own local knowledge, "to give an opinion upon a subject in which all the friends of the country have a common interest." Gouveneur Morris in the Senate solicited similarly: "your ideas [as between Jefferson and Burr] will have weight on the minds of many here, should you think proper to transmit them. . . . The subject is certainly of high consideration."

McHenry informed Rufus King that Federalists with whom

he had talked "think they understand Burr, and that he will not be very angry at being aided by the Federalists to outwit the Jeffersonians . . . the opposition are in . . . violent . . . apprehension lest Mr Jefferson should not be chosen." George Cabot, when the campaign was warming, reported that faltering Federalists favored making common cause with Burr. They "conceive Burr less likely to look to France for support than Jefferson, provided he could be supported at home. They consider Burr as actuated by ordinary ambition, Jefferson by that and the pride of the Jacobinic philosophy. The former may be satisfied by power and property, the latter must see the roots of our society pulled up." And Pickering reported that "There are said to be many ingenious reasons why the federalists at Washington . . . prefer Mr. Burr . . . they probably suppose that the federal interest will not be so *systematically* opposed under Mr. B. as under Mr. J." He hinted at a bargain: "Perhaps this may be *previously understood.*"

If others did not know how to estimate Aaron Burr, Hamilton was fully aware of his failings. He did not need to be urged to warn against the folly of any bargain with Burr. He immediately began a pointed correspondence with reliable Federalist leaders and others who were wavering. His pleas, to whomever addressed, were on the same theme as that he expressed to Gouverneur Morris: "His [Burr's] elevation can only promote the purposes of the desperate and profligate. If there is a man in the world I ought to hate, it is Jefferson. With Burr I have always been personally well. But the public good must be paramount to every private consideration."

Hamilton had recovered from the dissonance and confusion of mind that had marked his attack on John Adams. He was now collected and in dead earnest. He canvassed every unworthy feature of Burr's character and conduct. To James A. Bayard, in the House, who became the key figure in Hamilton's campaign to defeat Burr: "I . . . am sure there is no means too atrocious to be employed by him. In debt vastly beyond his means of payment, with all the habits of excessive expense, he cannot be satisfied with the regular emoluments of any office of our government. Corrupt expedients will be to him a *necessary* resource, Will any prudent man offer such a President to the temptations of foreign gold?" Any deal with Burr would be violated. "No engagement that can be made with him can be depended upon; while making it, he will laugh in his sleeve at the credulity of those with whom he makes it. . . . Disgrace abroad, ruin at home, are the probable fruits of his elevation. To contribute to the . . . mortification of Mr. J., would be, on my part, only to retaliate for unequivocal proofs of enmity; but in a case like this, it would be base to listen to personal considerations."

Hamilton, calling Burr "the most dangerous man of the community," exhorted Representative John Rutledge, "You cannot . . . render a greater service to your country than by exerting your influence to counteract the . . . impure idea of raising Mr. Burr to the chief magistracy." And to Senator James Ross he wrote that Burr was dishonest, bankrupt, intriguing for his own advantage, "will court and employ the worst men of all parties as [his] most eligible instruments. . . . Let the Federalists vote for Jefferson. But, as they have much in their power, let them . . . obtain assurances from him." Jefferson, if voted into the presidency by Federalists, should promise to preserve public credit, gradually increase the navy, maintain neutrality, and not make a sudden wholesale ouster of Federalists in minor offices. There was no reason to suppose Jefferson "capable of being corrupted." His Gallicism would cool as popularity of that cause waned. And, again to Bayard, he insisted that if the Federalists adopted Burr, he, Hamilton, would consider himself "an isolated Man," refusing to be one of a party that degraded itself. Elsewhere he exclaimed, "Adieu to the Federal Troy, if they once introduce this Grecian horse into their citadel." Hamilton had helped build a nation, and a political party incidentally. He would not permit the political instrument to destroy his master work.

Hamilton regularly requested his correspondents to make discreet use of his denunciations of Burr. John Adams after his defeat sulked and exerted no influence when the election of Jefferson or Burr hung in the balance in repeated votes in the House. Hamilton had sinned politically by his attack on Adams, which had put his party out of the running, but he was still the moral leader of the Federalists—vocal, unselfish, unafraid.

Bayard, under Hamilton's urging, tipped the scales. The vote was by states, and Bayard was a fortunate instrument since he was the sole representative of Delaware and had influence with other Federalists as well. Bayard reported to Hamilton, after the long struggle, "I came out with the most explicit and determined declaration of voting for Jefferson." It was a close thing, for Bayard confessed that he might have chosen Burr had Burr chosen the Federalists. But Burr was "determined not to shackle himself with federal principles." Burr was excoriated by others besides Hamilton, but actually, as a candidate, he disavowed, with apparent sincerity, any competition with Jefferson. Before the vote of electors he believed that "as to the V.P.—Adams & P[inckney] appear to have about equal chances." Hamilton and the Federalists generally had no doubt that Jefferson would maintain the authority of the Chief Executive. Federalists could not quarrel with his idea of the role of the central government, expressed to Governor Fenner of Rhode Island shortly after he became President: "to the United nation belongs our external and mutual relations; to each state severally the care of our persons, our property . . . and religious freedom."

Of course the build-up for Jefferson had been long and was nourished by various causes, but Hamilton at the dramatic moment determined his accession. To say that it was an unselfish act diminishes Hamilton's commitment to the public good, for not his personal comfort, but the welfare of the nation was his abiding concern. A generation later Bayard's son referred to Hamilton's letters to his father preferring Jefferson over Burr: "they do him infinite honor, exhibiting the sincerity of his attachment to the existing institutions[,] his discrimination of character and loftiness of mind." Hamilton could not have known that by his magnanimous plea for Jefferson's success he was preparing the way for the sacrifice of his own life.

Hamilton offered "a public declaration of . . . approbation of [the] contents" of Jefferson's inaugural speech. He viewed it "as virtually a . . . retraction of past misapprehensions, and a pledge to the community, that the new President will not lend himself to dangerous innovations, but in essential points will tread in the steps of his predecessors." This was not entirely altruism toward Jefferson, for Hamilton would discredit the violent Republicans who were supporting the effort of George Clinton to regain the governorship of New York following Jay's term. Jefferson, in his inaugural, had allowed that the Federalists brought the Republic to "the full tide of successful experiment." If Jefferson, by his moderation, alienated his more dogmatic followers, "in the talents, the patriotism, and the firmness of the Federalists, he will find more than an equivalent for all that he shall lose."

From his youth Hamilton had eagerly expressed himself in newspapers and pamphlets. He had a sympathetic relationship with Fenno's Philadelphia *Gazette of the United States,* but not until the election of Jefferson did he sponsor a newspaper, the *New York Evening Post,* with his friend William Coleman as editor. Hamilton gave character to the *Post*'s columns by interviews which Coleman took down in shorthand. Noah Webster's *Commercial Advertiser* had declared certain disagreements with Federalist policy and was losing subscribers whom Coleman's paper attracted. The first issue of the *Post*, dated November 16, 1801, declared a more democratic purpose than most readers expected in a paper promoted by Hamilton, Troup, Varick, Gracie, and their friends. "Though we openly profess our attachment," said the prospectus, "to that system of politics denominated Federal, because we think it most conducive to the welfare of the community . . . yet we . . . believe that honest and virtuous men are to be found in each party."

While Hamilton made the best of the political change-over, his eldest son, Philip, would not leave well enough alone, and he got into youthful mischief that led to tragedy. Evidently he had read the Fourth of July oration of Captain George I. Eacker, an attorney who celebrated Jefferson's victory with expected aspersions on the Federalist record. In the following November, young Hamilton, with a companion named Price, entered the theater box occupied by Eacker and friends. Philip in loud conversation made rude remarks about Eacker's oration. Eacker affected not to hear the taunts, but when Philip persisted Eacker invited the youngsters to the lobby, where he exclaimed that he would not be insulted by a set of rascals. Price challenged Eacker, and four shots were exchanged, but both came off unscathed. John(?) Lawrence, acting as the friend of Eacker, was equally the intimate of the Hamilton family. He, remarking on Philip's youth and the political nature of the quarrel, proposed mutual apologies. However, Eacker was stubborn, Philip sent his challenge, and next day they met on the Jersey shore. Had Philip kept his resolve, enjoined by his father, to discharge his pistol at the ground and let his antagonist decide whether to resume, all might have been well. Both drew up their weapons at the same moment and Philip Hamilton fell with a wound of which he died that night.

The distress of the family was unrelieved except by religious resignation. Philip had recently been graduated from Colum-

bia College and was of much promise and his parents' special
pride. Friends thought that Hamilton never quite recovered
from this sorrow. The effect of the shock on Mrs. Hamilton
was feared because she was pregnant; the Schuylers brought
her to Albany for a change of scene.

In a slump of spirits after his son's death, and after having
seen the federal government captured by the opposition party,
Hamilton complained to Gouverneur Morris: "Perhaps no man
in the U States has sacrificed or done more for the present
Constitution than myself—and contrary to all my anticipations
of its fate . . . from the very beginning. I am still labouring to
prop the frail and worthless fabric. Yet I have the murmurs of
its friends no less than the curses of its foes for my reward.
What can I do better than withdraw from the Scene? Every day
proves to me more and more that this American world was not
meant for me."

Never was a lament more false. Within a week he was alert-
ing Morris, who had succeeded Schuyler in the Senate, to support amendments to the Constitution proposed by the New
York legislature. One was to designate candidates for President and Vice President separately. The recent protracted contest between Jefferson and Burr was illustration that "the people should know whom they are choosing." The other
amendment would have electors chosen by the people in districts under the direction of Congress. This "removes thus far
the intervention of the State governments, . . . strengthens
the connection between the federal head and the people."

Soon he was further propping the Constitution in admonitions to Morris; "there must be a systematic . . . endeavor to
establish the fortune of a great empire on foundations much
firmer than have yet been devised." The "structure of our national edifice" must be fitted "to control eccentric passions and
. . . to keep in check demagogues and knaves in the disguise
of patriots."

He wished that Rufus King, our minister in England, would

come home to lend a hand in preventing mischief in the Federalist party. "There is certainly a most serious schism [then, June 1802] between the chief [Jefferson] and his heir-apparent [Burr]; a schism absolutely incurable, because founded in . . . the rivalship of an insatiable . . . ambition." This was "ripening into a . . . bitter animosity between the partisans of the two men." Federalist support of Burr for the presidency, which Hamilton had blocked the year before, did not end there. "Several men of no inconsiderable importance among us like the . . . adventurous character of [Burr], and hope to soar with him to power." It would be folly in the Federalists, eager to regain the reins, to adopt Burr as their candidate in the next election.

In the first years of establishing the national government the Federalists had enjoyed popular support. Opposition had been diffused and repelled by the imperative of events. But now, if they were to return to office, they must refer more decisions to citizens in the mass. Hamilton sought to enlist their wisdom, not their caprice; "unless we can contrive to take hold of, and carry along with us . . . strong feelings of the mind, we shall in vain calculate upon any . . . durable results . . . the present Constitution is the standrad to which we are to cling. Under its banners, *bona fide,* must we combat our political foes." Hamilton was never contemptuous of the people, much less willing to abuse their soverignty.

Chapter 22

DUEL

The Hamiltons, after renting for years, bought a home at 58 Partition Street, but their increasing brood outgrew it. Having enjoyed country life in a place he had leased with the Churches the year before, Hamilton, in 1799, decided to purchase upwards of thirty acres in Harlem, land adjoining his friend Ebenezer Stevens, which was eight miles from the city. It ran down to the Hudson River from a wooded height. John McComb, the architect of City Hall and other notable buildings, designed the house, and it was completed in 1802 by Ezra Weeks, brother of the Levi Weeks whom Hamilton had defended against a murder charge. The property was called "Grange," perhaps after the family plantation of the Lyttons on St. Croix. General Schuyler, always the generous *pater familias*, had lumber cut to size and seasoned at Saratoga, advised that brick be laid up between the studs, and said that the partitions should be of solid plank so they would furnish no space for rats and mice. The many fireplaces—that in the kitchen had an iron fireback five feet long, two cranes, and an oven—were on the approved design of Count Rumford. Much of Schuyler's correspondence with his daughter was about the larder; meat from his farms was a welcome addition to the yield of garden and orchard at Harlem.

Hamilton, who delighted in his rural adventure, applied to the notable horticulturist Richard Peters for advice on red clover and to General Pinckney in Charleston for melon seeds. On his way to and from town he stopped at the botanical gardens of his physician, Dr. David Hosack, whence came plans for bulb beds and shrubbery. Hamilton sometimes ranged the woods with his fowling piece, a break from long application in the office. The house cost more than was originally planned, but Hamilton's law practice, now producing around $14,000 a year, warranted a modest mansion. (The house, which was moved a couple of blocks from its first site, stands on Convent Avenue above 141 Street; it was shorn of porches to permit it to be squeezed between buildings on either side. Hopes are entertained for its restoration.)

One case Hamilton was involved in near the end of his career had a permanent effect in American jurisprudence. That was the defense of Harry Croswell, in February 1804 against the charge of libeling Thomas Jefferson, President of the United States. Croswell edited a little Federalist paper, *The Wasp*, at Hudson, New York. He copied into it, with remarks of his own, tart comments on Jefferson made by John Holt in the *Evening Post*. "Holt says . . . that Jefferson paid Callender for calling Washington a traitor, a robber, a perjurer; for calling Adams a hoary-headed incendiary and for most grossly slandering the private characters of men he well knew were virtuous. These charges not a democratic Editor . . . ever will dare to meet."

The indictment averred, in the unfailing legal style, that Croswell, printer, "being a malicious and seditious man, of a depraved mind, amd wicked and diabolical disposition; and also deceitfully, wickedly, and maliciously devising, contriving, and intending Thomas Jefferson, Esq., President of the

United States of America, to detract from, scandalize, traduce, vilify, and to represent him, the said Thomas Jefferson, as unworthy of the confidence, respect, and attachment of the people of the said United States," and to withdraw from him the odedience of the citizens of New York to the evil example of all others in like case offending.

Croswell sought in vain to have the trial put off until he could call James Thompson Callender as a witness to the truth of his, Croswell's, charge. This was that "Callender was the writer of a certain pamphlet, called the 'Prospect before us.' . . . That Thomas Jefferson . . . well knowing the contents of said publication, . . . paid or caused to be paid, to the said . . . Callender, the two several sums of fifty dollars . . . for the purpose of aiding and assisting him . . . in the publication. . . ."

Croswell was convicted, and the case came into the Supreme Court of New York on a motion for a new trial on the ground of a misdirection of the judge "that the only Points for [the jury's] consideration were . . . whether the Deft [defendant] published the Paper stated in the Indictment, & . . . whether the innuendoes were true [i.e., whether Croswell made these innuendoes], & that if they were satisfied of those two Points, it was their Duty to find the Deft guilty." Also that the judge had "denied to the Deft the opportunity of producing Testimony to prove the Truth of the libel, on the Ground that the Deft could not be permitted to give [, in] the evidence to the Jury, the Truth of the charges contained in the Libel."

Hamilton had reason to respond to Croswell's appeal to defend him, which he did without fee. Holt's piece had appeared in the *Evening Post,* which Hamilton patronized, and Callender, represented as Jefferson's hireling to traduce leading Federalists, had published insinuations of Hamilton's malfeasance in the Treasury. Hamilton, more than most of his party, had been the target of unprincipled attacks by Republican editors. He was unable to come into the case at the earlier stage, but argued it before a full bench—Chief Judge Morgan Lewis and Justices Brockholst Livingston, Smith Thompson, and James Kent—in Febrary 1804. Associated with Hamilton for the defense were his friend Richard Harison and William W. Van Ness. For the people were Attorney General of New York Ambrose Spencer and George Caines.

Hamilton's long concluding speech is known in several versions. As Judge Kent described the performance, Hamilton "had bestowed unusual attention on the case, and he came prepared to discuss the points of law with a perfect mastery. . . . He was, at times, highly impassioned and pathetic. His whole soul was enlisted in the cause. The aspect of the times was portentous, and he was persuaded that if he could overthrow the high-toned doctrine of the judge [Lewis] it would be a great gain to the liberties of this country . . . He never before, in my hearing, made an effort in which he commanded higher reverence for his principles, nor equal admiration for the power . . . of his eloquence." After Hamilton's death Ambrose Spencer, his antagonist in this case, said of him, "I was in situations often to observe and study him. I saw him at the bar and at home. He argued cases before me while I sat as judge on the Bench. Webster has done the same. In power of reasoning, Hamilton was the equal of Webster; and more than this can be said of no man. In creative power Hamilton was infinitely Webster's superior."

Hamilton's persuasiveness in Croswell's appeal for a new trial contained moving allusions to the contemporary scene. His citation of precedents, Roman and British, was incidental to his discussion of the developing history of the law and of government as they involved civil rights. He often conceded the ostensible application of authorities relied on by his opponents, only to nullify them as Star Chamber declarations.

His theme was that "The liberty of the press consists in the right to publish with impunity truth, with good motives, for justifiable ends, though reflecting on government, magistracy, or individuals." The allowance of this right is essential to preservation of free government. In guarding against abuse, the jury must not be confined to the mere question of publication of opprobrious terms (as Judge Lewis, relying on Lord Mansfield, had held). The jury must be allowed to pronounce upon "the construction, tendency, and intent of the alleged libel . . . the intent . . . or *quo animo*, is an inference of fact to be drawn by the jury." This is because a libel is not susceptible of statutory definition or judicial precedent that would limit fact, as found by the jury, to a pat recognition. Guilt or innocence depends upon circumstances and motive. These are comprehended in the fact, which falls in the province of the jury. Then, "in determining the character of a libel, the truth or falsehood is in the nature of things a material ingredient." This is not to say that the truth always excuses, for it may be told for evil purpose.

Hamilton lifted his argument into the sphere where the attorney is truly an officer of the court: "whether the truth be a justification will depend on the motives with which it was published." If one "uses the weapon of truth wantonly; if for the purpose of disturbing the peace of families; if for relating that which does not appertain to official conduct, so far . . . the doctrine of our opponents is correct." But it was error to contend that the truth cannot be material in any respect; always "the truth may be given in evidence."

On the last day of the term Chief Justice Lewis announced that the Court was equally divided on the Croswell case (Lewis and Livingston against, Thompson and Kent for) so the motion for appeal was lost. Though entitled to move for judgment, the prosecutor did not. Croswell was left at large. But the sequel was what Hamilton argued for. The public was aroused, and in 1805 a law on libel, sponsored by W. W. Van Ness, was passed unanimously by both houses of the legislature. It was followed by words set out in the state constitution of 1821: "In all criminal prosecutions . . . for libels, the truth may be given in evidence to the jury; and if it shall appear to the jury, that the matter charged as libellous is true, and was published with good motives, and for justifiable ends, the party shall be acquitted; and the jury shall have the right to determine the law and the fact." Other states, before and after, adopted similar provisions, so Hamilton's position (which was Jefferson's also) settled the law of libel in this country.

A quarter-century after Hamilton's death John Quincy Adams tried to connect him with a plan of disunion. New England and as many of the middle states as it could get to go along—New York, New Jersey, Pennsylvania—would form a separate confederacy. Aaron Burr would be the head of it, and if military action was necessary, Hamilton would lead the army of secession.

It is true that Timothy Pickering meditated such a withdrawal of Northeastern states in 1804 and proposed a meeting of select Federalists of the "Essex Junto" in Boston to forward it. He was irked by the Louisiana Purchase, which was said to be unconstitutional and sure to increase the representation of Southern states in Congress. Passing through New York, Pickering broached his project to Rufus King and Hamilton, who emphatically turned him down. If Hamilton had consented to attend the meeting in Boston—of which there is no independent evidence—it would have been to dissuade his Federalist friends from such a repugnant undertaking.

Hamilton's whole life was a refutation of the charge that he would be a party to weakening, much less breaking up, the Union. His last political letter, to Sedgwick of Massachusetts, written the day before the duel, concentrated his advice in "one sentiment, which is, that Dismemberment of our empire will be a sacrifice of great positive advantages without any counter-balancing good." The notion that Hamilton would have fought to place Burr in a position of power is outlandish. John Quincy Adams shared his father's enmity to Hamilton, which made him credulous of a report of William Plumer, old-

time New Hampshire Federalist turned Democrat. Adams said
that the meeting of conspirators was not held because of Hamilton's death.

Only the passage of time, and ignorance, and Adams's hostility could so distort the last events of Hamilton's life. His
policy for the Federalists was to remain faithful to their principles, where necessary to support the most eligible candidates
of the opposing party, and to bide their time until they should
be called back to authority. Governor George Clinton having
declined to stand for re-election, the majority of Democrats in
New York nominated Chancellor John Lansing, Jr., for governor, with Senator John Broome for lieutenant governor. After
accepting, Lansing unaccountably withdrew, and his party
nominated Chief Justice Morgan Lewis and Broome. Burr's
friends at Albany, dissenting Democrats mostly, announced a
rump caucus, February 18, 1804, to support Burr for governor.

Hamilton was in Albany on the Croswell case and met with
the Federalists to decide where they would throw their minority strength. What an enemy called "General Hamilton's ha-
rangue at the city-tavern" surely followed the advice he had
drawn up beforehand when the contest was expected to be between Lansing and Burr. His aim was to detach the Federalists
from Burr. If Burr were elected governor, Federalist votes in
New York would further commend him in New England.
There he would propagate the "opinion, that a dismemberment of the Union is expedient." Using his vantage in New
York, he would become chief of a Northern secession. Burr, "of
irregular and insatiable ambition," would debase democracy
into dictatorship. Federalists had best support the Republican
candidate; Burr's party, already divided, might split wide,
give an opening for Federalist resurgence. Hamilton himself
recognized that it would be hard to shift Federalists from Burr
in any event, especially after Lewis was substituted for the
Republican candidate after Lansing quit the ticket.

Handbills tossed about New York City, issued mostly by the

"regular" Jeffersonian Republicans, damned Burr for everything from malpractice of the law to seduction of "unhappy wretches who have fallen victims to this accomplished debaucher." Burr, or someone acting for him, rebutted the attack on his professional conduct and quoted Richard Harison and Hamilton as approving his administration of an estate. The pamphlet war was equally virulent. Cheetham was in his element in accusing Burr. First "a coadjutor to General Hamilton," Burr soon attached himself to the Republicans because he could not match Hamilton's distinction. "Your jealousy of General Hamilton afterward ripened into implacable hatred." Burr's fast friend William P. Van Ness, writing as "Aristiades," defended him all along the line. Burr, by his diligence for the Republicans in 1800, had won them New York City, the state, and thus the nation. He cited Burr's denial that he had "proposed or agreed to any terms with the federal party" in hopes of topping Jefferson in the election, which appears to have been true.

Fearing the defeat of Morgan Lewis, the Federalists considered running Rufus King, but King was unwilling to be a third candidate even though the Republicans were split. Not in letters or speeches, but undoubtedly in personal contacts, Hamilton urged Federalists to vote for Lewis, the majority Republican candidate. Burr carried the city by a slim margin, but in the state as a whole Lewis won, 30,829 to 22,139.

Burr's political ambition was wrecked. He had been repudiated by the party in national power. Now he had failed to win the governorship of New York, which might have been a stepping stone to chief of a secessionist Northern confederacy. In both contests, for the presidency and the governorship, Hamilton had stood astride his path. Burr's bitter disappointment rankled to personal revenge. While hope of preferment had remained he had not challenged what he must have known was Hamilton's too free language condemning him. Now his resentment was uppermost.

The correspondence during the nine days that led to the duel commenced between the principals, then was transferred to their seconds. Burr's opening letter, June 18, 1804, enclosed a newspaper statement signed Charles D. Cooper, published some time before, but which "has . . . very recently come to my attention." Van Ness, who was Burr's messenger, would point out the offending passage. Reporting a dinner conversation at the home of Judge John Tayler at Albany the previous winter, Dr. Cooper had said that "General Hamilton and Judge Kent . . . declared in substance, that they looked upon Mr. Burr to be a dangerous man . . . who ought not to be trusted with the reins of government." This was not out of the ordinary, but Cooper's further remark provoked Burr's ire: "I could detail . . . a still more despicable opinion which General Hamilton has expressed of Mr. Burr." Hamilton must perceive, said Burr, "the necessity of a prompt and unqualified acknowledgment or denial of the use of any expression which would warrant the assertions of Dr. Cooper."

As Hamilton later said, he would avoid extremities "if it could be done with propriety," and he repeated that wish in a letter left for his wife. After two days' reflection, he rejected Burr's demand as too vague, without specification of time, place, or person supposed to have been addressed. If Burr accepted the description "dangerous man" as within the limits of political contest, why should he bristle at an unspecified further comment alleged to be "more despicable"? Hamilton could not answer for irresponsible construction of his language over many years. He stood ready to avow or disclaim at once "any precise . . . opinion which I may be charged with having declared of any Gentleman." "If not, I can only regret the circumstance and must abide the consequences."

Burr rejoined that Hamilton must disown Dr. Cooper's dishonorable epithet. Hamilton told Van Ness that this rude letter could draw no reply except that Burr should take what steps he liked. Van Ness, later not so prudent, cautioned Hamilton against rashness. Hamilton consulted with his friend Nathaniel Pendleton, to whom he referred Van Ness.

Pendleton first tried conversations with Van Ness. Hamilton was prepared to say that his remarks to Dr. Cooper "turned wholly on political topics, and did not attribute to Colo Burr, any instance of dishonorable conduct, nor relate to his private character." With this Burr might have been satisfied, but he demanded, through Van Ness, whether Hamilton had ever set afloat rumors derogatory to Burr's honor. This was refused, whereupon Burr's friend had a message to deliver when Hamilton's friend would receive it. Hamilton and Pendleton made another effort. Hamilton had circulated one charge against Burr, but that had long since been explained between them. To hold him indefinitely responsible for ill opinions was to betray "predetermined hostility." If this was the case, Van Ness could deliver his message.

Van Ness issued Burr's "invitation." It was accepted and Pendleton would communicate the necessary arrangements. Hamilton, hastily informed, was not sure whether the seconds had committed them. He gave Pendleton, on June 28, a last letter calling on Burr to be specific, not to insist on an "abstract inquiry" to which Hamilton would not submit. Van Ness would not accept this letter, holding that the meeting had been agreed to. Hamilton needed a short delay until the Circuit Court rose, then required a few days to settle his private affairs. The duel was set for the morning of July 11.

Hamilton, to outward appearance nothing perturbed, a week before the duel called on William Short (who had been agent of the Treasury in negotiating Dutch loans a decade earlier) "to request the pleasure of his company at a Family Dinner in the country, on Saturday next three oClock." Hamilton made his will, penned for his executors a list of his liabilities, wrote farewell letters to his wife, left a grateful note for his friend Pendleton, and drew up an explanation of his motives in meeting Burr. This would be expected of him as a public man.

From the time of Burr's first remonstrance, Hamilton knew the duel was fated. The disavowal required by Burr "in a general and indefinite form, was out of my power . . . because . . . my animadversions on the political principles, character, and views of Col. Burr, have been extremely severe; and on different occasions I . . . with many others, have made very unfavourable criticisms on . . . the private conduct of this gentleman." His distrust of Burr, urged for what he believed the public good, was difficult of apology. Hamilton could understand Burr's resentment when these detractions came to his ears.

Hamilton's moral principles condemned the practice of dueling. To shed a fellow creature's blood in a private combat forbidden by the laws was abhorrent to him. He had resolved to throw away his first fire, "and I *have thoughts* even of *reserving* my second fire—and thus giving a double opportunity to Col. Burr to pause and to reflect."

Love for his family and duty to his creditors restrained him. But "all the considerations which constitute what men of the world denominate honour, imposed on me (as I thought) a . . . necessity not to decline the call. The ability to be in future useful, whether in resisting mischief or effecting good, in those crises of our public affairs which seem likely to happen, would probably be inseparable from a conformity with public prejudice in this particular."

He repeated this solemn decision in letters to be given his wife if he should fall in the duel. "If it had been possible for me to have avoided the interview, my love for you and my precious children would have been alone a decisive motive." And, again to Elizabeth, the night before he met Burr, "The scruples of a Christian have determined me to expose my own life to any extent, rather than subject myself to the guilt of taking the life of another. This much increases my hazards, and redoubles my pangs for you."

He rejected the plea of Rufus King that he refuse to go to the field. King lamented, "with a mind the most capacious and discriminating that I ever knew . . . he had laid down for . . . himself certain rules upon the subject of Duels, the fallacy of which could not fail to be seen by any man of ordinary understanding[;] with these guides . . . he could not have avoided a meeting with Col. Burr, had he even declined the first challenge." Egbert Benson and John Jay had advance word of the duel from King, but not from Hamilton, and they made no attempt to intervene. His trusted brother-in-law, Church, surely knew, for it was his pistols which Pendleton borrowed for the encounter, but there is no record of Church's advice, if asked or offered.

Hamilton's views had changed from years before when he had disclaimed, to Dr. Gordon, any intention of fighting a traducer, for "we do not now live in the days of chivalry . . . *The good sense of the present times has happily found out, that to prove your own innocence, or the malice of an accuser, the worst method you can take is to run him through the body or shoot him through the head.*"

He had permitted his son Philip to meet Eacker; the revulsion he felt at the fatal result must have been in his heart when, nevertheless, he accepted Burr's challenge. On principle he could not apologize for possible injuries to his adversary unless he learned that his censures had been unfounded. Further, to preserve his public influence he must bow to prevailing prejudice. He must not be suspected of cowardice. Some have supposed that Hamilton, as chief of the Federalists, was scornful of public opinion. In fact he believed that the body of citizens wanted unselfish guidance. That he was in turn respectful of their views is evident in the last act of his life. Tensions within the country and in our foreign relations doubtless influenced him to protect at all cost the confidence in which he was held.

Possibly the strain he was under had the compensating effect of marked joviality in his manner. At the meeting of the Society of the Cincinnati, of which he was president general, he saluted the company with a song, while Burr is said to have looked fixedly at him. He spent the evening of Monday, July 9, at Wolcott's house in a circle of friends. Wolcott recorded afterward that "He was uncommonly cheerful and gay."

Probably he had been with his whole family at the Grange over the weekend, came into town Monday morning, and spent the night before the duel at his house in town, 54 Cedar Street. He would not have returned to the Grange because he was to "leave town" for the dueling ground "about five o Clock" the next morning. The "place agreed on" was Weehawken, New Jersey, on the west bank of the Hudson opposite the end of 42d Street, New York.

The boat carrying Hamilton, Pendleton, and Dr. Hosack arrived at about seven o'clock. Burr and Van Ness were already on the ground, which was a shelf or terrace part way up the Palisades. Casting lots for choice of position and whose second should give commands, both fell to Hamilton, the last luck he was ever to have. The seconds loaded the pistols in each other's presence, then measured ten paces. The duelists being ready, Pendleton cried "Present!" Both pistols were discharged, which first the seconds did not agree. Pendleton's description was that Hamilton's weapon went off after he was struck by Burr's bullet.

When Hamilton fell, Burr approached him with a gesture of regret, but was then hurried from the field so Dr. Hosack could not see him. Dr. Hosack related, "When called to [General Hamilton] I found him half sitting on the ground . . . in the arms of Mr. Pendleton. His countenance of death I shall never forget—He had at that instant just strength to say, 'This is a mortal wound, Doctor;' when he sunk away, and became to all appearance lifeless." However, he slowly revived in the boat. Seeing his pistol he warned, " 'Take care of that pistol; it is undischarged, and still cocked . . . Pendleton knows, (attempting to turn his head toward him) that I did not intend to fire at him.' " He was then silent, except to say that he had lost all feeling in his legs. As they approached the shore he begged that Mrs. Hamilton be sent for; the news must be broken to her gradually, "but give her hope."

At the foot of Horatio Street Hamilton's friend William Bayard, whose house was at hand, was alarmed to see Hamilton lying in the bottom of the boat. He had been told of the crossing to New Jersey and had guessed the errand. He and his family were so distressed that they could hardly obey the doctor's direction to get a bed ready.

In spite of being given an ounce of laudanum, his sufferings were "almost intolerable." Dr. Hosack was joined by his colleague Dr. Wright Post, and by surgeons from French frigates in the harbor, who had experience in gunshot wounds, but all thought Hamilton's case hopeless. Mrs. Hamilton arrived from the Grange, entirely ignorant of what had happened. "My sister bears with saintlike fortitude this affliction," Angelica Church wrote to her father at Albany. "The town is in consternation" with grief and anger.

Burr, in his home near by, had the grace to inquire of Dr. Hosack for Hamilton's condition, as did Van Ness of Pendleton. Van Ness, though, was fearful for Burr and himself; he cautioned Pendleton not to publish anything without consultation.

Wolcott informed his wife that Hamilton "has of late years expressed his conviction of the truths of the Christian Religion, and has desired to receive the Sacrament." (Hamilton's return to religion—he had been pious as a youth—is also known from other sources). Episcopal Bishop Benjamin Moore came to see him, but went away without administering the rite, implying that the stricken man needed time to reflect on the sin that had brought him low. Hamilton persisted; his old friend Dr. Mason, following the rule of his Dutch Reformed Church, felt obliged to refuse to give the communion privately. He assured the dying man that the sacrament was only a sign of the forgiveness he could claim from his expressions of repentance—"I went to the field determined not to take *his* life." Hamilton still wanted the sign; Bishop Moore returned, heard that the sufferer forgave Burr and would, if he lived, always testify against dueling. Hamilton received the sacrament with gratitude. Actually, in dying Hamilton gave the code its severest blow to that time.

That night he slept fitfully, and next day he was manifestly sinking. At his bedside were his wife and seven children, the youngest only two years old. Wolcott was there, as were the doctor and Bishop Moore, and doubtless the Churches, when Hamilton breathed his last about two o'clock, July 12, 1804.

Bulletins on Hamilton's worsening state aroused the city to menace against Burr, but the first particulars of the duel were not published until the following week, and then in words that relieved Burr of special blame. Though Pendleton, anxious to have the facts known, was not careful of his own safety, Burr and Van Ness kept to their houses.

Immediately it was known that Hamilton had died, civic organizations, and the military, led by the Society of the Cincinnati, made plans to participate in the public funeral, which was to take place on Saturday, July 14. The Common Council recommended a suspension of business. Muffled bells tolled, British and French frigates in the harbor peaked their yards and fired minute guns, as did the forts, and merchant vessels flew their colors at half mast. The funeral procession required two hours to move from Church's house in Robinson Street to Trinity Church. There Gouverneur Morris pronounced a eulogy.

Coroners' juries in New York and New Jersey gave verdicts

of murder against Burr and the seconds, and grand juries indicted them. After eleven days Burr was rowed at night to the home of Commodore Truxton at Perth Amboy, and from there he made his nervous way to Philadelphia and temporary safety. He visited his daughter Theodosia in South Carolina, then returned to the Senate to preside over the impeachment trial of Judge Samuel Chase. The Republicans rallied to Burr's support and succeeded in freeing him of legal charges.

On the eve of the duel Hamilton had expressed the "ardent wish" that he was mistaken in his antagonist's demerits and that Burr might yet "prove an ornament and blessing to his country." It was not to be, for the bullet that killed Hamilton also killed Burr, politically. His fortunes declined; though tried and declared not guilty of treason, suspicions drove him to penurious exile, from which he returned to lasting disrepute.

Encomiums on Hamilton were widespread through the states, and included retractions of ill opinions by such slanderers as Cheetham. Fisher Ames was among the discerning in saying that Hamilton "had not made himself dear to the passions of the multitude by condescending . . . to become their instrument . . . it was by loving his country better than himself, preferring its interest to its favor, and serving it" that homage followed him. His last political counsel has been misunderstood. He had warned Sedgwick against the project of New England's secession. Separation would administer "no relief to our real Disease; which is *Democracy,* the poison of which by a subdivision will only be the more concentered in each part, and consequently the more virulent." From many other contexts it is plain that by "poison" of "Democracy" he meant not the rights of the people, but unworthy designs of demagogues in deceiving them.

For his young nation Hamilton recommended associated effort to produce a stable political structure and a rounded economy. He rejected the individualist method—born in France, propagated by Adam Smith, the inspiration of Thomas Jefferson. For him the means of improvement was the will of the community. Active, planful government was the prompter of private initiative which would develop the country in agriculture, industry, and commerce. In his view, passive government, laissez faire, indeed, democracy in pure form, could not serve until the preparatory stage of stability had been accomplished.

There were departures from his principles after his death, but recent years have witnessed the resurgence of government. How much that was once regarded as private dependence has become public responsibility! The notion of an agricultural society, resting on self-sufficiency of the individual and preferring local government, has long faded. Hamilton's projection of a many-sided, often corporate economy and central political authority has come to pass. Could Hamilton revisit the American scene he would be the first to warn against an excess of paternalism, which now threatens to inhibit democratic control.

After Hamilton's death friends subscribed a sum to pay his debts and give Mrs. Hamilton possession of her Grange home and assistance in bringing up her two girls and five boys. Resourceful, courageous, and loyal, she deserves all praise in Hamilton's story. In the fifty years that she outlived her husband she devoted herself to gathering his papers, which are the memorials of his greatness.

BIBLIOGRAPHY

Readers wishing documentation are referred to my *Alexander Hamilton*, 2 vols. (New York: Macmillan, 1957, 1962; republished, New York: Farrar, Straus & Giroux, 1976).

The principal source is Harold C. Syrett (ed.), and Jacob E. Cooke *et al.* (assoc. eds.), *The Papers of Alexander Hamilton* (New York: Columbia University Press, 1961—; the last two volumes of this twenty-six-volume work will be published in 1977). Indefatigably collected, and edited with specialized scholarship, these volumes contain all that has been discovered and is available of Hamilton's writings, letters to him, and related materials. Detailed editorial introductions shed light on chief reports and episodes. Similar is Julius Goebel, Jr. (ed.), *The Law Practice of Alexander Hamilton, Documents and Commentary*, 2 vols. (New York: Columbia University Press, 1964, 1969).

Many letters written by Hamilton for Washington's signature are identified in J. C. Fitzpatrick (ed.), *Writings of George Washington*, 39 vols. (Washington, D.C.: Government Printing Office, Bicentennial Edition, 1931–44).

Biographies of Hamilton
and some of his contemporaries:

Alden, John Richard, *General Charles Lee, Traitor or Patriot?* (Baton Rouge, Louisiana State University Press, 1951).

Anderson, D. R., *William Branch Giles* (Menasha, Wis.: Geo. Banta, 1914).

Berkeley, Edmund, and Dorothy Smith Berkeley, *John Beckley: Zealous Partisan in a Nation Divided* (Philadelphia: American Philosophical Society, 1973).

Bernhard, Winfred E., *Fisher Ames, Federalist and Statesmen, 1758–1808* (Chapel Hill, University of North Carolina Press, 1965).

Beveridge, A. J., *Life of John Marshall,* 4 vols. (Boston, Houghton Mifflin, 1916–19).

Boyd, G. A., *Elias Boudinot* (Princeton, 1952).

Brant, Irving, *James Madison* 6 vols. (Indianapolis: Bobbs-Merrill, 1941–61).

Burns, Edward McNall, *James Madison: Philosopher of the Constitution* (New York: Octagon Books, 1968).

Callahan, North, *Henry Knox, General Washington's General* (New York: Rinehart, 1958).

Chinard, Gilbert, *Honest John Adams,* new introduction by Douglas Adair (Boston: Little, Brown, 1964).

Cooke, Jacob E. (ed.), *Alexander Hamilton, a Profile* (New York, Hill & Wang, 1967).

Cresson, William P., *James Monroe* (Chapel Hill, University of North Carolina, 1946).

Davis, Joseph S., *Essays in the Earlier History of American Corporations,* esp. "William Duer, Entrepreneur, 1747–99," and "Society for Establishing Useful Manufactures, Paterson, New Jersey," 2 vols. (Cambridge, Mass.: Harvard University Press, 1917).

Ernst, Robert, *Rufus King, American Federalist* (Chapel Hill, University of North Carolina Press, 1968).

Flexner, James T., *George Washington,* 4 vols. (Boston: Little, Brown, 1965–72).

Freeman, Douglas S., *George Washington, A Biography,* 7 vols. (New

York: Scribners; last vol. by John A. Carroll and Mary W. Ashworth, 1948–57).

Greene, George W., *The Life of Nathanael Greene,* 3 vols. (New York: Hurd and Houghton, 1971).

Hacker, Louis M., *Alexander Hamilton in the American Tradition* (New York: McGraw-Hill, 1957).

Hamilton, Allan McLane, *Intimate Life of Alexander Hamilton* (New York: Scribners, 1910).

Kapp, Friedrich, *The Life of William Von Steuben,* 2nd ed. (New York: Mason Bros., 1859).

Kent, William (ed.), *James Kent, Memoir and Letters* (Boston: Little Brown, 1898).

King, Charles R. (ed.), *Life and Correspondence of Rufus King,* 6 vols. (New York: Putnams, 1894–1900).

Kline, Mary-Jo (ed.), *Alexander Hamilton, a Biography in his Own Words* (New York: Harper & Row, 1973).

Koch, Adrienne, *Jefferson and Madison, the Great Collaboration* (New York: Oxford University Press, 1964).

Larson, Harold, "Alexander Hamilton; the Fact and Fiction of His Early Years," *William and Mary Quarterly,* 3d. ser., No. 9, pp. 139–51.

Lodge, Henry Cabot, *Life and Letters of George Cabot* (Boston: Little, Brown, 1878).

Lossing, B. J., *Life and Times of Philip Schuyler,* 2 vols. (New York: Sheldon, 1873).

Loth, David, *Alexander Hamilton, Portrait of a Prodigy* (New York: Garrick & Evans, 1939).

Malone, Dumas, *Jefferson and the Rights of Man* (1951), and *Jefferson the President, First Term* (1970), both in the series *Jefferson and His Time* (Boston: Little, Brown).

Miller, John Chester, *Alexander Hamilton: Portrait in Paradox* (New York: Harper, 1959).

Mitchell, Broadus, *Alexander Hamilton, the Revolutionary Years* (New York: Crowell, 1970).

———, "The Man Who Discovered Hamilton," 69, *New Jersey Historical Society Proceedings,* pp. 88–114.

———, *Heritage from Hamilton* (New York: Columbia University Press, 1957).

Monahan, Frank, *John Jay, Defender of Liberty* (Indianapolis: Bobbs-Merrill, 1935).

O'Brien, Michael, Jr., *Hercules Mulligan* (New York: P. J. Kennedy, 1937).

Oliver, Frederick Scott, *Alexander Hamilton, An Essay on American Union* (New York: Putnam, new ed., 1918).

Patterson, Samuel White, *Horatio Gates, Defender of American Liberties* (New York: Columbia University Press, 1941).

Peterson, Merrill D., *Thomas Jefferson and the New Nation: A Biography* (New York: Oxford University Press, 1970).

Pickering, Octavius, *The Life of Timothy Pickering*, 4 vols. (Boston: Little, Brown, 1867–73).

Robertson, Wm. Spence, *Life of Miranda*, 2 vols. (Chapel Hill: University of North Carolina Press, 1929).

Schachner, Nathan, *Aaron Burr, A Biography* (New York: Stokes, 1937).

———, *Alexander Hamilton* (New York: A. S. Barnes, 1961).

Sedgwick, Theodore, *A Memoir of the Life of William Livingston* (New York: J. and J. Harper, 1833).

Smith, Page, *John Adams*, 2 vols. (Garden City, N.Y.: Doubleday, 1962).

Spaulding, E. W., *His Excellency George Clinton, Critic of the Constitution* (New York: Macmillan, 1938).

Swiggett, Howard, *The Extraordinary Mr. [Gouverneur] Morris* (Garden City, N.Y.: Doubleday, 1952).

Ver Steeg, Clarence I., *Robert Morris, Revolutionary Financier* (Philadelphia: University of Pennsylvania Press, 1954).

Wallace, David Duncan, *The Life of Henry Laurens, with Sketch of the life of Lieutenant-Colonel John Laurens* (New York: Putnams, 1915).

Welch, Richard E., *Theodore Sedgwick, Federalist; a political portrait* (Middletown, Ct., Wesleyan University Press, 1965).

Whiteley, Emily S., *Washington and His Aides-de-Camp* (New York: Macmillan, 1936).

Wilkinson, James, *Memoirs of My Own Times*, 3 vols. (Philadelphia, A. Small, 1816).

Works bearing on Hamilton's career in various ways:

Alexander, DeAlva S., *A Political History of the State of New York*, 4 vols. (New York: Holt, 1906–23).

Baldwin, Leland D., *Whiskey Rebels* (Pittsburgh, University of Pittsburgh Press, 1939).

Boyd, Julian P., *Number 7, Alexander Hamilton's Secret Attempts to Control American Foreign Policy* . . . (Princeton University Press, 1964).

Brant, Irving, *The Bill of Rights; Its Origin and Meaning* (Indianapolis: Bobbs-Merrill, 1965).

Callahan, North, *Flight from the Republic; the Tories of the American Revolution* (Indianapolis: Bobbs-Merrill, 1967).

Charles, Joseph, *The Origins of the American Party System* (Williamsburg, Va.: Inst. of Early American History and Culture, 1956).

Cole, Arthur H., *Industrial and Commercial Correspondence of Alexander Hamilton Anticipating his Report on Manufactures* (New York: Kelley, n.d.).

Coleman, William (ed.), *A Collection of Facts and Documents, Relating to the Death of* . . . *Alexander Hamilton* (New York: Hopkins and Seymour, 1804).

Cooke, Jacob E. (ed.), *The Federalist* (Middletown, Conn.: Wesleyan, 1961).

DePauw, Linda G., *Eleventh Pillar; New York State and the Federal Convention* (Cornell Univ. Press, 1966).

East, Robert A. and Jacob Judd (eds.), *Loyalist Americans* (Sleepy Hollow, 1974).

Farrand, Max (ed.), *The Records of the Federal Constitution of 1787*, 4 vols., rev. ed. (New Haven, Yale University Press, 1937).

Feltman, William, *Journal* . . . *1781–82, including the Siege of Yorktown* (Philadelphia, H. C. Baird, 1853).

Flexner, James T., *The Traitor and the Spy* (New York: Harcourt, Brace, 1953).

Flick, Alexander C., *Loyalism in New York During the American Revolution* (New York: AMS Press, 1970).

Forman, Sidney, *West Point: A History of the United States Military Academy* (New York: Columbia University Press, 1956).

Gibbs, George, *Memoirs of Administrations of Washington and Adams*, 2 vols. (New York: W. VanNorden, 1846).

Gurney, Gene, *The United States Coast Guard* . . . (New York: Crown Publishers, 1973).

Jensen, Merrill, *The New Nation: A History of the United States During the Confederation, 1781–1789* (New York: Knopf, 1950).

Koch, Adrienne (ed.), *Notes of Debates in the Federal Convention of 1787, Reported by James Madison* (New York: Norton, 1969).

List, Friedrich, *The National System of Political Economy*, trans. from German by S. S. Lloyd (London: Longmans, 1855).

Looze, Helen Johnson, *Alexander Hamilton and the British Orientation of American Foreign Policy, 1783–1801* (The Hague, Mouton, 1969).

Miller, John C., *The Federalist Era, 1789–1801* (New York: Harper & Row, 1960).

Nevins, Allan, *History of Bank of New York and Trust Company . . .* (New York: privately printed, 1934).

Paltsits, V. H. (ed.), *Washington's Farewell Address in Facsimile, with Transliterations of all the Drafts* (New York: New York Public Library, 1935).

Pennsylvania Archives, 2d. ser, Vol. IV, ed. by J. B. Linn and Wm. H. Egle (Harrisburg: B. F. Meyers, 1878; pp. 5–550 devoted to Whiskey Insurrection).

Syrett, Harold C., and Jean G. Cooke (eds.), *Interview in Weehawken, the Burr-Hamilton Duel as Told in the Original Documents;* Introduction and Conclusion by W. M. Wallace (Middletown, Conn.: Wesleyan, 1966).

Smith, Darrell H., and F. W. Powell, *The Coast Guard; Its History, Activities, and Organization* (Washington, D.C.: Brookings, 1929).

Society of the Cincinnati, *Institution of*, with list of members of New York State Society (New York: J. M. Elliott, 1851).

Stryker, W. S., *The Battle of Monmouth*, W. S. Myers (ed.) (Princeton, N.J.: 1927).

Taylor, George R., *Hamilton and the National Debt* (Boston: Heath, 1950).

Van Tyne, Claude H., *The Loyalists in the American Revolution* (New York: Burt Franklin, 1968).

Ward, Christopher, *War of the Revolution*, 2 vols. (New York: Macmillan, 1952).

White, Leonard D., *The Federalists, a Study in Administrative History* (New York: Macmillan, 1948).

William and Mary Quarterly, 3d. ser., Vol. 12, No. 2 (April 1955) Bicentennial Number, *Alexander Hamilton, 1755–1804*).

Index